THE LEGACY
of the
LIBERAL SPIRIT

THE LEGACY
of the
LIBERAL SPIRIT

MEN AND MOVEMENTS IN THE
MAKING OF MODERN THOUGHT

BY

FRED GLADSTONE BRATTON

NEW YORK

CHARLES SCRIBNER'S SONS

1943

TO MY WIFE

Preface

TODAY, MORE THAN EVER before, an author is required to "show cause" for using valuable paper. The present volume is felt to come under the category of "necessary" work because it attempts to describe the spirit or tradition for which the allied nations are at the present moment fighting, because it seeks to interpret the history of freedom in its most critical stages, to distinguish between the incidental forms of liberalism as a way of life and its essential soul, and finally to show that the liberal spirit is neither dated, dead, nor dying, but passing into a new form of life, the nature of which is herein prefigured.

The title of this book implies, admittedly, a point of view on the part of the author. A thorough-going objectivity has its dangers and professorial fence-sitting, if carried to extremes, results in the flabby notion that everybody is right. Such a type of broad-mindedness neither serves the ends of scholarship nor makes for good reading. But while confessing to a point of view, the author hopes that he is not like the Cheerful Cherub's dogmatist who said:

> "In controversial moments
> My perception's rather fine;
> I always see both points of view:
> The one that's wrong—and mine."

Many thoughtful people today, infected with the virus of questionnaire-education and the discussional method, can hardly bring themselves to end a sentence with a period. They are not sure of anything. Like Pilate, they ask:

vii

"What is Truth?" They remember too well the witticism of Justice Oliver Wendell Holmes that "no generalization is wholly true, including this one." Not wishing, therefore, to appear dogmatic, they refuse to take sides. They belong to what Dean Willard Sperry used to call the "Yes, but—" group. To go about at this late date raising the question, "Yes, but what *is* Liberalism?" is to be living intellectually on borrowed time. This deliberate haziness has helped to bring on our present moral paralysis.

On the other hand, there is an understandable ambiguity about such words as Humanism, Democracy, Pacifism, Socialism, and even Liberalism. It is desirable in the interests of semantics that an author define or qualify the terms he uses. That is the purpose of this Preface.

The word "liberal" as herein used refers to a way of life which emphasizes the primary importance of the person, the freedom of the individual, free press, free speech, constitutional government, tolerance, the scientific spirit of inquiry, the rational outlook, social reform, popular education, a relativistic philosophy, and an ethico-social religion.

The legacy of the liberal spirit in its organized forms of political democracy, civil liberties, and religious freedom is the way of life that is at stake in the present world struggle. A proper defense of that tradition is unintelligible without a knowledge of its history and pedigree. The purpose of this book is to trace the course of the liberal tradition in its critical phases. Among other things the author attempts to establish the connection between religious liberalism and political democracy, especially as found in eighteenth-century France and America. During that period "democracy" was a philosophical term with certain religious, social, and political implications, all of which centered in one principle: the importance of the individual, his reason and conscience, his freedom and responsibility.

One reason for the present confusion about the term Liberalism is that we have not distinguished between its passing and permanent phases. Liberalism is an idea, a principle, not a platform or a party. Laissez-faire, for instance, coming from the eighteenth-century emphasis on individualism, was once a liberal method. The fact that for certain people it has now become obsolete is no reason for giving up the whole concept of Liberalism. The liberal spirit of any given age, in other words, cannot be frozen into any transient form.

Liberalism is not to be viewed as a nineteenth-century phenomenon ending with the second world war. As an attitude towards life it has a history of 2500 years. As an organized cultural movement it might be said to have started with the French Enlightenment, which gave birth to the spirit of Rationalism and naturalistic philosophy. But back of the Age of Reason was the Renaissance-Reformation, which shifted men's attention to man. Even before that there were many expressions of the liberal outlook, abortive but nonetheless distinct attempts to establish intellectual freedom and the life of reason. The endeavor is here made to bring fresh light to the pregnant periods in the development of liberal thought and to paint in true form and color the most representative thinker of each period. These men—misunderstood and mistreated—will probably never be given their proper place in history but it is hoped that the present volume will make some contribution towards their rehabilitation—which is long overdue.

The use of the biographical method should reveal the author's belief in the inadequacy of economic determinism as a key to history. Institutions, as it is often remarked, are the lengthened shadows of great men, and it does not take an astute observer to recognize the significant rôle of the individual for good or evil in world affairs today. The theory of economic determinism, for that matter, has been worked for more than it is worth. There is no single cause for history, Marxists to the contrary. Moral values and human decisions have turned the tide as much as, if not more than, the economic factor. History in the final analysis is the constant interplay of men and movements. This periodic interplay is the plot of the story related here.

This interpretation of the seven ages of liberal thought is offered both as a timely tribute to our heritage and as a summons to a more articulate faith in the way of life therein described. If it points any one to a more accurate knowledge of those values about which we feel strongly but at times incoherently, it will have been of some service in these turbulent days. And finally, it may help to remind us of what will be lost if this heritage is destroyed.

FRED GLADSTONE BRATTON.

Springfield, Massachusetts
September 1943.

Contents

I

Origen

Life

EVERY CREATIVE AGE in history has given birth to a few individuals whose voluminous literary output has staggered the imagination of the modern reader. Such an intellectual superman was Origen to whom are credited no fewer than 6000 works. If this statement of Epiphanius be not too exaggerated, we must assume that it refers to rolls and short documents. The brilliant scholar Jerome exclaimed: "Which of us can read all that he has written?"

Origen kept seven amanuenses busy and in addition employed a dozen copyists and expert calligraphers. All this activity was made possible by his friend Ambrose who subsidized in Medicean fashion Origen's work, prodded him on, and circulated his books. Origen, in fact, called Ambrose a slave driver.

This ancient combination of H. G. Wells, Harry Elmer Barnes, and Adolf Harnack was not only the most prolific writer but the most liberal thinker in the first thousand years of Christian history. Product of the Alexandrian and Antiochian schools, he represented the more rationalistic and less dogmatic interpretation of Christianity and today stands as the fountain-head of the liberal tradition.

Origen was born in Alexandria in 185 A.D. and sat at the feet of Clement in the famous school of theology in that city. His education was of the best both in science and theology. Brought up on the Scripture, he could recite most of it from memory, but he was eager to pursue the study of biblical literature more comprehensively. In the persecution of Christians under Septimus Severus, Origen's father, Leonidas, was arrested and thrown into prison. Origen, who was seventeen at the time, ardently desired to die a martyr's death along with his father but his mother prevented his leaving the house by hiding his clothes. This seemed to be sufficient deterrent for the boy and he contented himself with writing letters to his father, urging him to keep the faith.

Leonidas' death left the widow with seven children and no property, as that had been confiscated by the state. Origen, the oldest, was given a home by a wealthy lady of Alexandria, a prominent convert to Christianity. Another protégé of Origen's patroness was Paul of Antioch, a Gnostic, whose views Origen thoroughly repudiated as anti-Christian and unsound. Rather than continue to take meals and prayers with this teacher, Origen left and started "on his own." He helped to solve the problem of living by selling his library of Greek classics, most of which he had transcribed himself. The money realized in this way gave him a certain independence and meanwhile he continued to teach in the daytime and study at night. He was not long in making his reputation as a teacher and in attracting pupils. Starting as an instructor in rhetoric, he plunged into an attack on pagan theology. Many converts came to him for instruction in the Christian faith. He insisted that, while intellectualism was no substitute for piety, faith and knowledge were not antagonistic and it was necessary for the true Christian to achieve a sound liberal education.

He continually expressed his sympathy for those who

were being persecuted and his open admiration for these martyrs incurred the displeasure of the pagan authorities, with the result that he was often stoned and publicly humiliated. The systematic persecution put an end to the Catechetical School of Clement and the teachers were forced to flee.

By the time he was eighteen years of age, Origen had attracted such widespread attention even among pagans that Demetrius, the Bishop of Alexandria, made him president of the famous school, an office which could be held without ordination or even formal authorization from the Church itself. In spite of persecution and grave danger the young lecturer held forth and won respect as a man of wisdom, skill and religious zeal, and students thronged to hear him. He required no fees from his pupils, claiming that it was contrary to Scripture to charge tuition. In his lectures he demonstrated that the Christian faith was thoroughly compatible with the best philosophical and scientific learning. He taught logic, geometry, astronomy, and the various systems of philosophy as a preparation for instruction in Christian doctrine and morals. In teaching the Greek literature and philosophy, Origen differed from other fathers of the Church, for as Farrar says, "He never shared the bigotry of the narrower-minded Christians, who discouraged or even forbade the study of pagan literature." [1]

Influenced by the prevailing ascetic ideals of Stoicism, neo-Platonism, and nascent monasticism, Origen at this time carried the principle of self-discipline to an incredible degree—even to the extent of self-mutilation—so eager was he to be above suspicion and to avoid indulgence. It seems inconsistent and certainly unfortunate that Origen should find it necessary to apply the Scripture literally in

[1] Frederic W. Farrar: *Lives of the Fathers*, p. 294.

this instance (Mt. 19:12), while otherwise he spurned literal inspirations and resorts to allegory. Since he was
thrown in with young women as well as men in his teaching
he felt perhaps that emasculation was necessary in order to
be free from charges of impurity, and they were common
enough in third-century Alexandria. It was an "error of
judgment" for which he afterwards repented, an error
which assuredly sprang from noble motives.[2]

On the death of Severus, Origen, then in his thirtieth
year, visited Rome, but the trip was of little importance in
his career. Returning to Alexandria, he resumed his lecturing at the School of Theology. With the rapid growth
of the student body, he was able to place the beginners
under his former pupil, Heraclas, and he then took only the
advanced students. Thus relieved, he commenced his exegetical studies in the New Testament, at the same time
perfecting his knowledge of Hebrew so as to enable himself
to work also in the Old Testament.

One of Origen's converts to the Christian faith was the
rich Alexandrian, Ambrose, who became his firm friend.
This friendship was one of the reasons for Origen's tremendous literary production. The wealthy patron not only
encouraged him in his studies but supplied the funds for
the purchase of manuscripts and for the publication of his
writings. Equipped with trained helpers and spurred on by
his gracious friend, Origen now entered a period of unbe-
lievable literary activity. He scarcely took time out for
meals and sleep. After wearying his scribes with his rapid
fire of dictation during the day, he spent the evening dis-
cussing exegesis with Ambrose. Working under pressure
militated against quality; his aim, however, was not pol-

[2] Some authorities have questioned the story—Baur, Schnitzer, Farrar—
but Redepenning and others, following Eusebius, regard it as true.

ished writing but an effective propaganda against Gnosticism. The part played by Ambrose cannot be exaggerated, for most of Origen's commentaries and apologetics were written at the instigation of this "taskmaster."

Origen received many requests to lecture abroad, one of which was from the governor of Arabia. His visit to Arabia was a brief one and soon after his return he received from Julia Mammaea, the mother of the emperor Alexander Severus, an invitation to visit Antioch. He was given a military escort from Alexandria to Antioch, where he was entertained at the royal palace. He lived here for a brief period and then, according to Eusebius, "after bearing powerful testimony to the glory of the Lord and the worth of divine instruction, hastened back to his accustomed duties."

Origen's next flight from Egypt was occasioned by the persecution under Caracalla in 216. Offended by some reference to the murder of his brother, a criticism which he thought came from Alexandria, Caracalla took an army to that city and massacred thousands of people. Origen escaped to Palestine where he was received by Alexander, Bishop of Jerusalem, and Theoktistus, Bishop of Cæsarea. (Apparently the years with their added responsibilities and hopes for the future had changed his attitude regarding personal martyrdom.) The two bishops arranged for Origen to lecture in their churches. This seems to have been an ecclesiastical *faux pas* since laymen were not permitted to preach in a church and Origen had never been ordained. At any rate, the procedure aroused the displeasure of Demetrius, a stickler for propriety, and he promptly ordered Origen back to Alexandria. The pagan persecution in the meantime having stopped, he was able to resume his work at the Catechetical School.

In 228 Origen was sent on a mission to Greece to pacify the Achaian Christians who were disturbed by heretical teachers. He had to go through Cæsarea where his friends naturally wanted to hear him preach. In order to avoid further trouble with his own bishop and probably also to approach his mission to Greece with a greater degree of authority, Origen permitted the Bishop of Cæsarea to ordain him a presbyter. This action was interpreted by Demetrius as an infringement on his prerogatives and, being by this time somewhat jealous of his favorite professor, he took steps to have Origen banished and unfrocked. Meanwhile Origen arrived at Athens and there distinguished himself as an orator. Returning by way of Ephesus, he attended a theological conference in that city and helped to settle a troublesome dispute.

His success in Greece and Asia Minor further incensed Demetrius, who made it so uncomfortable for Origen upon his return that he had nothing to do but leave Alexandria. He decided to go to Cæsarea. It is an evidence of his greatness that he left without raising his voice and, surrounded as he was in Cæsarea by powerful friends, it is also to his credit that he refused to lead an opposition party to fight Demetrius but at great sacrifice to himself insisted on preserving Christian unity. Few people would have been able to resist a "parting shot" at least. In spite of Origen's conciliatory attitude, Demetrius called a meeting of the Egyptian bishops, who formally deposed him from his office as teacher and nullified his ordination as presbyter. The latter action was based on alleged heretical statements. According to Jerome, his writings were corrupted and his opinions considerably garbled even in his lifetime. The statement of his excommunication was circulated by letter to many foreign Christian centers and most of them, Rome in particular, hastened to confirm it. The Roman Bishop, Fabian, was vehement in his condemnation and even his friend Heraclas deserted him.[3] It was rumored that he was an apostate and arch heretic, whereas the only charge that could honorably be made concerned the regularity of his ordination. According to Harnack, Origen's ordination was "undoubtedly an infringement of the rights of the Alexandrian bishop; at the same time, it was simply a piece of spite on the part of the latter that had kept Origen so long without any ecclesiastical consecration." [4]

Demetrius died a year after this episode and was succeeded by Heraclas, who had supported the bishops and presbyters in the banishment of Origen. There may be no connection between this attitude and his appointment to the bishopric but the fact remains that as bishop he made no effort to have the former action against Origen rescinded.

Origen's removal to Cæsarea had its advantages. Here he was near the biblical scene and also in a cultural center. Here he found peace and was honored by his friends. He resumed his work on the Hexapla and commentaries. Not content with research alone, he again became the teacher and established a school of theology at Cæsarea. One of his pupils was Gregory Thaumaturgus, who happened to be visiting Cæsarea but after meeting Origen stayed five years to complete the course. In his "Panegyric" Gregory pays a great tribute to his teacher as a scholar and as a Christian, and helps us to appreciate the unusual charm of his personality.

What promised to be a peaceful life in Cæsarea was suddenly disturbed by the renewal of persecution, this time

---

[3] The Bishops of Achaia, Palestine, Arabia, and Phoenicia completely exonerated Origen.
[4] Article in *Encyclopaedia Britannica*: "Origen."

by the cruel and barbarous Maximin. During this persecution (235) Origen lived secretly for two years in the home of a Christian lady named Juliana. Fortunately for Origen this lady had fallen heir to the writings of Symmachus, who had made a Greek translation of the Old Testament. These manuscripts proved to be of great value to Origen in his preparation of the Hexapla which will be referred to later.

The murder of Maximin in 238 put an end to the persecution in Cæsarea, so Origen returned to his lecturing and critical work, which continued uninterrupted except by occasional visits to Greece and Arabia. His last years were overshadowed by the persecution under the Emperor Decius which was more severe and systematic than any previous one. Since the authorities were instructed to seize all teachers, officials, and prominent Christians, it was not to be expected that Origen would escape this time. From Eusebius we learn that he was thrown into a dungeon where he had to wear a heavy iron collar. His legs were stretched on the rack for days at a time and he was threatened with being burned at the stake, but he refused to recant.

This persecution ceased with the death of Decius but, while Origen survived and was released, he was so weakened by his sufferings that he lived only three years. During this time he wrote letters and continued his theological and exegetical writings. The death of his benefactor, Ambrose, reduced him in his last days to poverty. He died in 254 at the age of seventy.

Personality

From the standpoint of charm and versatility, Origen is one of the most appealing characters in history. His independence of mind prejudiced orthodoxy against him so that he was never beatified, but not all saints are canonized. Owing to his comparatively liberal views, the historic Christian Church has never given him his rightful place either as a thinker or as a Christian character. Today, however, we are able to appraise him more dispassionately.

He possessed a balanced mind in which the intellectual did not destroy the spiritual. From his youth to his last hour he showed an uncommon fearlessness. His restraint under the treatment given him by Bishop Demetrius and the Egyptian Church stands as an example of Christian grace that is rare even among the saints. His rigorous self-discipline and impeccable moral life furnish a strong contrast to the lustful career of the better known Saint Augustine. It would appear that canonization has often been a matter of theological orthodoxy rather than exemplary conduct.

He had the conscientiousness and patience of the true scientist and went to great length to ascertain the exact word or phrase. He had all the admirable qualities of a good teacher and his students worshipped him. He knew how to clarify a problem and could stir his listeners emotionally as well as challenge their intellects. From Gregory Thaumaturgus we learn of his personal magnetism and ability to inspire: "He stimulated us by the deeds he did more than by the doctrines he taught." His critical judgment, creative energy, and catholicity of knowledge are not equalled in any Christian thinker before Erasmus. Intellectually, Erasmus was his equal, no doubt, but the Renaissance scholar lacked Origen's generosity of mind and affectionate disposition. It is, therefore, a pity that so noble a character and so complete a man should be only a name in the annals of Christian history.

Writings

There has never been a genius or a prophet who was not to a greater or less degree a child of his own age. No great thinker has been able to free himself completely from the ideology of his day. This is no less true of Origen. He regarded the Scripture, for instance, as "the divine writings," although he qualifies his infallible view by his discussion of the difference in quality and degree of inspiration. He uses the allegorical method in interpreting the mysterious passages but even that was due to his disbelief in the miraculous and represents a modern (though unsound) compromise. He used the allegorical method to expound the deeper sense of the Scripture. Allegory, of course, has the shortcomings of all argument by analogy and is just as fruitless. His Alexandrian partiality to Gnosis with its esoteric revelations and his Platonic idealism seemed to incline him to the mystical interpretation. As used in the nineteenth century, allegory was simply a rationalization of the miraculous element, which the scientific and critical schools had discredited; it was a justification of biblical material that obviously could not be taken literally. Such a view presupposes an impossible subtlety on the part of the Old and New Testament authors. In using allegory as a weapon to fight heresy, Origen anticipated to a certain degree an all-too-prevalent tendency today to teach superstitious beliefs because they are useful in keeping people in line, but which the teachers themselves know to be untenable. But Origen's use of allegory, as Dean Inge says, was not only "an instrument of apologetics" but was "at the same time a device to gain freedom of thought." Even so, his interpretation was more scientific than post-Reformation literalism, for often he refused to admit the literal validity of Scripture.

But in spite of Origen's partial dependence on the ideology of his time, his differentiation from that age predominates over his likeness to it. In this respect he was a great modern and the oft-repeated saying that "the ancients have stolen our thunder" can with all aptness be applied to him. This modernity is seen first of all in his exegetical and expository writings where he is recognized as the forerunner of modern textual criticism. His greatest contribution in this field is the Hexapla. The Septuagint had by this time become a polemic in the hands of Christians against Jews and both sides constantly argued over the accuracy of the text. It was clear to Origen that the then-current form of the Septuagint was unreliable, owing to the haste and ulterior motives with which copyists transcribed it. He dedicated himself to the task of restoring the original text of the Septuagint, an assignment which consumed twenty-eight years. "As an example of sheer pluck and monumental industry," writes Professor Fairweather, "there is perhaps nothing in the annals of scholarship to compare with this first achievement in the field of biblical criticism." [5] His aim was to secure a text that would be more reliable than any recension then in existence, thereby putting Christians on a par with Jews. To accomplish this task he proceeded to collect and collate all the Septuagint manuscripts. These showed hopeless discrepancies; the Hebrew text itself was replete with interpolations and faulty reconstructions. To ascertain the original text was obviously impossible but he was certain that a comparative study of these Greek manuscripts and the Hebrew Old Testament would result at least in a superior text.

His edition of the Old Testament is commonly called the Hexapla because each page consists of six parallel columns: the Hebrew text, a transliteration of the same into Greek,

[5] W. Fairweather: *Origen and Greek Patristic Theology*, p. 100.

the Greek translation of Aquila, that of Symmachus, the Septuagint, and the version of Theodotion. The differences between these texts were appropriately indicated in marginal notes, some of which apparently contained a Greek version of the Samaritan text. The Hexapla was known and used by Eusebius and Jerome. The original document was probably lost in the destruction of Cæsarea by the Arabs in 653.

Origen's exegetical writings, covering both Old and New Testaments, comprise grammatical notes, commentaries, and expository lectures, a field in which his work was equally voluminous. Little remains in the Greek original but many of the commentaries and homilies are found in the Latin translations of Jerome and Rufinus. As the first exegete, Origen served as a model for all later interpreters and even comparatively modern commentators have revealed their indebtedness to him. His knowledge of the Greek grammar and language was unsurpassed in his day. His most important commentaries are those on the Fourth Gospel, Matthew, and Romans. These expositions start with an introduction to the whole book and then follows a critical analysis of each verse. The homilies were expository sermons delivered for the most part at Cæsarea and taken down by shorthand writers. They are intellectual rather than sentimental in their appeal, and reveal their author as one of the great preachers of antiquity.

To Rufinus also we owe the preservation of Origen's chief dogmatic opus, De Principiis ("On the Fundamentals"), a philosophy of the Christian religion. Conspicuous in his treatment of man is his insistence on free will. Man has the power of choice between good and evil, a choice which entails both the possibility of achieving divinity of character and personal blame for failure. Like Jeremiah, he sees man's potentialities as independent of environment and like Ezekiel, he preaches individual responsibility. Origen stood opposed to the later Christian dogmas of inherited guilt and human depravity, teaching that man can, in spite of hostile powers, rise to the divine likeness.

Faithful follower of Plato, Origen defined God as "Spirit" and "Light," "the Source of all Mind." [6] As pure spirit God is without corporeal existence; he is not to be thought of as physical. "It is not to be supposed then that God is either a body or in a body; He is a simple intellectual nature." [7] Origen anticipated Spinoza in conceiving the world as the manifestation of God but he steers clear of pantheism by his assertion that God is spaceless and timeless. Contrary to certain passages of Scripture, says Origen, God is merciful and does not punish; punishment is a consequence of sin and is self-inflicted. God is self-limited by virtue of his own love and wisdom and can do nothing contrary to natural law.[8]

The doctrine of the Trinity had become by the beginning of the third century the central problem of Christianity. While Origen followed the prevailing trinitarian theology, he insisted on the Son's subordination to the Father, a differentiation which was at least an incipient unitarianism and which furnished a background for the Arian position in the next century.

Origen's great apologetic work was *Contra Celsum* ("Against Celsus"). Celsus, a pagan philosopher who was well informed both on Greek and Christian thought, had written an attack on Christianity called *The True Dis-*

[6] *De Principiis.* 1:1.
[7] *Ibid.*, 1:1.
[8] *Cf.* the "finite-god" theory of the present liberal school.

course. It was an able document and on close inspection appears to be not far from Origen's own theology. Although both wrote on the background of Platonism, which made their metaphysical premises somewhat similar, their ethical conclusions were diametrically opposed. Celsus bitterly denounced Christianity, Christians, and Christ. Origen's reply in eight books lacks system, is unduly emotional and prejudiced in places, and unnecessarily tedious, but it became the most complete and definitive apologetic of the early Church. Compared with fourth-century theologians, Origen was a liberal, but compared with Celsus, he naturally appears conservative. The twentieth-century religious humanist would probably find more in common with the pagan Celsus than with the Christian Origen and not all of that common ground could be called un-Christian in the light of modern criteria.

Maker of the Modern Mind

Earlier in this chapter it was conceded that Origen was in many respects a child of his age. Much of his theology was in line with the normal belief, as might be expected. The amazing thing is that he should have given expression to as much heterodoxy as he did; and here he reveals his contemporaneousness. We can be sure that his liberalism was much more articulate than the extant form of his works indicates, for Rufinus, through whose Latin translations most of his dogmatic and interpretative writings are preserved, expressly stated that he would translate Origen's books only with the understanding that he, like Jerome, would excise or amend all heterodox statements so as to protect Origen from slander and charges of heresy.

Origen was the first scientific theologian, and as William

Fairweather says, "Within the sphere of Christian dogma he was the first, and he has been the only independent, builder." [9] That he was the watershed of early Christian thought, and represented its most progressive expression, is also attested by Harnack: "Orthodox theology of all creeds has never yet advanced beyond the circle first mapped out by his mind. She has suspected and corrected her founder, and she has thought she could lop off his heterodox opinions as if they were accidental excrescences." [10]

The soil having been prepared by the Greek-writing Jew, Philo, it was Origen's purpose to sow the seed of Hellenism on a Jewish field, to make a philosophical statement of Christianity that would counteract extreme Gnosticism and also harmonize the apostolic tradition with Judaic-Greek philosophy. Following in the steps of Clement, his teacher, he recognized the necessity of finding a philosophy for Christianity that would meet the intellectual demands of that day, a theology that would ally itself with Greek culture and the scientific spirit. Tertullian, on the other hand, stoutly opposed such a cultural development. Clement meant to endow Christianity with the spirit of Plato; he saw in the Greek philosophy a preparation for the Gospel similar to that of the Law for the Jews. Origen went still farther in his advocacy of reason, tolerance, and cultural adjustment. "Il est encore un vrai fils de la Grèce. Il a leur curiosité d'esprit. Comme eux, il éprouve un besoin irrésistable de poser des questions." [11] Like Spinoza, he discarded everything that could not be reconciled with reason. Contrast Origen's rationalism with the blind belief of Ter-

[9] *Op. cit.*, p. 212.
[10] *History of Dogma:* Vol. 2, p. 334.
[11] E. de Faye: *Origène*, 1, p. 220.

tullian: "I believe it because it is absurd" or the authoritarianism of Augustine: "I would not believe the Gospel if the authority of the Catholic Church did not compel me."

His idea of faith is distinctly Protestant. He anticipates Luther's belief in justification by faith alone but combines with it the teaching of Jesus that a faith which does not express itself in ethical conduct is invalid. It is this ethical emphasis in contrast to sacramentalism that stamps him as a modernist. The ethical criterion with him was no mere theory but found direct application in his own life, which was pure and blameless. "There have been few fathers of the church," writes Harnack, "whose life-story leaves such an impression of purity behind it as that of Origen." Another great Church historian who penetrated the mists of orthodoxy to see the greatness and the goodness of Origen was Mosheim, who wrote: "Certainly if any man deserves to stand first in the catalogue of saints and martyrs and to be annually held up as an example to Christians, this is the man; for except the apostles of Jesus Christ and their companions, I know of no one among all those ennobled and honored as saints who excelled him in virtue and holiness."

It is in his biblical criticism particularly that Origen's anticipation of modern liberal study is most clearly seen. In denying the literal validity of Scripture, he says, "What man of sense will suppose that the first and second and third day, and the evening and morning existed without sun, moon, and stars? Or that God walked in a garden in the evening, and that Adam hid himself under a tree? Or that the devil took Jesus into a high mountain, whence he could see the kingdoms of the Persians and Scythians and Indians?" [12] In the same work he writes: "There are some passages which are not literally true, but absurd and impos-

[12] *De Principiis*, IV, 1:16.

sible." [13] Regarding some of the so-called laws of Moses, he comments: "I should blush to admit that God has given such commands which are inferior to many human enactments." He revolted against the anthropomorphism of the Old Testament and referred to such stories as Moses' seeing God as "old wives' fables." [14] He designated as immoral and unfit to read such material as Lot's intercourse with his daughters, Abraham and his licentious conduct, and Jacob's amours.[15] He regarded as barbarous the command in Genesis 17:14 to do away with uncircumcised children. His treatment of the New Testament from the critical standpoint is remarkably advanced, for he calls attention to various discrepancies and contradictions in the Gospels.[16] Origen was one of the first to escape from the Jewish and Zoroastrian eschatology, and for him, as for Paul, immortality was a spiritual continuity and not a resurrection of the body.[17] His eschatology was at variance with the current thought on judgment, heaven, and hell. The modern relegation of miracle to a secondary and non-important rôle was also anticipated by this great third-century teacher. "Even were I going to admit that a demon named Aesculapius had the power of healing bodily diseases, I might still remark to those who are amazed at such cures or at the prophecies of Apollo, that such curative power is of itself neither good nor bad but within reach of godless as well as of honest folk; while in the same way, it does not follow that he who can foretell the future is on that account an honest and upright man. . . . The power of healing diseases is not evidence of anything specially divine." [18]

His views on salvation and the sacraments differ materi-

[13] *Ibid.*, IV, 1:18.   [14] *Ibid.*, II, 4:3.
[15] *Ibid.*, IV, 1:9.
[16] *Commentary on John*, X, 2–3; *de Prin.*, IV, 1:18.
[17] *Contra Celsum*, VI, 29.   [18] *Ibid.*, III, 25.

ally from the later Augustinian thought. He recognized
that the sacraments were not magically efficacious and re-
gretted that "not all those who are baptized in water are
forthwith bathed in the Holy Spirit." [19] He declared that
men are saved by living spiritual lives, not by the perform-
ance of sacramental acts. He had a justifiable interest in
dogma but he renounced dogmatism and despised shibbo-
leths.

The Forgotten Man of Christianity

Origen is the forgotten man of Christianity. He is forgotten because orthodoxy suppressed his teaching and outlawed him as a heretic.

If Christianity had followed Origen instead of Augustine, Hellenism rather than Africanism, its history would
have been more prophetic and less legalistic, more liberal
and less authoritarian, more eclectic and less exclusive.
Constantine's imperial decree in 313 A.D., by which the
Christian Church went quantitative, was the ratification of
the Latin credo and in purging itself of Origenism, the
Church succumbed to a devitalized and stilted orthodoxy.

The reaction against Origen received its greatest impetus
from the Christological controversies in which the Arians
claimed Origen for their party, followed by the unorthodox Pelagians and the Nestorians. This alignment threw
the weight of the orthodox leaders inevitably and permanently against Origen. His condemnation was shared in
the fourth century by Bishop Theophilus of Alexandria
and in the sixteenth by Luther, who questioned whether he
was not "doomed to endless torment" for his impiety. The
great humanist Pico della Mirandola was practically con-

[19] *Homily on Numbers*, III, 1.

demned for declaring that it was more reasonable to
believe that Origen was saved. Since the seventh century
he has received the eternal condemnation of the papacy.
On the other hand, few men in the history of Christianity
have received such superlative tributes as those paid to
Origen. Jerome called him "the greatest master of the
Church after the Apostles" and fifteen hundred years later
Bishop Westcott was to honor him by saying: "His life was
an uninterrupted prayer." His real worth was also perceived by Canon Farrar who said: "In the history of the
early Church there is no name nobler or more remarkable
than that of Origen. Few men have rendered to the cause
of Christianity such splendid services, or lived from child-
hood to old age a life so laborious and so blameless. Anathematized for centuries by the ignorance and prejudice of
men incomparably his inferiors in learning and saintliness,
he has exercised an influence deeper in many respects than
that even of Augustine." [20]

Fresh evaluations of the past must now be made; new
definitions of greatness must be found. A just recognition of
Origen as a greater figure than Augustine, both in intellect
and character, is long overdue. To arrive at such an appreciation is to imagine what Christianity might have been
rather than to view it in the light of what it became. For
those who value the Greek spirit above the Latin spirit,
Origen should indeed take on the halo of a saint. He was
the first Christian liberal.

[20] *Op. cit.*, p. 291.

Early Christian Radicalism

Heredity and Environment

THE FIRST PREREQUISITE for a study of Christian history is the unqualified recognition of the syncretistic nature of early Christianity. The traditional view holds that the Christian religion is a revelation, unique and independent. It assumes that Christianity was not historically conditioned but was a divine essence, supernaturally revealed and unaffected by previous deposits or contemporary conditions.

The critical view, favored by progressive scholarship, might be called the evolutionary or genetic approach, which takes into account social and cultural forces, antecedent factors and environmental influences. This theory states that Christianity cannot be properly understood independent of its early milieu. Christianity was born in a Jewish home and grew up in a Greek household; or, to change the figure, its roots were Jewish and the environment that influenced its growth was largely Hellenistic.

The issue can be stated thus: Is Christianity static and quantitative or developmental and qualitative? Considered as a unique revelation, Christianity becomes a quantity, something to accept or reject *in toto*, an entity immune to cultural change. Considered as a growth, it becomes an assimilative religion in which change is primary and modification is not only possible but necessary for life.

As the offspring of Judaism the Christian religion received three abstract or philosophical conceptions: monotheism, ethics, and teleology, or faith in a divine goal. From the institutional standpoint Israel bequeathed the Synagogue, the Sabbath, the Canon, and the Diaspora, or Dispersion communities. The former group of principles became the essential religious philosophy of Jesus; the latter group of institutions had an indirect influence in the formation of Christianity.

While the legacy of Israel is generally admitted today, many would still be reluctant to concede the second phase: the environmental factor. It must be recognized, of course, that here the influence is not so demonstrable, and if present, is in most instances only indirect. But it is inconceivable that the Jewish ethic of Jesus could survive and dominate the Graeco-Roman world, as it did in the first three hundred years of its history, without accommodating itself to the thought-forms of that world. This modification is usually referred to as the Hellenization of Christianity. Such ideas as the supernatural birth of a religious hero, deification, Lord, Savior, miraculous resurrection, Last Supper, baptismal rites, divine healing, and mystic union with the deity were widespread in the religions of Mithras, Attis, and other Mysteries. Some authorities are unwilling to see in these pagan forms anything more than analogies, but the fact remains that in the critical period of Christian history the religion of Jesus became the religion about Jesus; the informal community of "The Way" became a complex ecclesiastical institution with sacraments, which were believed to be magically efficacious, with divinely ordained officials, a rigidly defined creed, and an infallible canon of Scripture. Where did all this originate? Those who hold to the developmental theory feel that these changes represent an assimilative process in which pagan thought-patterns, and perhaps sacramental practices themselves, were gradually taken over by the Christian leaders.

For the first three hundred years of its history Christianity was in a state of flux and could have become something quite different from its normative form. If Arius, for instance, had had a larger following at Nicea, would not Christianity have become unitarian instead of trinitarian? If Constantine had not made Christianity compulsory, would it have become the "ghost of the Roman Empire," an authoritarian system? If Augustine had not been converted to the Catholic Church, which he resisted till he was thirty-two, would it have assumed the same theological features?

The Graeco-Roman world, in which Christianity took form, teemed with all kinds of religious philosophies. To recognize the religious and cultural atmosphere as essentially Hellenistic is to concede the possibility of pagan influences in both the mystical and institutional aspects of early Christianity. This interpenetration, beginning with the Gentile expansion under Paul, is a primary factor in the divergence of the organized Church from the simple Gospel of Jesus. It is hardly likely that the Jewish ethic of Jesus could be propagated in the Gentile world without recourse to pagan terms and thought-patterns. Added to the Greek mysticism was the Latin institutionalism. The result was an externalism quite as spiritually devitalizing as the older Jewish legalism. The dogmatic, legalistic, and sacramental character of fourth-century Christianity came largely through the influence of three Africans: Tertullian, Cyprian, and Augustine. They cast the Christian religion into a mould of unreason, superstition, and static quiescence.

But the Greek culture had other legacies to bestow upon nascent Christianity beside pagan myths. There were teachers who would have baptized Christianity with the Hellenic spirit of free inquiry and enlightenment. There were schools which would have enriched it with the spirit of rationalism. Two such schools were Alexandria and Antioch.

The Alexandrian School

Cosmopolitan Alexandria had achieved an undisputed preeminence in the cultural world and could boast of the greatest library in existence. It had been the center of Greek and Jewish learning and in the Graeco-Roman age became the rival of Antioch and Rome as a seat of Christian scholarship. It was the meeting place of many streams of thought, a channel where cross currents met, and the resulting syncretism produced an unusual tolerance. Here, Greek and Jew, Christian and pagan, sat side by side to hear the lectures; here, diverse philosophies intermingled and colored each other. It was Alexandria that produced the Septuagint, which included the "Wisdom of Jesus, son of Sirach" and other excellent books rejected in the more conservative Palestinian circles. This inclusiveness made itself felt also in the case of the prominent authorities on the New Testament canon, where the accepted lists were invariably longer than those of Gaul, Italy, Asia Minor, or Syria. Eclectic Alexandria gave birth to Philo and the Jewish-Greek rapprochement on the background of which was built the Johannine Christology and Christian Platonism. It was at Alexandria too that the necessity was first seen for systematizing Christian theology and reconciling the apostolic tradition with Greek thought.

The Alexandrian School of Theology was a well-established institution by the middle of the second century with Pantaenus as its president. Instruction was given in natural science, astronomy, geometry, philosophy, ethics, and theology. The theological school developed from an earlier catechetical school which prepared neophytes for baptism. Pantaenus was succeeded by his famous pupil Clement, who also became presbyter of the church at Alexandria.

Clement, a Greek both by birth and philosophical training, envisaged the happy union of Hellenism and Christianity. He appreciated the contribution of secular learning and made room for reason along with revelation. This tempering of mysticism with rationalism was the secret of the Alexandrian spirit passed on by Clement to his disciple and successor, Origen. Just as Philo had attempted to fuse Judaism with Hellenism, the Alexandrian School under Clement and Origen aimed to apply Greek culture to Christianity, to combine faith with reason. Philosophy, said Clement, should not be the enemy but the handmaid of Christian truth. This harmony was attempted within the bounds of revelation and assumed highly speculative forms, but it was broader and more tolerant than the orthodoxy which later prevailed.

Clement's system was a synthesis of biblical and philosophical learning and represents the beginning of the transformation of the ecclesiastical tradition into a philosophy of religion. He tried to adjust the Gospel to the spirit of the times, which is a mark of liberalism.[1] Clement's contribution is well stated by Adolf Harnack: "Here then is found, in form, and content, the scientific Christian doctrine

---

[1] Any reference to liberalism in the first four centuries of the Christian era must be thought of as relative to that age, a comparative liberalism that usually went under the label of heresy.

of religion which, while not contradicting the faith, does not merely support or explain it in a few places, but raises it to another and higher intellectual sphere, namely, out of the province of authority and obedience into that of clear knowledge and inward intellectual assent emanating from love to God." [2]

Clement legitimized the Greek culture within Christendom and through this amalgamation found intellectual freedom, all of which contrasts strongly with the narrow authoritarianism of Tertullian, Cyprian, and Augustine. His eclecticism was accomplished without betraying the original Gospel; in fact, his emphasis on the goodness of God and the moral responsibility of man is central in the teachings of Jesus.

The Antiochian School

The Antiochian School was not a formal institution like Alexandria with a faculty, student body and succession of presidents so much as the center of a certain system of interpretation, or a school of thought. The school of Antioch followed the historical and exegetical method in contrast to the Alexandrian emphasis on allegory. Theologically, the two schools were rivals for two centuries. Paul of Samosata, an earlier teacher in Antioch, had championed the Monarchian theory that Christ was only human until visited by the Holy Spirit. Adherents to the Monarchian view held that the deity of Christ as viewed by the more orthodox theologians implied polytheism (monarchianism —the government of one God). This anti-trinitarian tendency was typical of the Antiochian School and produced the Arian and Nestorian heresies. At Antioch also was

[2] *History of Dogma:* Vol. 2, pp. 324, 5.

developed the historical method in biblical criticism. Both of these progressive tendencies point to the influence of Lucian (d. 312), the founder of the Antiochian School. Along with Origen, Lucian initiated the direct exegetical treatment of the Bible and prepared the way for the textual criticism.

It remained for one of Lucian's pupils, Arius, to bring the Christological controversy to a head. Arius, as presbyter of the church at Baucalis, was well known for his learning and courage. The dispute between Arius and his Bishop, Alexander, began about 320. Arius represented the teaching of Lucian and Origen that Christ was a created being, not of the substance of God, and not eternal. However superior to other created beings, the Son remains nevertheless a creature and is inferior to the Creator. This was the only position he could take and be clear on the unity and self-contained existence of God. Of course, he did not achieve a satisfactory theology because he placed Jesus somewhere between God and man, a lower god. Like Origen, he was unable to penetrate completely the ideology of that age and take the unequivocal stand that Jesus was strictly human. But the distinction which he initiated was enough to precipitate debate and lay the foundation for later unitarian thought.

The Emperor Constantine was ill-informed in such matters but he knew that it was to his advantage to keep the Church intact and not divided by heresy. So he called an ecumenical council at Nicea in 325 to decide the Christological question and formulate a creed. The unitarian party at the council was naturally outnumbered. Arius was struck in the face when he stood up to speak. Many of the delegates left the hall immediately so as not to hear the heretic's words. Constantine presided but had no idea as to what it was all about and came to a decision by simply counting hands. The conclusion read that "Jesus Christ was Son of God, the only begotten of the Father, God of God, Light of Light, Very God of Very God, begotten and not made, consubstantial with the Father." Such a statement obviously protests too much. Arius was anathematized and excommunicated. But the battle continued to rage even after the Nicene Council: the followers of Arius contending that the trinitarian formula was polytheistic, and the orthodox party under Athanasius fighting the heresy until it was practically stamped out.

Another thorn in the flesh of the Church was the British monk Pelagius (360–420), whose advocacy of free will and individual freedom aroused a violent controversy in the early part of the fifth century. Pelagius was a man of great learning and moral earnestness. We discover him first in Rome, denouncing public and private morals and preaching an ethical religion. By 400 A.D. the process of formalization had set in; the ethical content of Jesus' teachings had been sacrificed to the theological method of the organized Church; the emphasis on human perfectability had been given up in favor of total depravity.

The clergy in Rome rationalized the excesses of immorality on the grounds of human weakness. Pelagius on his part was convinced that the doctrine of human depravity and original sin undermined the human will and insulted God. We are born, he argued, with no bias towards good or evil and there is no such thing as original sin, "sin being a thing of will and not of nature." If sin were natural and innate it would be chargeable to God, the Creator. The heresy of Pelagius lay in his assertion that the determining factor is the human will which takes the initiative. The orthodox position was that the initiative was taken by the divine will which offered grace to fallen man. Using as his motto the words "If I ought, I can," Pelagius maintained that man is able to live without sin, if he wills it, because God gave him this ability. In denying original sin and the fall of man, Pelagius came into conflict with Augustine, whose own experience had probably satisfied him that man is inherently sinful and can be saved only by reason of a special act of divine grace. Pelagius replied that men are not necessarily evil and that salvation or destiny depends on the free choice of the individual. Augustine went to work. In addition to writing a dozen books against the rapidly growing heresy, he called two councils and with them secured the papal condemnation of Pelagianism.

Africanism *versus* Hellenism

By the fifth century the Christian Church had decided which way it would go. It chose the formalism of the Latins rather than the rationalism of the Greeks. Christianity from the first had been exposed to the Greek culture in the Alexandrian school, just as Judaism had, but it did not take full advantage of the contiguity. In rejecting Origen, Arius, and Pelagius and accepting Tertullian, Cyprian, and Augustine, Christianity turned its back on tolerance, culture, and rational thinking and embraced dogmatism, legalism, and sacramentalism. Christianity could have profited by the wisdom of the Greeks, but instead it cast its lot with the supernaturalism of the Latins. Had it appropriated some of the pagan culture of the Graeco-Roman world, it would have been spared many of its modern ideological troubles. The rejection of Hellenism brought on a thousand years of darkness, broken only by the Renaissance. Greek paganism, being assimilative and eclectic, attempted to absorb the worthy elements in its environment; African Christianity, ascetic and exclusive, scorned the life of culture. Paganism had medicine and physicians; Christianity, believing in demon possession, resorted to incantation. Paganism, with its profound belief in man, would have benefited Christianity a thousand times more than African sacramentalism, with its distrust of man. When Christianity turned a deaf ear to Origen, who would have baptized religion with reason, and elected instead to follow Augustine, who plunged it into the dark night of superstition, it stooped to conquer.

Since Christianity catered to the masses, it had to submit itself to their mentality, a phenomenon recognized in a saying of Dean Inge: "A religion succeeds, not because it is true, but because it suits its worshipers." Latin Christianity with its infallible authority was welcome to the populace; it was an opiate; it enabled the people to conduct themselves with a "maximum of intellectual frugality." Religion paid the price of success when it coincided with the prevalent antipathy of the lower classes towards mental activity. It was easier to partake of the benefits of religion by participation in mysterious rites than by moral self-realization. It was easier to believe in the worthlessness of man than in his divinity. Myths are more romantic than cold facts. Pageantry, miracle, and magic are visible and therefore (to the untrained mind) *real*.

The most significant contribution of the Hebrew prophets and Jesus to civilization was the belief in the divine worth of human personality. Practically all of Jesus' principles and parables revolve about this axis. But when the religion of Jesus became the religion *about* Jesus, and Christianity had changed from a personal, moral experience to a theology, the divine in man was lost sight of.

The victory of Carthage over Alexandria for the hand of Christianity meant a defeat for the *genus homo*. Enter Augustine with the official pronouncement that "God created man upright, but man having of his own free will become depraved and having been justly condemned, begat a posterity in the same state of depravation and condemnation." Christianity preferred Tertullian's delight in the torture of the damned to the universalistic faith of Pelagius. It adopted Cyprian's dictum that "without the church there is no salvation" rather than the heretical teaching of Antioch that all pre-Christian souls who loved God were redeemed. In the victory of Carthage over Alexandria the Christian Church chose to be sensational and morbid rather than rational and sane.

Africanism won over Hellenism for the hand of Christianity but the Greek spirit reasserted itself from time to time within Christendom, and those recurrences through the centuries tell the story of liberalism.

III

Erasmus

Citizen of the World

RABELAIS SAID that Erasmus defended his convictions "this side of burning." The same can be said, for that matter, of Rabelais himself, as well as of Galileo and Voltaire. Without detracting too much from the glory of the martyr, something must be said for the genius who is clever enough to say the same things the martyr said and remain alive. Erasmus, for one, thought he could do more for the world alive than dead.

Thereby hangs a riddle. When the evidence is all in and the verdict is ready, who will be acclaimed—the impassioned reformer or the prudent scholar?—the militant prophet who storms the enemy's gates and carries the day, or the pacifistic philosopher who refuses to take sides openly and by his writing appeals to time? The revolutionist or the evolutionist? Luther or Erasmus? The answer, of course, depends on the philosophy of the judge. There will always be pacifists and interventionists and it is unfair to say that one is right and the other wrong. A glance backward shows that both types have been necessary for progress. Every creative period of history has had its fanatical reformer and its dispassionate humanist. It is idle to lament that the one could not have become like the other.

Frail of body and supersensitive in nerves, Erasmus was

too cautious a soul to be a hero. In times of grave decision he sidestepped the issue, fearing to commit himself. Yet his aloofness was at once his failure and his success. With him freedom of mind was everything. He refused to be a slave to any party or cause. The concept of democracy, viewed from any angle, can be reduced to one word—*freedom*. This was the ideal nearest the heart of Erasmus and an examination of his works today reveals him as the true prophet of the modern spirit. Therein lies his greatness as a liberal.

The pen of Erasmus more than anything else in the world precipitated the Reformation and with it, religious freedom. And yet, it was Luther's rebellion alone that made it possible for lesser men than Erasmus to enjoy the freedom which he preached. Both were right and both were radical in their way. Erasmus gave his life to the cause of peace, unity, and tolerance. Hating violence and fearing schism, he stayed in his study—not from cowardice but from a deep-seated conviction that through education and enlightenment, the regeneration of the Church and universal religion would come. His aim was political and religious unity, and he was the first one to envisage a "United States of Europe."

His failure to take sides actively in the Reformation is readily understood in the light of his life-purpose. Erasmus represented an attempt to amalgamate the Greek and Hebraic streams, the Classics and the Gospel. Visualizing a synthesis of the two cultures, he typified in essence both the Renaissance and the Reformation; if, for the moment, the two movements can be considered separately. As H. A. Brautigam puts it: "As much opposed to the excesses of a pleasure-bent life as to the irrationalities of theology, he conceived it his mission to Christianize the Renaissance and to humanize Christianity." [1] This was precisely the ideal of his ancient prototype, Origen.

Erasmus' birth in cosmopolitan Holland fitted him well for the task of combining the Hellenic and Christian traditions. "I wish to be called a citizen of the world," he said, "the common friend of all states, or, rather, a sojourner in all." To Budde, the French Humanist, he wrote: "That you are very patriotic will be praised by some and easily forgiven by every one; but in my opinion it is more philosophic to treat men and things as though we held this world the common fatherland of all."

Early Studies and Writing

Erasmus was born in Rotterdam in 1466, the illegitimate son of the priest, Gerard.[2] His elementary education was received at the well-known school of Deventer, from which Thomas à Kempis had once graduated. At one time the school boasted some 2000 students. The principal subject in the curriculum was Latin, which, according to Erasmus, was taught in a barbarous and silly manner.

In 1484 Erasmus was presented to Rudolph Agricola, a famous Humanist, as the top ranking student of the Deventer School and author of the prize poem. He strongly desired to go on to the university but his guardian practically forced him to enter a monastery, the priory of Emmaus at Steyn. In the cloister he reveled in the Latin authors and was greatly impressed by the anti-clerical and undogmatic writings of Lorenzo Valla, an early contemporary, who scorned asceticism and scholasticism.

---

[1] Eugene E. Bewkes: *Experience, Reason, and Faith*, p. 435.
[2] Charles Reade's *The Cloister and the Hearth* is based on the life of Gerard and his son, Erasmus.

Erasmus himself began his career as a writer at this time, pleading for a union of religion and culture and foreshadowing the satirical jibes of his later *Praise of Folly.* His early literary efforts won for him a position as secretary to the Bishop of Cambrai. Shortly after taking this office he was ordained priest at Utrecht by Henry of Burgundy. Of his life in the episcopal residence, we know nothing except that he soon tired of it and in 1495 contrived to enter the University of Paris.

He matriculated in the College of Montaigu where he entered upon the scholastic studies of Duns Scotus. Nauseated by the unhygienic conditions as well as by the barren sophistries of scholasticism, he soon returned to Holland to recuperate. Back again in Paris, he boarded with a friend and continued his studies. He made many friends, among them the scholars Faustus Andrelinus and Robert Gaguin. While Paris was a corrupt city, there seems to be no evidence that Erasmus at any time yielded to its pleasures. He received financial help from the Bishop of Cambrai and also took pupils, one of whom was William Blount, Lord Mountjoy, later tutor of Henry VIII and father of Charles Blount, the early English Deist.

When a writer or speaker in the present pragmatic times quotes or alludes to Horace or Vergil, he is apt to be called "a gentleman of the old school." With the decline of the classics it is difficult for moderns to appreciate the relish with which each morsel of antiquity was received at the peak of the Renaissance. A Humanist validated his argument by quoting chapter and verse from Tacitus, Seneca, or Livy, just as a theologian used the Bible. Erasmus was one of the first to fall heir to the wealth of ancient wisdom, for his birth coincided with that of the printing press, and during the first half of his life most of the Latin literature was printed for the first time. Erasmus himself edited many of the Greek and Latin classics.

Returning to Paris from his first short visit to England in 1499, he was confined with an attack of fever. He spent his convalescent days in the enjoyable and not too irksome task of selecting epigrams from the Latin authors and commenting upon them. From this pastime emerged the *Adages* or *Familiar Quotations from the Classics*, which he dedicated to Lord Mountjoy. New editions of the *Adages* appeared from time to time and the final redaction contained 4,151 proverbs. Many of the quotations were accompanied by lengthy homilies in which Erasmus amplified these quotations and traced their history. In his comment on the adage "Evil communications corrupt good manners," for instance, after assigning the verse to Menander, he quoted Paul, Tertullian, Aristotle, Seneca, and his own contemporary, John Colet, all of whom had made use of the expression. The *Adages* went through sixty editions during the author's life-time and in the century that followed no fewer than seventy-five editions were demanded. Translated from the Latin into English, German, Italian, and Dutch, it became a standard work and influenced the thought and style of Montaigne, Bacon, and Shakespeare.

It was at this time that Erasmus discovered Greek and settled down to a study of the language. As the foremost Greek scholar of his day, he later remarked: "We have in Latin at best some small brooks and turbid pools, while the Greeks have the purest fountains and rivers flowing with gold." He began to perceive that Greek was indispensable for an accurate knowledge both of the Old and New Testaments and the early theological works. As the original editions of the Hellenic philosophers and dramatists came off the presses of Aldus and Froben, Erasmus read and mastered their contents—Homer, Hesiod, Aristotle, Aristophanes, Herodotus, Plutarch, Plato, Pindar, Pausanius and the rest. His Hebrew studies were also begun at this time but he did not go far into that field. He saw little in the Old Testament that had permanent and universal value. "Would that the Christian Church did not rely so much on the Old Testament," he wrote to a friend, "which, although it was only given for a certain time and is full of shadows, is almost preferred to the Christian writings. And thus we turn from Christ, who alone suffices us."—an observation that might well be applied to many modern Christians who, in many instances, are more concerned with the mythical stories of the Old Testament than with the ethical teachings of the Sermon on the Mount.

Erasmus left Paris in 1501 and for three years sojourned in his native land and in Louvain, where he was offered a university instructorship but declined. While in Holland he produced a small devotional book called *Enchiridion Militis Christiani* or *Handbook of the Christian Knight*. This was his first definition of the religious life. The religion of Erasmus, like that of Origen, was based on the Sermon on the Mount and the Greek tradition. The sixteenth-century expressions of these two traditions, the German mystics and the Florentine Platonic Academy, were the immediate sources for the Erasmian ideal. Worlds apart in many respects, they agreed in their opposition to sacrament and their emphasis on personal, moral living. The mystics of Northern Europe, sensing the externalism of organization, creed, and ceremony, taught the life of the spirit. The Christian Platonists, such as Pico della Mirandola, placed reason above dogma and asserted that religion was a life, not a set of rules.

"External worship is not condemned," wrote Erasmus in his *Enchiridion*, "but God is pleased only by the inward piety of the worshiper." As part and parcel of the Renaissance (much more a part of it than the Reformers), he ignored cult and sacerdotalism, scorned the life of meticulous religiosity, and always placed right above rite. Much of the *Enchiridion* was a rehearsal for his *Praise of Folly*, as the following passage reveals: "The true way to worship the saints is to imitate their virtues; they care more for this than for a hundred candles. . . . You venerate the bones of Paul laid away in a shrine, but not the mind of Paul, enshrined in his writings."

England

When Erasmus crossed the English Channel he was cured of the Middle Ages and was intellectually reborn. His first visit was at the invitation of his pupil, Lord Mountjoy, who introduced him to the two leading English Humanists, Thomas More, the author of *Utopia*, and John Colet. Erasmus' enthusiasm for England led to several additional visits from 1505 to 1517. His friendships in educational and religious circles multiplied and in 1511 he was appointed lecturer in Greek at the University of Cambridge. Later he accepted the Margaret Tudor chair of divinity, an appointment made possible through his friendship with John Fisher, Chancellor of the University. The Archbishop of Canterbury granted him numerous benefices and a pension for life.

Among his appointments was an honorary or nominal rectorship at Aldington in Kent. Whatever supervision he gave to this parish was *in absentia*, for he probably never saw the place except on a visit to the shrine of Saint Thomas

of Canterbury, described by Erasmus and also reproduced
by the biographer, Preserved Smith. Erasmus' description
of the idolatry of Pre-Reformation England—a humorous
preview of things to come—shows how far he and Colet
were from being devout believers.

"On the altar is the point of the sword with which the
archbishop's skull was cloven. We religiously kissed its
sacred rust, on account of our love for the martyr. Entering
the crypt, the skull itself was displayed to us, incased in
silver, though with a part at the top left bare to be kissed.
There also are hung up in the dark the hair shirts, girdles,
and bands with which that prelate used to subdue the flesh.
The very appearance of them made us shudder, such a
reproach were they to our luxurious softness. Thence we
returned into the choir, on the north side of which are
repositories for relics. When these were unlocked, from
them were produced an amazing quantity of bones: skulls,
jawbones, teeth, hands, fingers, and arms, all of which we
adoringly kissed, until my companion, a man less well
disposed to this department of religion than I could have
wished, not over politely refused to kiss an arm which had
bleeding flesh still attached to it . . ."

Upon being shown the wealth of vestments and money
placed on the shrine by pious devotees, Colet remarked to
the attendant that since the saint was so liberal to the desti-
tute when he himself was poor, now that he was so rich he
might not care if some poor woman took a small part of the
great riches for the relief of her family. In the sacristy
where more relics were exhibited, the guide, relates Mr.
Smith, "had the poor judgment to offer Colet as a souvenir
a handkerchief once used by the saint to wipe the sweat
from his brow and to blow his nose, and showing plainly
signs of the use to which it had been put. Colet regarded it

with a derisive whistle and turned contemptuously away. As they were leaving, an old man offered them St. Thomas's shoe to be kissed, whereupon Colet flared up with: 'What do the dolts mean? Next they will bring us his excrements to kiss.' "

Erasmus also described in the *Colloquies* a visit to the shrine of Our Lady of Walsingham, where he was shown Saint Peter's knuckle and the milk of the Virgin still liquid and saw her statue nod. Instead of bestowing gold on the altar he composed a Greek poem and left it as a votive offering.

Such incidents together with the impressions gained on his first visit to Italy, where superstition was more rampant than in England, had much to do with the preparation of his mind for *Praise of Folly*. Arriving in Bologna in 1506 he witnessed the triumphal entry of Pope Julius II after conquering the city. Rather than being awed by the spectacle of the Vicar of Christ marching at the head of his army and hierarchy, Erasmus could be impressed only by the discrepancy between the bloody exploits of the Prince of the Church and the sacrificial life of the Prince of Peace. His year in Italy was occupied with study, travel, and the friendship of scholars. The art of Bellini, Titian, and Giorgione at Venice; the Duomo, the Baptistry, Santa Maria Novella, and the Piazza Signoria at Florence; the paintings of Michelangelo and Raphael at Rome—all this was lost on the Humanist scholar, who had an aesthetic blind spot. The libraries and universities of Italy sufficed for him and he would have settled permanently in Rome or Florence if he had not been living in high hopes of a preferment from the new King of England, Henry VIII.

After returning to England, while resting at the home of his friend, More, Erasmus dashed off *Praise of Folly*, the

most effective of all his writings. The title in Latin is a pun
on the name of his host: *Encomium Moriae*.[3] This sketch
is a Voltairean satire on the manners of the day. Dame
Folly passes in review the rhetoricians, the lawyers, the
philosophers, the landlords, the scholars, the military, and
the divines, each one the object of jest and coarse invective.
Through Dame Folly Erasmus facetiously mirrors the corruption of the Church, the vice of the clergy, and the stupidity of the theologians, but behind the trifling pasquin-
ades of the jester are the bitter arrows of the critic; behind
the mask of the clown are the true features of the serious
scholar. Luther's tirades against Romanism were tame by
comparison. His favorite object of ridicule were the Scholastics.

"They will tell you how the world was created. They
will show you the crack where sin crept in and corrupted
mankind. They will explain to you how Christ was formed
in the Virgin's womb; how accident subsists in synaxis without domicile in *place*. . . . Like the Stoics, they have their
paradoxes—whether it is a smaller crime to kill a thousand
men than to mend a beggar's shoe on a Sunday; whether it
is better that the whole world should perish than that a
woman should tell one small lie. Then there are Realists,
Nominalists, Thomists, Albertists, Occamists, Scotists—all
so learned that an apostle would have no chance with them
in argument. They will tell you that although St. Paul
could define what faith is, yet he could not define it ade-
quately as they can. An apostle might affirm the synaxis;
but if an apostle was asked about the *terminus ad quem* and
the *terminus a quo* of Transubstantiation, or how one body
could be in two places at once, or how Christ's body in
heaven differed from Christ's body on the cross or in the

---

[3] More's defense of *Praise of Folly* is a classic in its own right. It is
given in condensed form in Froude's *Life and Letters of Erasmus*, pp. 143 ff.

sacrament, neither Paul nor Peter could explain half as
well as the Scotists. Doubtless Peter and the other apostles
knew the mother of Jesus, but they did not know as well as
a modern divine how she escaped the taint of Adam's sin.
Peter received the keys of knowledge and power, but Peter
did not comprehend how he could have the key of knowledge and yet be without knowledge."

Dame Folly hurls her darts at the friars:

"They call it a sign of holiness to be unable to read. They
bray out the Psalms in the churches like so many jackasses.
They do not understand a word of them, but they fancy the
sound is soothing to the ears of the saints. The mendicant
friars howl for alms along the street. They pretend to
resemble the apostles, and they are filthy, ignorant, im-
pudent vagabonds. They have their rules, forsooth. Yes,
rules—how many knots, for instance, there may be in a
shoe-string, how their petticoats should be colored, how
much cloth should be used in their hoods, and how many
hours they may sleep. But for all else—for conduct and
character, they quarrel with each other and curse each
other."

With Luther, he held in horror the commercialization of
religious practices:

"What shall I say of such as cry up and maintain the
cheat of pardons and indulgences? that by these compute
the time of each soul's residence in purgatory, and assign
them a longer or shorter continuance according as they
purchase more or fewer of these paltry pardons? By this
easy way of purchasing pardons, any notorious highway-
man, any plundering soldier, any bribetaking judge, shall
disburse some part of his unjust gains and so think all his
grossest impieties atoned for. So many perjuries, lusts,
drunkennesses, quarrels, bloodsheds, cheats, treacheries, de-

baucheries, shall all be, as it were, struck a bargain for; and such a contract made as if they had paid off all arrears and might now begin a new score."

Nor do the popes escape this determined assault of Dame Folly:

"Now, as to the popes of Rome, who pretend themselves Christ's vicars: if they would imitate his exemplary life by preaching incessantly, by taking up with poverty, nakedness, hunger, and contempt of the world; if they did but consider the import of the word pope, which signifies 'father' . . . there would be no such vigorous making of parties and buying of votes in the conclave; . . . and those who by bribery should get themselves elected would never secure their sitting firm in the chair by pistol, poison, and violence. How much of their pleasure would be abated if they were endowed with one dram of wisdom? Wisdom, did I say? Nay with one gram of that salt which our Saviour bid them not lose the savor of. In place of their riches, honors, jurisdictions, Peter's pence, offices, dispensations, licenses, indulgences, would succeed watchings, fastings, tears, prayers, sermons, hard studies, repentant sighs, and a thousand such severe penalties; nay, what is yet more deplorable, it would follow that all their clerks, notaries, advocates, grooms, ostlers, lackeys, pimps, and some others whom for modesty's sake I shall not mention . . . would all lose their employments."

How could the author of such strictures escape the Inquisition? One reason for Erasmus' safety lay in the ambiguous position which he assumed. Were these insolent jests the ravings of the Fool or the serious personal opinion of Erasmus? If accused of heresy, the author could simply reply that he himself had not said such things; it was Dame Folly who spoke, and one cannot take a fool too seriously. This was not the first instance—nor the last—of a prominent satirist deftly utilizing symbol, allegory, and the mask of the fool. Rabbi Ben Ezra, Swift, and Voltaire resorted to the same method of criticism. In the second place, such a satire was tolerated simply because Erasmus was Erasmus. All the Pope could say, upon reading *Praise of Folly*, was, "Here is our old friend again." The Dutch Humanist by this time wielded too much power to risk rebuke. He must be won over rather than antagonized. In this small book, and other works that were to follow, Erasmus smuggled into the cloister enough heresy to send a thousand men to the stake. But the book was not unopposed. Clergy clamored for the fagots, bishops fulminated, university authorities banned the book and prohibited students from reading it.

At the same time, Erasmus was not interested in mere negation. His criticism—never arrogant or carping—was always accompanied by positive suggestion. True prophet that he was, he never denounced the status quo without pointing to the ideal. As a Christian Humanist he was irrevocably opposed to an open schism and forever feared revolution. What he wanted was reform from within, a transfiguration of the Church and a rediscovery of the essentials of Christianity beneath the crust of dogma and superstition. Later when he heard the remark that he laid the egg that Luther hatched, he said: "Yes, but the egg I laid was a hen, and Luther hatched a game-cock." The essence of Christianity, said he, lay not in outward observance but in a faith within, not in sterile scholasticism but in cultivating the life of integrity. More important than attendance at Mass or visiting shrines is the ordering of a life in the spirit of Jesus.

With this small book Erasmus conquered Europe. Its

publication gave him an international reputation equalled only by Voltaire 250 years later. Everywhere men turned eagerly to the one person who would lead them back to the Gospel, to the free study of truth, to universal religion. All Europe looked to this man for a sign but a sign was not for him to give. Erasmus was not a man of action. As Stefan Zweig says: "Erasmus could clarify but not shape, he could prepare the ground but not garner the harvest. His name does not adorn the annals of the Reformation; another was to reap where he had sown." [4]

Simultaneously with *Praise of Folly* appeared an anonymous publication under the title *Julius Excluded from Heaven*. Informed opinion, however, was not long in proving Erasmian authorship. This dramatic dialogue became so popular that it was brought to the Paris stage in 1514. Julius II appears at the gate of heaven, demanding entrance.

Julius: What the devil is this? The gates not opened! Something is wrong with the lock.

Spirit: You have brought the wrong key perhaps. The key of your money-box will not open the door here. You should have brought both keys. This is the key of power, not of knowledge.

Julius: I never had any but this, and I don't see the use of another. Hey there, porter! I say, are you asleep or drunk?

Peter: Well that the gates are adamant, or this fellow would have broken in. He must be some giant or conqueror. Heaven, what a stench! Who are you? What do you want here?

Julius: Open the gates, I say. Why is there no one to receive me?

[4] *Erasmus of Rotterdam*, p. 97.

Peter: Here is fine talk. Who are you, I say?

Julius: You know this key, I suppose, and the triple crown, and the pallium?

Peter: I see a key, but not the key which Christ gave to me a long time since. The crown? I don't recognize the crown. No heathen king ever wore such a thing, certainly none who expected to be let in here. The pallium is strange too. And see, there are marks on all three of that rogue and impostor Simon Magus, that I turned out of office.

Julius: Enough of this. I am Julius the Legurian, P.M., as you can see by the letters, if you can read.

Peter: P. M.! What is that? Pestis Maxima?

Julius: Pontifex Maximus, you rascal.

Peter: If you are three times Maximus, if you are Mercury Trismegistus, you can't come unless you are Optimus too.

Julius: Impertinence! You who have been no more than Sanctus all these ages—and I Sanctissimus, Sanctissimus Dominus, Sanctitatas, Holiness itself, with Bulls to show it.

Peter: Is there no difference between being Holy and being called Holy?

St. Peter continues to cross-question the Pope who naïvely boasts of his military power, intrigue, incest, and countless other crimes. At the conclusion of the conversation Julius is refused admission into Paradise.

"Prince of Learning"

Declining the flattering offers of Henry VIII, Erasmus left England in July 1514. *Praise of Folly*, the *Adages*, and the *Enchiridion* had brought him such fame that he was recognized as the leading Humanist on the Continent and his visits to the cities of the Rhine country and Belgium were a continual procession of triumph. Nominally he was still a monk at large, enjoying the special dispensation granted him many years before. Now the episcopal authorities thought it was time that this heretic-priest should be brought to account. But Erasmus had advanced beyond the point in his thinking where a bishop or prior of a convent could demand of him confession of sin and obedience to monastic rules. With a long dissertation to the prior about the casuistry of the laws regarding clerical dress and monastic profligacy in general, he went on his way.

In Brussels, Strassburg, Frankfurt, Basel, and Antwerp, Erasmus was welcomed as the "Prince of Learning," "*doctor universalis*," "father of study," "the light of the world." The name of Erasmus stood for the highest and the best, the alpha and omega in learning. Camererius, a contemporary Humanist, wrote: "Every one who does not wish to remain a stranger in the realm of the Muses admires him, glorifies him, sings his praises. He who is capable of extracting a letter from Erasmus has already achieved fame and can celebrate a veritable triumph. But he who is allowed converse with Erasmus may count himself among the blessed that walk this earth." Such veneration was enjoyed not even by Leonardo or Michelangelo. Emperors and kings, popes and cardinals vied with each other for his favor. Charles V, ruler of two worlds, offered him a position on his Council; Henry VIII promised him a palace and a pension if he would reside in England; Ferdinand offered similar inducements if he would go to Vienna; the same proposal came from Holland, Brabant, Hungary, Poland, and Portugal; five universities tempted him with professorships. Countless gifts came to him and bribes were ever dangling before his eyes. He accepted gifts and praise as a matter of course, but Erasmus was not for sale and he preserved his independence as long as he lived.

How account for such hero worship? Erasmus made no appeal to the people; he ignored them. He shouted no slogans or battle cries; he pleaded no popular cause. The answer can only be the one word *Zeitgeist*. Erasmus was the personification of all that the Renaissance stood for. The new spirit of Humanism born in Europe found in him its true expression. "For the first time," says Stefan Zweig, "intellectual authority was given precedence over inherited or transmitted authority; and that the change was brought about rapidly is shown by the fact that the wielders of authority submitted voluntarily to the new order of things." [5] It is an acknowledgment that creative thought, works of art, and the intellectual life were considered more significant than the mailed fist of power politics. Erasmus therefore become the spiritual champion of Europe, the prophet of a new day of freedom and tolerance, the herald of a united civilization.

An integral part of this new spirit was the study of Greek and Hebrew. As the leader in the battle of languages, Erasmus now jumped to the defense of John Reuchlin, the celebrated Hebraist, who was being charged with heresy. It mattered little if the Bible had originally been written in Hebrew and Greek; the sacred text of the Church was Latin. The clerical forces, led by the chief of the German Inquisition, had demanded that all Hebrew books except the Bible be destroyed. Reuchlin, who produced the first Hebrew grammar and introduced the study of that language in Europe, persuaded the Emperor Maximilian to suspend this edict. The Dominicans, resenting this interference, swore to bring Reuchlin to the stake. The

[5] *Op. cit.*, p. 103.

Emperor failed to hold his ground under Inquisitorial pressure and imprisoned Reuchlin, pending judgment from the Pope. It was at this point that Erasmus jumped into the fray. He wrote memorable letters to the authorities at Rome and enlisted the support of all Humanists in Germany. The opposition thus aroused was sufficient to delay final action and the case ultimately was forgotten in the turmoil of the Reformation.

Meanwhile Erasmus, recognizing the imperfections of Jerome's Vulgate New Testament, made a fresh translation and, when completed, dedicated it to Pope Leo X. To effect such a revolutionary change was heresy in itself, but in dedicating the translation to the Pope, Erasmus not only conciliated the Vatican in a delicate matter but won Leo to his side and the side of Humanism. With the Pope as his patron, Erasmus envisaged a peaceful and effective reformation of the Church from the inside. He had visions of a revitalized Christianity in which superstition and scholasticism would be absent, the Scripture used as authority, the clergy educated, and the unified, free society of Colet and More becoming a reality. But reform was not so easy and its leadership passed into the hands of another as evolution gave way to revolution.

The Greek New Testament

The revision of the Vulgate was only a preliminary phase of Erasmus' program of rational religion. Far more important for purposes of reform as well as for scholarship was his edition of the Greek New Testament which appeared in 1516. His collation of the best available manuscripts and the exegetical notes accompanying the Greek text mark the real beginning of modern biblical criticism. Under his criti-

cal eye the text of the New Testament was substantially
improved. He detected many theological emendations and
dogmatic interpolations such as I John 5:7; "For there are
three that bear record in heaven, the Father, the Word, and
the Holy Ghost: and these three are one." Not finding this
verse in any Greek manuscript, Erasmus ruled it out as an
early trinitarian interpolation. (The words were first used
and probably inserted in the text by Priscillian, 380 A.D.)
Later exegesis bears out Erasmus' verdict, for the verse is
lacking in all the fourth and fifth century codices which
later came to light, notably Vaticanus, Sinaiticus, and Alex-
andrinus. Erasmus was the first also to label as editorial
insertions the last twelve verses of Mark's gospel (the story
of Jesus' resurrection) and John 7:53–8:11 (the story of
the woman taken in adultery). The more scientific labors of
Tischendorf and of Westcott and Hort in the nineteenth
century confirmed these findings and extended technically
the biblical research so well initiated by Erasmus.

His critical notes show a fine discrimination and helped
to lay the foundation for the Higher Criticism of a later
day. He did not hesitate to place the ethical portions of the
New Testament above the silly and indecent fables of the
Old Testament. One would be better off, he remarked, to
read Livy rather than the book of Judges. His discriminating approach is seen in a paragraph from the *Adages*:

"If in the Old Testament you read that Adam was made
from mud, that his little wife was unobtrusively drawn
from his side while he slept, that the serpent tempted the
little woman with forbidden fruit, that God walked in the
cool of the evening, and that a guard was placed at the gates
of Paradise to prevent the fugitives returning, would you
not fancy the whole thing a fable from Homer's workshop?

If you read of the incest of Lot, the whole story of Samson, the adultery of David, and how the senile king was cherished by a maiden, would that not be to chaste ears repulsively obscene?"

Such comments manifest the liberal spirit in spite of the fact that Erasmus often resorted to allegory or figurative interpretation when he came upon a passage that violated reason or was plainly immoral. If he had lived in the twentieth century he would not have faced the necessity of preserving the infallibility of the Scripture and would no doubt have assigned such passages to ignorance, primitive mentality, or early stages of development. Even so, he far surpassed in fine perception any other exegete of his century.

Among the books of the New Testament Erasmus questioned the canonicity of Hebrews, James, Revelation, II and III John and II Peter, which classification was held by most of the bishops in the third century. Erasmus rejected emphatically the Augustinian doctrine of original sin and total depravity. He took the more rational view that whatever wrong Adam may have done, it did not involve posterity. He was the first great scholar after Origen to apply the rational criterion to the whole Bible and to apply to every aspect of life the principle of spirit rather than letter. He was forever distinguishing between the "philosophy of Christ" and the externalism of the Church, between the simple teachings of Jesus and the dogmas, sacraments, and institutionalism of organized religion. The purpose of the New Testament, he said, was to give to the world the character of Jesus. "If any one shows a relic of Christ's clothes we fall down, adore it and kiss it; but it is only the Gospels and the Epistles that efficaciously bring back to us the whole Christ."

The Greek New Testament of Erasmus was hailed by liberals in every country and roundly condemned by reactionaries—as has been the case with every new thing in the history of civilization. The Erasmian text was the basis for the German translation of Luther and the English of Tyndale, the first translations of the Bible from the original tongues into the modern vernacular and in each case the greatest single influence in the formation of modern German and English. All previous translations—from the Anglo-Saxon attempts to the work of John Wycliffe—were made from the Latin Vulgate, itself a translation and replete with errors. Only when a reputable Greek text was assembled through a comparative study of the earliest manuscripts available could the New Testament be translated with any degree of accuracy. Erasmus was thoroughly Protestant in his belief that the Bible should be in the hands of all the people. As to the blasphemy of turning the sacred books into English or German, he said that "the Evangelists turned into Greek what Christ spoke in Syriac, nor did the Latins fear to turn the words of Christ into the Roman tongue." The exegetical notes accompanying the New Testament were welcomed and widely used by the leading scholars of Europe. Luther at first leaned rather heavily upon them but later, resenting their humanistic and rationalistic flavor, spurned them as thoroughly distasteful.

From the standpoint of style and originality Erasmus' most representative work was the *Familiar Colloquies*. This book was nominally for the instruction of youth in religious questions and one edition was subtitled: "Useful not only for polishing a boy's speech but for building his character." It took the form of a dialogue dealing with manners and speech but was also an attack, like *Praise of Folly*, on the superstitions and pagan practices of the

Church. The *Colloquies* went through many editions and had much to do with the liberalizing of sixteenth-century Europe. "The spread of the Reformation in particular," writes Preserved Smith, "and of ideas still more liberal for that day and generation, was due more to this text-book of style than to any other one volume. Among the Anabaptists and among the Arminians, in Franck and in Acontius, the Erasmian liberalism obtained a full evaluation; in Rabelais and Montaigne it reached a still higher plane of expression." [6]

The *Colloquies* constituted the last popular work penned by the Dutch scholar. More important for scholarship was his editing of the classics, where his work reached its highest peak of quality. His detection of forgeries and his textual corrections have never been excelled in point of accuracy. He corrected four thousand corruptions in the text of *Seneca* alone. Perhaps his best work was in the field of patristics. His edition of Jerome—the life and nine volumes of his works—is a masterpiece. Erasmus' attachment to Jerome was logical enough. The hermit of Bethlehem had translated the Scriptures, specialized in Greek and Latin, and in his untheological, anti-Augustinian mind was closer to the Erasmian ideal than any other Church father except Origen.

In addition to his original editions of fifteen Latin and twelve Greek classics—the work of a life-time for any scholar—Erasmus is also remembered for his political writings (especially the *Institution of a Christian Prince*), *Method of Theology, Paraphrases, Method of Study, Method of Preaching,* and an enormous output of correspondence. The *Opus Epistolarum* embraces letters to and from the most famous personages of his time, including

[6] *Erasmus, A Study of His Life, Ideals, and Place in History,* p. 301.

four popes, all the kings and emperors of Europe during his life-time, and all the leading thinkers on both sides of the Reformation. These letters in Latin, witty, brilliant, and epigrammatic, are a study in prose style.

The Reformation

History offers no greater contrast than those titanic opponents, Erasmus and Luther—Humanist and Reformer, working for the same ends but using dissimilar methods. Their names were invariably linked together and their paths crossed frequently but they were never destined to meet each other. Physically and temperamentally they were diametrically opposite; Erasmus—sickly, hypersensitive, gentle of voice, and physically inactive; Luther—robust, domineering, loud, and full of surplus energy. Erasmus the cosmopolitan, being a man of universal interests, treated everything objectively; Luther, the nationalist, living in a more circumscribed world, vitalized and personalized whatever came within his horizon. Erasmus, the man of the study, was conciliatory, rational, tolerant; Luther, the man of action, was fanatical, passionate, intolerant. There seemed to be no common meeting ground for these two organically different souls.

And yet, back of these personal differences there was the similarity of purpose as seen in the resemblance of the two movements they represented: the Renaissance and the Reformation. Both of these movements were revolts against Medievalism and Scholasticism; both stood for a new individualism; both emphasized the claims of this world rather than the next, and both were the outgrowth of the middle-class capitalistic revolution. The conflict between the Reformers and the Humanists arose, in fact, out of their identity of purpose and their difference of method. The Reformers were interested primarily in the spiritual life; the Humanists, in the intellectual life. The Reformation was a popular movement; the Renaissance, an aristocratic one.

Erasmus had expostulated against the sale of indulgences and had satirized the practices of the Roman Church in a more caustic manner than Luther had ever dared to employ. But satire does not reach the people; Luther nailed his ideas to a door! Erasmus, living only in the stratosphere of the intellect, was content in satisfying the mind of the scholar; Luther, penetrating the folk-passion, appealed to the common people. With the nailing of the Ninety-five Theses, Luther became the leader of the Reformation. At first, he had no desire to form a rebellion but after his debate with Eck, the die was cast and he welcomed the fight. Erasmus feared his tone and said: "If only Luther could be more moderate." Luther begged for the Humanist's support but received only words of caution in return. Frederick the Elector visited Erasmus to elicit from him an unequivocal verdict but Erasmus did not deal in categorical answers. His lengthy dissertation, written for the Elector, showed that he was on Luther's side, at least in aim if not in method.

The conspicuous thing about the Diet of Worms was the absence of Erasmus. That was probably his last chance to effect a reform from within the Church. But he preferred to stay in his attic in Basel, where he secretly sympathized with the cause of the Reformation and openly lamented the fanaticism of rebellion and the increasing violence of the Peasants' Revolt. A final plea came from Luther: "I have been sitting quiet long enough, my dear Herr Erasmus, and though I have been waiting for you, as the greater man and the elder of us twain, to make the first move to break the silence between us, yet, after so long a wait, my love urges me to make a beginning myself, by writing to you. . . . For since it is obvious that the Lord has not yet endowed you with such constancy, such courage, and such sense, as should lead you to fight against this monster boldly, shoulder to shoulder with us, I would not expect of you what is too much for my own strength. . . . I should, however, have preferred it had you thought fit to refrain from devoting your gifts to mingling in our affairs; for although, with your standing and your eloquence, you might achieve much, yet it would be better, since your heart is not with us, for you to serve God only with the talent he confided to your safe keeping." This all too human exhibition of sycophancy combined with bitterness on Luther's part brought from Erasmus the reply: "I shall never admit that the evangel shall be sacrificed on the altar of human passion." Finally, exasperated by Erasmus' aloofness, Luther became vehement in his outbursts: "He who crushes Erasmus cracks a bug which stinks even worse when dead than when alive. . . . I hold Erasmus to be the greatest enemy of Christ, such an enemy as does not appear more than once in a thousand years. When I pray, 'Blessed be thy holy name,' I curse Erasmus and his heretical congeners who revile and profane God."

A Free Soul

Erasmus was forced to leave Basel because it was too Protestant and he was forced to leave Louvain because it was too Catholic. An independent mind is not thoroughly at home in any environment. A fugitive from the war-torn world, he found asylum in Freiburg. Here he continued his

literary studies. As he grew older and became more mellow, he grew somewhat critical of the Humanists as well
as the Reformers. He had never served the cause of classicism for its own sake. The classical studies, in his mind,
would save civilization only when they served the interests
of essential Christianity, the "philosophy of Christ." A
slavish imitation of the ancients was sterile, and the
pedants, he said, had no soul. He attacked Humanistic pur-
ism in a treatise called *Ciceronianus*, in which he warned
against being Christian in pagan clothes. But it can hardly
be maintained with some authorities that in taking this
stand he "foreshadowed a Christian Puritanism." [7]

It was a disillusioned, heart-broken Erasmus who settled
down in Freiburg to await the end. Estranged from the
cause of the Reformation, disappointed as he saw his dream
of Christian Humanism being smashed on the rocks of violence, and physically worn out, he withdrew even from his
loyal friends. He continued doggedly to write letters, re-
vise former editions of the Classics, and compose new
works. Rather than participate in a war of fanaticism, he
continued to stand aloof, appealing to time. In his despair
he sighed: "May God gather me soon unto Himself so
that I may quit this mad world."

What then shall we say of Erasmus' atittude of independence? Throughout his life he had been consistent in
his pacificism but can the same be said of his liberalism?
Can his noncommittal attitude be justified when others—
Berquin, John Fisher, Thomas More, Zwingli, Münzer,
Tyndale, and the Anabaptists—gave their lives for the
cause of intellectual and religious freedom? Was he a John
the Baptist for Luther now turned Judas? Did he kindle
the fire of the Reformation and then run away?

[7] *Cf.* J. Huzinga: *Erasmus*, p. 219.

This much is clear: Erasmus chose to remain forever the Humanist rather than the Reformer. He was unwilling to assume the rôle of martyr, or even of prophet, as far as the Reformation was concerned. He differed from the Reformers only in the matter of method. As the centuries pass, the tragedy of his life becomes his genius. His vice takes on the aspect of virtue, namely, his unswerving insistence on freedom. He was beholden to no man or party, but kept himself free at all times to form his own opinion. As the smoke of battle clears, his liberalism becomes increasingly transparent. If any doubt should exist as to that, one need only note the source of opposition to his teaching on the one hand, and the character of his followers on the other. Branded by the Catholic Church as a heretic and atheist and his complete works placed on the *Index Expurgatorius*, Erasmus has become in the minds of all liberal-minded individuals not only the most brilliant star of the Renaissance but, as Andrew D. White writes, "one of the two men of letters who have taken a stronger hold and exercised a wider influence on the thought of the civilized world than any others, from the Roman Empire to this day." [8]

Erasmus at the last desired to return to his homeland to die. He set out for Brabant but he was not destined to see the land of his birth again. He was compelled to stop at Basel. Here he met some of his faithful friends who attended to his needs, and here he passed his last days. Deserted now by both religious parties, he felt utterly alone and made the remark: "My foes increase in number, while my friends become fewer."

As he lay dying, a messenger arrived from Rome with

[8] Charles Dudley Warner (Ed.): *Library of the World's Best Literature*, Vol. 14, p. 5509.

the Pope's offer of a red hat. As with Voltaire, who received the same offer, such a bribe carried certain concessions which neither man was willing to make. Erasmus the independent, who had steadfastly refused bishoprics, deanships, and all such sinecures, pushed this also aside. "Shall I, a dying man," he said, "burden myself with something which I have hitherto invariably refused to shoulder?" He would die a free soul.

His body a pile of bones and dry skin, Erasmus wrote to the last and died with his pen—his sixth finger—in his hand.

IV

Renaissance Humanism

Greece Reborn

THE RENAISSANCE-REFORMATION set in motion two great forces which fashioned the modern world: realism and individualism. These two forces took diverse forms but, however and wherever expressed, they spelled the downfall of medievalism and laid the foundations of modernism. The Copernican theory revolutionized man's conception of the universe and shook to the core biblical cosmology, Aristotelian logic, and medieval supernaturalism. The explorations of da Gama, Magellan, and Columbus proved the sphericity of the earth and shifted world trade from the Adriatic to the Atlantic. The flow of gold from the Americas and the theology of thrift in Calvinistic Switzerland combined to overthrow the economic status quo and introduce the capitalistic system. The invention of the printing press in Germany made possible the circulation not only of ideas but of exchange rates, bank cheques, and commercial bulletins, thus facilitating a complete change in commercial enterprise. The houses of the Medici, the Fuggers, and the Chigi created the art centers of Florence, Augsburg, and Rome, encouraged the revival of learning, and called into play the artistic and literary genius of the time.

Realism to the Italian meant a new and elemental appreciation of the natural world and a return to the Hellenic ideal of the abundant life. The famous saying of Pope Leo X (a Medici) illustrates the pagan response of Renaissance Italy to the liberated spirit of naturalism: "Let us enjoy the Papacy," he said, "now that God has given it to us." Zeus and Jehovah, Isis and Mary, pagan rites and Christian sacraments—all were synthesized in Medicean Italy. The enigmatic smile of Mona Lisa, the mischievous cupids of Raphael, the sumptuous scenes and sensuous nudes of the Venetians, the boasted crimes of Cellini, the blackmailing verses of the scourge Aretino, the gargantuan canvases of Michelangelo—all typify the exuberant revolt against the medieval morality.

In Holland the masters translated realism into barnyards and kitchens, homely women and sprawling drunkards—art for life's sake and not for the church. The contagion spread to the northern countries in the form of nationalism and a revolution in religion. Here the impulse of humanism represented a more ideational break with the past, a break which was more fundamental than that of the Italians because of its educational, moral, and economic character.

Such was the spirit of the Renaissance in its multifarious effects. It was the birth of the middle class. It brought a new exaltation of the individual, a new trust in human nature. It meant the end of ancient dualism with its ascetic practices and brought to life the belief in man as a unified and potentially good personality. It gave birth to science and the life of reason. It proved the fallibility of absolutism and validated the philosophy of relativism.

In the larger sense—including causes and effects—the Renaissance-Reformation might be said to extend from 1350 to 1700, a period which represents the transition from medieval to modern times, a transition from authority to freedom, from Aristotelian logic to the empirical method. The Renaissance is described by Ralph Roeder as "one of those recurring crises in the annals of the race when a ferment of new life, like a rising sap, bursts the accepted codes of morality and men revert to Nature and the free play of instinct and experience in its conduct." [1]

Leonardo—L'uomo Universale

The example par excellence of this eclectic, universal vitality which was the Renaissance is Leonardo da Vinci, "the most resplendent figure in the history of the human race," as Thomas Craven calls him. When Leonardo died, his faithful disciple, Melzi, said: "It is not in the power of Nature to produce such another man" (the chances physiologically speaking are, for that matter, probably one in ten billion). Long remembered as the painter of a dozen pictures, he has emerged from the last half century of research as the finest product of the Renaissance, the most versatile and capacious mind in all history. Here was a man who saw the whole world as his province and yet could penetrate to the utmost point of specialization and spectroscopic analysis.

Leonardo was both skeptic and mystic. In him were combined the scientific and aesthetic, qualities rarely present in one personality. Challenged by the potentialities of mechanical invention, he directed his attention to the release and multiplication of power. He invented the first self-propelling vehicles with differential gear. His notebooks contain drawings of cranes, boring machines, armored tanks, and flying machines. He was always haunted by the dream of men flying in the air. He left many pages of specifications for airplane construction. Most of the designs call for

[1] *Man of the Renaissance*, Preface, vii.

wings or sails that can be beaten, birdlike, up and down on the air. Following the laws of avian flight, he indicated that the relation between the weight to be borne and the span of the wings must be the same as in birds.

He was the first to make records of the internal structure of the body in drawings not excelled in accuracy for centuries. Having dissected some thirty corpses, he was able to describe death by arteriosclerosis and tuberculosis. He made drawings of embryos at different stages; also skulls, muscles, and various organs. He anticipated Harvey in the discovery of the circulation of the blood. He planned cities with sewage systems, underground sanitation and air conditioning. He experimented with steam and recorded his use of this new power; helped to design the Milan Cathedral and Saint Peter's in Rome; constructed a camera; organized festivals and staged great theatrical productions; designed a spinning machine and looms; surveyed Italy from coast to coast and made relief maps of the country; erected an astronomical observatory; discovered the laws of inertia; and wrote a volume on the anatomy of the horse. He drained marshes, built canals, devised locks to control water; established the laws of petrifaction; invented roller bearings, the diving bell, the dulcimer, and the submarine.

Even in his painting his approach was that of experimentation. With Leonardo came the earliest independent landscape in western art and the first use of chiaroscuro. He was interested not in making a photographic likeness but in studying and portraying emotional states, optical phenomena, atmospheric effects, divisions of tones, and colors of shadows. He was attracted by unusual heads and searched the city for the oddest, ugliest and most grotesque faces, which he reproduced in caricature form.

Much has been made in recent studies of Leonardo's

inventions and scientific observations [2] but his biographers have never done him justice as a philosopher. His notebooks reveal him to be the same prophetic spirit in the philosophic world as in the realm of science. Thoroughly religious, he was opposed to fanaticism, superstition, and magic. As an enemy of clericalism and dogma, he may well be considered a precursor of modern liberal thought. His interest in religion was ethical rather than mystical. "Whoever in discussion," he wrote, "adduces authority uses not his intellect but rather memory." Following the implications of humanism more critically than his fellow Italians, he anticipated Erasmus and Luther in his denunciation of ecclesiasticism, and he disapproved strongly of such practices as the sale of indulgences, worship of saints, Mariolatry, and confession. He was vehemently opposed to astrology, witchcraft, and alchemy.

The conflict between freedom and authority finds Leonardo always on the side of freedom. "When besieged by ambitious tyrants," he wrote, "I find a means of defense in order to preserve the chief gift of nature which is liberty." His recognition of the "cultural lag" sounds strangely appropriate for our day: "How by an appliance many are able to remain for some time under water. How and why I do not describe my method for remaining under water; for this I do not publish or divulge on account of the evil nature of men who would practice assassinations at the bottom of the sea by breaking the ships in their lower parts and sinking them together with the crews who are in them."

The clue to Leonardo's religious liberalism is discovered in the nature of the opposition. His clash with Thomism

[2] Attention is called to the most satisfactory biography in English to date: Antonina Vallentin: *Leonardo da Vinci* (1938), and to the authoritative translation and editing of the notebooks: Edward MacCurdy: *The Notebooks of Leonardo da Vinci* (1939).

and Scholasticism provoked the enmity of both ecclesiastical authorities and orthodox scientists. The Church, for instance, placed a ban on his anatomical studies on the grounds that the human body is a sacred mystery and dissection is a sacrilege. Using the empirical method before Copernicus, Galileo, and Bacon, he can be considered, to use a phrase from Emil Ludwig, "the greatest pathfinder of the new occident." "Those sciences are vain and full of errors," wrote Leonardo, "which are not born of experience, mother of all certitude, and which do not terminate in observation; that is, whose origin or middle or end does not come through one of the five senses. . . . I will make experiment before I proceed because my intention is first to set forth the facts and then to demonstrate the reason why such experience is constrained to work in such fashion. And this is the rule to be followed by the investigators of natural phenomena: while nature begins from causes and ends with experience, we must follow a contrary procedure, that is, begin from experience and with that discover the causes." [3]

Leonardo was the Renaissance. His life is the story of Florence and Rome, Milan and Venice, Lorenzo the Magnificent and Michelangelo, Leo X and the Borgias, Mirandola and Ficino, political intrigue and ecclesiastical corruption, city rivalries and foreign invasions—a kaleidoscopic scene, dominated by the titanic figure of Leonardo da Vinci. His life is the story of a mind that grew with the world in the most pregnant period of human history.

The Humanists

Individualism is at once the central emphasis of the Humanists and the Reformers. In the medieval world the

---

[3] *Trattato della Pittura* (*Treatise on Painting*) Ch. 29. (Quoted in part by Kenneth Clark: *Leonardo da Vinci*, p. 86.)

individual was nil and the authoritarian scheme of the Roman Catholic Church dovetailed perfectly with feudalism. Humanism stood for self-expression in art, literature, and religion. Lippo Lippi, Raphael, Michelangelo, and da Vinci threw off the conventional requirements of the church and impressed upon their paintings their own individual personalities. Erasmus, Rabelais, Mirandola, and Ficino were free souls, untrammelled, delighting in the full range of the physical life, describing it in their own fearless way. Luther, Tyndale, and Servetus insisted on the expression of free conscience and the right of private judgment.

As an attempt to recover the Greek way of life, Humanism is known for its re-discovery of the classics. The Humanists went back to the Greek and Roman authors because paganism was anthropocentric whereas medieval ideology was theocentric. They were interested in the Greeks because they believed in the well-ordered life of freedom. Pico della Mirandola set forth the Humanist manifesto and rang the bell of freedom in his *Oration on the Dignity of Man.*

"Thou, restrained by no narrow bonds, according to thy own free will, in whose power I have placed thee, shalt define thy nature for thyself. I have set thee midmost the world, that hence thou mightest the more conveniently survey whatsoever is in the world. Nor have we made thee either heavenly or earthly, mortal or immortal, to the end that thou, being, as it were, thy own free maker and moulder, shouldst fashion thyself in what form may like thee best. Thou shalt have power to decline unto the lower or brute creatures. Thou shalt have power to be reborn unto the higher, or divine, according to the sentence of thy intellect." [4]

[4] From the works of Mirandola, quoted in J. A. Symonds: *The Revival of Learning*, p. 35.

Freedom had its risks, of course—license, intemperance, cruelty, anarchy, disorganization—but it was worth a trial. Men might fail to reach the higher or the divine, or, having reached it, fall back, but they should have the right to make their own mistakes. Freedom was better than blind obedience to authority. It was better than unreason, superstition, fear, and ignorance. It was better than the security of regimentation.

The Humanists inaugurated the study of classical philology by editing and collating the entire body of Greek and Roman manuscripts. They instituted a new system of education based on ancient literature in order to offset medieval Scholasticism. Rabelais was able to say: "Now discipline is restored and languages are in the curriculum: Greek, without which none can honestly call himself a scholar; Hebrew, Chaldean, and Latin. Books, inventions of God, as artillery is an invention of the Devil, are well and correctly printed." Old men, infected by this Humanist contagion, hurriedly began to study Greek and Latin before it was too late.

This momentous change, however, was achieved with certain losses. The devotion of the Humanists to the dead languages was in itself devitalizing when they concerned themselves with grammar, syntax, and metrical form to the exclusion of the weightier matters of the law. They became slavish imitators of the ancients, so intent on aping the Latin authors that they lost all originality. In repudiating the barren Scholasticism of the Church they made for themselves a new and still more barren Scholasticism of rhetoric. They replaced the authority of the Scripture with the authority of antiquity. "Latinizers" they were called. Italian and French were anathema; nothing but a barbarous idiom. Another defect of the Humanists was their tendency to divide society into two classes: the greater and the lesser. The common people clung to their superstitions and the Humanists wrote to each other in Latin, ignoring completely the "vulgum pecus." In general, the Humanists secluded themselves in their ivory towers and lost touch with the common herd and with the soil.

"To bring the dead to life" was Petrarch's reply when asked why he took the trouble of exploring through Greece, the islands of the Mediterranean, and the African coast for coins, inscriptions, and artifacts. For the Renaissance Humanists the ancient dead were more alive than their Scholastic contemporaries. To Ficino, the Humanist-priest, the resurrection of Plato rather than the resurrection of Christ was the proof of new life. Petrarch's communion was not with the living but with the saints, Cicero and Vergil. Ficino kept a lamp burning all the time before his bust of Plato, and Erasmus sighed: "Saint Socrates, pray for us." The myth of Helen had more attraction for the typical Humanist than the story of the Gospel. In Humanist Italy sermons were preached from Homer; the Virgin Mary was called a goddess and the Pope, Jupiter. It is related that a Parisian monk, translating Ovid's *Art of Love*, invoked the aid of the Trinity and dedicated the work to the Virgin Mary!

The leading exponents of the Christian-Platonist synthesis were Pico della Mirandola (1462–1494) and Marsiglio Ficino (1433–1499). These Neo-Platonists, reviving the ideal of Clement and Origen, aimed to reconcile Christian mysticism with Greek philosophy. They preached that religion and science were compatible and that philosophy and religion were supplementary. Their patron and supporter was Lorenzo de Medici (1449–1492) who followed his grandfather Cosimo's precedent of substituting

Plato for Aristotle. Lorenzo the Humanist made Florence the home of science, letters and the arts. As an artist and writer, he surrounded himself with genius—Michelangelo, Ghirlandaio, Botticelli, Luca della Robbia, Verocchio, Poliziano, Ficino, and Pico, all of whom ate at the magnifico's table and hailed him as their benefactor and friend. He was the most brilliant tyrant in the history of Florence, the personal embodiment of the Italian Renaissance in its release of energy and creative effort. "He had the happy gift," writes Ferdinand Schevill, "more characteristic of the fleet southern races than of the heavier northern breeds, to give himself, with entire surrender to his mind and senses and in swift succession, to the dictation of instructions to an ambassador departing on an important mission, to the examination of a newly discovered manuscript, to a discussion among experts of a mooted doctrine of Greek philosophy, and to the arrangements for a happy hunting expedition with a group of friends. Like his countrymen generally, he was not inhibited by an awkward self-consciousness but was of an open nature, courteous, and accessible to every one he met." [5]

Poliziano, Lorenzo's favorite companion, was the greatest poet of the Laurentian age, which is to say, the most successful imitator of the ancients. An expert philologist, he was made professor of Latin and Greek at the University of Florence and in that position did much for the advancement of linguistics and learning in general. But his poetry lacks distinction because the poet himself was too erudite and too far removed from people to have an inspiring message.

Marsiglio Ficino, another housemate of Lorenzo, gave himself to the translation of the Platonic dialogues, the

[5] *History of Florence*, p. 403.

completion of which coincided happily with the invention and commercial use of the printing press. He differs from Poliziano in being a thoroughgoing neo-Platonic mystic, translating Plato in terms of Alexandrian philosophy. Mirandola, Ficino, and Poliziano were the moving spirits of the Platonic Academy in Florence; Lorenzo was their champion and no less a poet, as is seen in his celebrated quatrain:

> "Fair is youth and free of sorrow,
> Yet how soon its joys we bury!
> Let who would be now be merry:
> Sure is no one of tomorrow."

Shifting our attention to France, we encounter François Rabelais (c. 1490–1553), friend and disciple of Erasmus. Like the Dutch Humanist, Rabelais was educated for the priesthood, abandoned the calling, and then devoted himself to satirizing it. Rabelais received the medical degree of Montpelier where he taught for a time. He is credited with introducing dissection before Vesalius. He was later appointed head of the hospital at Pont-du-Rhône. He called theology "nothingology" and declared that "Papimania" was sheer idolatry. The chief theme of his satire *Pantagruel* was tolerance, which the Sorbonne lacked in condemning both Rabelais and *Pantagruel*. His religion of reason was opposed by Calvinism just as vehemently as his anti-clericalism was repelled by Catholicism. His philosophy was a blend of Renaissance paganism, with its epicurean pleasure, and the life of reason.

Budé and Ronsard in France, Reuchlin and Hutten in Germany, Valla and Aldus in Italy, Colet and More in England complete the list of distinguished Renaissance Humanists. By reason of their efforts and those of their colleagues the beginning of the sixteenth century marks the beginning of the modern age. Reason had been substituted for revelation; knowledge and control of the natural world had supplanted a blind faith in the supernatural world. This shift would have been impossible, however, without the scientific revolution which was also the Renaissance.

The Scientists

The herald of the new age was Roger Bacon (1214–1294) who, as early as the thirteenth century, condemned belief based on authority and advocated experience as the test of validity as over against Scholastic disputation. Combining both the Humanistic and scientific ideas of three centuries later, this prophet of modernism defined the pragmatic method in unmistakable terms and established the primacy of mathematics in philosophy. "Experimental Science," he wrote, "has one great prerogative in respect to all other sciences, that it investigates their conclusions by experience. For the principles of the other sciences may be known by experience, but the conclusions are drawn from these principles by way of argument. If they require particular and complete knowledge of those conclusions, the aid of this science must be called in. It is true that mathematics possesses useful experience with regard to its own problems of figure and number, which apply to all the sciences and experience itself, for no science can be known without mathematics. But if we wish to have complete and thoroughly verified knowledge, we must proceed by the methods of experimental science." [6]

[6] *Opus Majus*, quoted in J. H. Randall, Jr.: *Making of the Modern Mind*, p. 211.

Later came Copernicus, Galileo, and Francis Bacon to give more systematic form to the inductive system.[7] Copernicus (1473–1543), however, did not arrive at his heliocentric theory through experimentation and induction but, curiously enough, by way of the Humanistic craze for the Greek and Roman classics. Plato had held that mathematics is the key to the universe; Cicero had maintained that the earth rotates on its axis every twenty-four hours; and Aristarchus had proposed that the earth revolves about the sun. The ancients had already stolen modern thunder but few were aware of it. Armed with these "new" ideas, Copernicus laid aside the Ptolemaic key to the heavens which made the earth the center of the universe. Shifting his point of reference to the sun, the Polish astronomer found that his rearrangement of the planets left fewer questions unanswered than the geocentric scheme. The revolutionary heliocentric theory was the result and a new theology was in the making. Confirmation of this theory came in the mathematical and empirical philosophy of Kepler, Descartes, Spinoza, and Newton. Ptolemaic astronomy and Scholasticism were dealt a blow from which they never recovered. The epoch-making character of Copernicus' discovery has been equalled in its theological consequences only by Darwin's theory of evolution three centuries later. But unlike the cultural adjustment of the nineteenth century, the Church of the sixteenth century was unable to assimilate such a far-reaching disclosure and retreated to its ancient cosmology.

The cult of Aristotle met another defeat at the hands of Galileo (1564–1642) who in 1590 conducted a practical experiment in falling bodies. The scene of the demonstra-

---

[7] The theory that knowledge is derived from particular observations which lead to generalizations.

tion was the leaning tower of Pisa. The young instructor from the University had announced that he would drop two unequal weights from the top of the tower and they would reach the ground simultaneously. This predicted phenomenon ran counter to Aristotelian physics and a good crowd was on hand to ridicule the young upstart who had assailed other dicta of long-standing authority. When the incredulous Aristotelians saw the two unequal weights strike the ground at the same time they suspected a hoax and continued to believe what they had always been told.

Galileo had proved that the time taken by an object to fall was not dependent upon the weight of the object but, as he said, "the distances traversed during equal intervals of time, by a body falling from rest, stand to one another in the same ratio as the odd numbers beginning with unity." So along with Galileo's falling weights fell Aristotle's physics as the experimental method received further impetus. Galileo agreed with Copernicus that the key to all natural law is mathematics and that the laws of the universe are unchangeable and orderly. With Bacon he believed that the first law of science is the observation and verification of facts and the second law is the reasoned conclusion based on mathematical experimentation. "The tempered combination of faith in the mathematical order of nature with the appeal to experiment, first achieved in the Western world by Galileo, brings us close to the assumptions and methods that have dominated modern science to this day. . . . The philosophical effects of Galileo's work were tremendous. Mechanical force—the tugs and thrusts of moving bodies—replaced divine purpose as the cause of natural events. The real world was henceforth held to consist of physical bodies moving in space and time according to laws capable of mathematical formulation." [8]

[8] Eugene Garrett Bewkes: *Experience, Reason, and Faith*, pp. 452–53.

We have seen how the heliocentric theory of Copernicus undermined the sway of Ptolemy. Tycho Brahe and Kepler with their calculations proved the theory to be a fact. Galileo confirmed their calculations by actual observations with his telescope. Thus reason was followed by mathematics and mathematics in turn was followed by experiment and the reasoned faith of one generation became the verified fact of the next.

Religious Change

From the standpoint of the Humanistic belief in man's dignity and perfectability, in reason and natural law, the Reformation has no place in the story of liberalism, for the Protestant Reform left untouched the supernaturalism of the Latin theologians and, in shifting the base of authority from the Pope to the Book, it was at best an appeasement. On the other hand, the Reformation cannot be separated from the essential spirit of the Renaissance. As a revolt from the absolutism of the medieval Church; as a rebellion against intolerance, commercialized religion, clerical immorality, and superstition, the movement set in motion by Huss and Wycliffe was just as liberal in its potentialities as the literary awakening of Petrarch, the economic awakening of John Ball, or the physical awakening of Galileo.

True, the Reformation merely changed the technique for the acquirement of salvation; it produced in the Bible just another external authority; the doctrine of private judgment applied to the Scripture bred division instead of unity; Calvinism exhibited an intolerance altogether as reprehensible as that of the Holy Inquisition; theological schisms created a multitude of rival sects; Genevese thrift resulted after three centuries in Wall Street capitalism; and the Calvinistic philosophy of individual freedom made it possible for twentieth-century industrialists in America simultaneously to send prayers to the Chinese and scrap iron to the Japanese. Yet it is also true that the Protestant Revolt gave birth to the most radical of modern forces (from the Church of England came American Congregationalism, from which came Unitarianism, from which came religious Humanism); the Protestant principle of private judgment resulted in the biblical criticism of the nineteenth century; the Protestant proclivity to division provided the backbone of the democratic system, namely, freedom to differ. There are no unmixed goods in this world; one must choose. Those who believe in democracy must accept its risks, the risks of chaos, mediocrity in office, and anarchy. The alternative is complete loss of freedom or totalitarianism.

In its revolt from the authority of the Catholic Church in matters of salvation the Protestant Reformation asserted the individual priesthood of all believers. Men have the right and the power to commune directly with God without any human mediation. The Reformation declared the individual's freedom and obligation. "Every man because of his faith," said Luther, "is a free lord of all things, subject to none; every man because of his love is in bondage, a servant of all." It declared that salvation or religious satisfaction is obtained by faith; it is a matter of mental attitude rather than of merit or "works." "Religiously," says Professor Randall, "the Reformation represented three things: first, a simplification of the body of Christian belief and an emphasis upon the doctrine of salvation and its means as the essentials; secondly, an individualistic emphasis upon salvation as a direct and immediate relation between the soul and God, on religion as inner and intensely personal; and thirdly, the consequent dropping away of the sacramental system of the medieval Church and its attendant hierarchy of priests." [9]

Like the Italian Renaissance itself, the Reformation was not a sudden or isolated event which took place in the early sixteenth century. There was nothing actually new in Luther's Reform. The re-discovery of individualism, freedom, and the simplification of religion had its prefigurement in the medieval heresies and the Pre-Reformers. Luther, a comparative late comer, simply rode on the tidal wave of social and political unrest which precipitated the actual break with Catholicism. Comparing the theological platform of Luther and Calvin with the more radical ideas of the earlier lower-class heresies, Ernest Sutherland Bates goes so far as to say that "in many ways they [Luther and Calvin] represented a betrayal of the Reformation, a counter-revolution which embodied an unstable compromise with the principles of Catholicism—a compromise eventually left behind in a further resurgence of the original anti-Catholic forces." [10]

Pre-Reformation Protestantism is found first in the Catharist movement, a lower class revolt against medieval authoritarianism. Adopting their name from the Greek *katharos* meaning pure, the Cathari attempted to revive ancient Manicheeism, a dualistic religion of Persian origin and an earlier rival of Christianity. They practiced outright pacifism, opposed the civil oath, rejected all the Old Testament but the Prophets, the Psalms, and the Wisdom Books, and replaced the Latin Vulgate with their own translation of the New Testament from Greek texts. They were Arian or semi-Unitarian in their Christology, sub-

[9] John Herman Randall, Jr.: *The Making of the Modern Mind*, pp. 144–45.
[10] *American Faith*, p. 34.

ordinating the Son to the Father. They rejected biblical miracles and vigorously denounced the sacerdotalism of the Catholic Church. They rejected the sacraments of baptism and the Eucharist in favor of a dedicatory laying on of hands and a memorial meal consisting only of the bread. They insisted on non-interference of civil authorities in matters of religion. In their belief in the separation of Church and State, their substitution of symbolic observances for sacraments, their anticlericalism, and their doctrine of pacifism, the eleventh-century Cathari appear to have been not only a form of medieval Protestantism but a harbinger of twentieth-century liberalism. Their hostility to the Catholic system challenged the common people and even won the favor of William, Duke of Aquitaine. In eleventh-century France they took the name of Albigenses (from the town of Albi, one of the strongest centers of the movement). In Milan they were known as Patarenes, and in Bulgaria, the Bogomiles. The prominence of the Cathari in the vicinity of Toulouse aroused the Church and, in 1208, Pope Innocent the Third's religious *blitzkrieg* practically wiped out all traces of the movement in Southern France. Survivors of the dreadful massacre fled to other countries. The heretics were killed but their heresy spread.

Similar in their anti-clericalism, their use of the vernacular New Testament, their opposition to sacramentalism and their strict morality were the Waldenses, followers of Peter Waldo, a merchant of Lyons who, in 1176, sold his business and began preaching to the poor. The "poor Men of Lyons," as they were called, were more distinctly Protestant than the later Lutherans. They repudiated indulgences, purgatory, the mass, and the sacrament of baptism. They defended lay preaching and held that prayer is more effective in secret than in church. They were opposed to capital punishment and oath-taking and were communistic in their social and economic organization.

Peter Waldo appealed to the Third Lateran Council for recognition but was refused and excommunicated. Then followed systematic persecution.[11] In spite of centuries of inquisitorial persecution the Waldenses thrived and by the end of the fifteenth century had at least two hundred thousand adherents in Europe. They are the only medieval sect to survive to the present day and are said today to number about 26,000.

Wycliffe and Huss

In his moral teaching and simplification of the Gospel, Saint Francis of Assisi deserves a place among the forerunners of the Reformation but since his reform failed to embrace any theological heresy and since it was merged with the Roman system even before he died, no organic connection can be made. But there was a lasting spiritual influence, as there was with the German mystics, especially Meister Eckhardt (1260–1327) and John Tauler (1300–1361). Pre-Reformation mysticism emphasized personal religious experience divorced from ecclesiasticism and "good works." The mystics' rejection of ritualism and belief in salvation by faith presaged the Protestant piety but did not constitute a rebellion against Catholicism.

"The Morning Star of the Reformation" was John Wycliffe (1324–1384), master of Balliol College, Oxford and leader of the Lollards. Wycliffe was opposed primarily to the temporal power of the Church and the character of the clergy. The momentous action of Henry the Eighth

[11] For a history of the Waldensian movement see Pius Melia: *Origin, Persecutions, and Doctrines of the Waldenses.*

in opposing the Vatican had its counterpart one hundred and fifty years earlier when Wycliffe influenced King Edward the Third to discontinue tribute to the Pope. This was supplemented by Wycliffe's preaching that the Church should be supported by voluntary offerings and that the Church service should be built around the sermon rather than ritual. Sacraments, declared Wycliffe, were invalid when administered by unworthy priests. The worship of relics and pilgrimages to shrines should be abolished. Papal supremacy was a case of foreign usurpation and bishops were merely ambitious politicians. He attacked the mendicant friars who wandered through the country hearing confessions, giving absolution "for a price," and exhibiting absurd and spurious relics. The Church was the landlord of over half the property of England.

Wycliffe's chief concern, however, was the authority of the Scripture. "If there were one hundred popes and all the friars were made cardinals, their opinion should carry no weight in matters of faith except it be based on Scripture." For substantiation of his doctrine of Scriptural authority, he translated the Bible from the Latin Vulgate into English, the first Bible to be translated into the native tongue for the people. Actually Wycliffe translated only the New Testament and his colleague Nicholas of Hereford was responsible for most of the Old Testament.

The "poor priests" whom Wycliffe sent out to distribute the Bible were called Lollards, because they were forever mumbling and singing (*lollen*, Low German or Dutch meaning "to sing in a murmuring strain"). In the hands of the commoners the Bible became an instrument of sedition against the State as well as the Church. Conscious of their own "lordship," they demanded their rights. Under John Ball and Wat Tyler they broke out in rebellion and marched on London where they burned the palace of the Duke of Lancaster, an enthusiastic patron of their own leader. Recognizing that they were riding for a fall unless they acted quickly, the nobility joined the clergy in resisting Lollardy. Wycliffe was dismissed from Oxford ostensibly for his disbelief in the doctrine of transubstantiation but in reality for his connection with the peasants' revolt. Although the authorities did not put Wycliffe to death, his followers were liquidated in much the same way as the Waldenses. An act of Parliament made the reading of the Wycliffe Bible a penal crime and all the copies that could be found were burned. But the heresy was not completely exterminated. In 1525 an English bishop testified to the continued influence of the Lollards in his statement that Luther's teachings "simply put new weapons into the hands of already existing bands of Wycliffe heretics."

The more immediate influence of the Lollards was felt in Bohemia which was just as ripe for heresy as England. The revolt was inspired by John Huss, a professor of philosophy at the University of Prague. Huss' ideas were drawn largely from Wycliffe's manuscripts but he paid a greater price for holding them. He made the mistake of thinking that the ecclesiastical authorities were sincere in guaranteeing protection and also a hearing at the Council of Constance where he was summoned to defend his teachings. After an eighteen-day journey with an imperial safe-conduct he presented himself for the hearing. The safe-conduct was merely a means to an end and instead of receiving a trial Huss found himself in a monastery dungeon where he was kept for seven months. The authorities demanded recantation but the prisoner replied that he could not recant when they had not informed him of his error. Finally, he was taken to the council to face the emperor, the princes, the cardinals, the archbishops, the bishops, the priests, and the monks. When the death sentence was read, Huss fell to the floor crying: "Lord Jesus, forgive my enemies!" He was unfrocked and his soul committed to the Devil. As he stood on the faggots, his neck chained to the stake, he was given a final chance to recant. "What shall I recant," he said, "when I have spoken naught save truth? I sought but to teach men repentance and forgiveness according to the Gospel of Jesus Christ. . . . I am not afraid to die!"

The religious rebellion initiated by John Huss and augmented by the growing national feeling was an anticipation of the Lutheran Reformation in almost every particular. Following the principles of their martyred prophet, the Bohemian Brethren, as they were called, instituted a separate religion and held to the Scripture as authority rather than the councils of the Church; rejected the primacy of the Papacy, the efficacy of indulgences, masses for the dead, and all non-biblical sacraments and ceremonies. The movement continued as the Moravian Church and as such was a definite influence in the career of John Wesley. It is not too much to say furthermore that the Hussite Reformation with its principles of freedom and democracy explains Masaryk and pre-Hitlerian Czechoslovakia.

The Protestant Revolt

The Reformation in its schismatic stage came only when other factors were present, namely, the growth of commerce and trade and articulate nationalisms. Emergent capitalism outmoded the feudal system and the religious revolt played into the hands of kings and nobles who craved independence from Rome. Thus were merged the economic, nationalistic, and religious factors. Those who claim that the ideational element played no causal rôle in the Reformation work the theory of economic determinism for more than it is worth. The currently popular view holds that the real point at issue was neither dogmas, morals, nor politics but economics and that the primary cause of the Reformation was "the great material prosperity of the age and its unequal distribution." [12] It is the fashion to regard the concepts of democracy and freedom as arising out of the industrial arena of the eighteenth century. But the real roots of democracy, as Ernest Sutherland Bates reminds us, "are to be found in the attempted revival of primitive Christianity by the radical lower-class sects of the Protestant Reformation, those peasants and yeomen who were our own ancestors, and who initiated the Reformation and eventually carried out its basic principles—especially in America—to conclusions undreamt of in the beginning. The ideal of local self-government was brought to America by the Pilgrims; the separation of Church and State was derived from the Baptists; the right of free speech was a development of the right to freedom of conscience established by Roger Williams and William Penn; the equality spoken of in the Declaration of Independence was an outgrowth of the equality practiced by the Quakers." [13]

As for capitalism, the monumental works of the economic historians, Tawney and Weber, testify to the causal significance of Calvin's theology. [14] "Above all," writes Lewis Browne, "Calvinism gave sanction to certain attitudes which in their zealous expression by increasing multi-

[12] Franz Funck-Brentano: *The Renaissance*, pp. 275–76.

[13] *Op. cit.*, p. 9.

[14] R. H. Tawney: *Religion and the Rise of Capitalism;* Max Weber: *The Protestant Ethic and the Spirit of Capitalism.* See also Troeltsch: *Protestantism and Progress* and *The Social Teaching of the Churches.*

tudes of men made for the revolutionizing of the basic character of society. Its doctrine of election made for democracy, its individualism encouraged the competitive spirit, and its emphasis on relentless industry and incessant thrift helped bring into being this whole capitalistic civilization we live in today." [15]

Wycliffe, Huss, and Luther were professors of philosophy. Their revolt was an ideological one and there would have been no Reformation without them. On the other hand, the Reformation would not have occurred when it did without the concomitant social, political, and economic factors. Along with all these elements was the corruption of the clergy and the commercialization of religious matters—the immediate cause of revolt. The unholy regimes of the Renaissance Popes, especially Alexander the Sixth and Julius the Second, were an important factor in provoking the Reformation and the consequent breakdown of Papal authority over Christendom. The practice of the sale of Church offices and pardons, the Papal policy of collecting revenue from foreign states by the sale of indulgences and recovery from debt by the imposition of exorbitant taxes have been dealt with too often to warrant detailed treatment here. The widespread popular discontent fomenting in Northern Europe for two centuries was finally focused in Martin Luther and then the storm broke. Denying the sacramental system of Rome as the means to salvation and the authority of the Pope, Luther defined salvation in terms of personal faith and rested authority in the Scripture.

As compared with the Lutheran Revolt, the Zwinglian Reformation made more drastic changes in the forms of worship but under Calvin the Swiss Reform took on a more

[15] *Since Calvary*, p. 322.

legalistic and doctrinaire character. God's absolute sovereignty, man's total depravity, and the doctrine of the elect characterized Calvinism. It must be conceded that the Calvinistic theocracy with its authoritarian ethics and the Lutheran separation of the religious from the secular were more Catholic than Protestant. Both were at best compromises with the old order, as was the Royal Reformation in England.

Far more radical in theory and practice than all three was the Anabaptist movement. Beginning in 1525 as a left-wing phase of Zwingli's anti-ritualistic reform in Zurich, the Anabaptists spread rapidly to Germany, Poland, Austria, Hungary, and Holland as a proletarian rebellion. The peasants were rabid in their repudiation of image worship, monasticism, veneration of saints, clericalism, the mass, and the whole sacramental system. Infant baptism especially was regarded as an abomination. Baptism, they claimed, was a seal upon one's faith and must be entered into voluntarily and with understanding. To administer baptism promiscuously to infants deprived the rite of its true significance and reduced salvation to an automatic routine. The nickname Anabaptists, or "rebaptizers," is partly misleading, for they rebaptized adults only when baptism had been administered at birth. A century later in England they took the more accurate title, the Baptists.

The Anabaptists preached the necessity of rebirth. Following what they felt were Scriptural injunctions, they refused to take oaths, bear arms, or participate in civil activities. Because of their advocacy of agrarian reform and their simplification of religious life they were severely persecuted by the more entrenched Catholic and Lutheran parties. Zwingli, who ranked second to Calvin in intolerance, drowned most of those who were in Zurich—total immersion with a vengeance, so to speak. Others were tortured on the rack, scourged, and buried alive. According to T. M. Lindsay, the famous historian of the Reformation in Holland, they were chained to a stake a short distance from a fire and slowly barbecued. But martyrdom was cheerfully endured and the Anabaptists thrived on this widespread persecution.

The original leaders, Hubmaier and Denck, were scholarly men but later propagandists became extreme, preaching the speedy return of Christ and the establishment of the New Jerusalem in Munster, Strassburg, and other communistic heavens. As the left-wing of the Reformation, the Anabaptists can be considered the forerunners also of the Quakers, the Congregationalists, and the Unitarians. Their advocacy of social amelioration was premature and their bid for a place on the religious map of Europe was repulsed by the rising bourgeoisie and nobility, but their assault on religious authoritarianism left its mark and the story of religious liberalism is not complete without them.

In Perspective

From the vantage point of the twentieth century the Renaissance-Reformation can best be viewed as a transition; not a complete or unified movement, but a vestibule from one world to another. The effect of Protestant theology on science, philosophy, and education was both progressive and reactionary, for it retained much that was medieval. But in spite of Luther's distrust of reason and the continuance of revelation, the Reformation opened the way for the Enlightenment. Luther and Calvin were necessary for Bayle and Locke. In spite of its half-way measures and its excesses of violence and intolerance, the Reformation marked the birth of a new authority in religion, that of individual thought. The cause of tolerance, liberty, and untrammelled inquiry was given a new lease on life. While Humanism and the Protestant Revolt both delayed the advent of the scientific revolution, Protestantism by its adherence to the biblical world view and Humanism by its reversion to the authority of the classics, together put an end to the medieval hegemony of the Church and accomplished the doom of Scholasticism. Nothing in the world today is more important than the one priceless contribution of the Reformation—the right of private judgment.

The Renaissance-Reformation contained both medieval and modern elements; it exhibited authoritarian as well as free concepts. It remained for later awakenings to clarify and extend the underlying principles of this epoch. It was left for the French and English Enlightenment to utilize the concept of freedom and with it to fashion modern democracy. Finally the nineteenth-century age of science and criticism was to apply the Baconian method to all of life and compel a vast reconstruction in theology and religion.

V

Voltaire

English Influences

THE REGENT OF FRANCE, meeting Voltaire in a park one day, said: "Monsieur Arouet, I'll bet I can show you something that you have never seen before." "What is that?" asked Voltaire. "The inside of the Bastille," came the quick reply. And Voltaire saw it the next day.

François Marie Arouet was a young man about town and perhaps somewhat more. His father had sent him to the Hague with the French Ambassador, requesting that he keep an eye on the young fellow. His flirtations, however, continued apace and at the age of twenty-one he was brought back to Paris.

Louis XV had just died and was succeeded by a regent. François' reputation for piety had not been enhanced by his Dutch sojourn and his subsequent antics in Paris were not calculated to help him any at the court. It is told that when the Regent for the sake of economy sold half the horses that filled the royal stables, François remarked how much more sensible it would have been to dismiss half the asses that filled the royal court. Certain poems suggesting that the Regent desired to usurp the throne were traced to M. Arouet. Then followed the incident in the park and the Bastille.

It was while he was in the Bastille that he adopted the

name Voltaire, the origin of which no one knows, but it may have come from his mother's family. His imprisonment bore other fruit in a work called *Henriade*, which was the story of Henry of Navarre. Not allowed writing paper during his twelve months' imprisonment, Voltaire wrote this lengthy poem between the lines of a printed book. The Regent suddenly relented (one year was punishment enough for writing a song) and released him with a pension. A few days after his liberation he met the Regent and facetiously remarked: "Monseigneur, I should be well pleased if His Majesty deigned to provide for my keep, but I beg Your Highness to make no further provision for my lodging."

Spurred on by this happy turn of fortune he wrote a tragedy called *Oedipe* which ran for forty-five consecutive nights, a record for those days. This play earned for him 4000 francs which he invested in a government lottery and from it realized a great sum. Voltaire became a matinée idol and a popular figure at the salons of Paris. It was at one of these dinners that Voltaire again struck a snag. The Chevalier de Rohan-Chabot asked: "What is the name of the young man who talks so loud?" The answer came fast. "My lord, he is one who does not drag a long name after him but does honor to the one he bears!" A few days later Voltaire was attacked by two hired ruffians while the Chevalier looked on. The day following, the poet appeared at the theatre, bandaged and limping. He approached Rohan's box and challenged him to a duel. The Chevalier was not expert with the sword. He avoided the duel and placed an order for Voltaire's arrest. On April 18, 1726, Voltaire was again on the inside of the Bastille but on May 2 he was freed on condition that he go into exile. This at 32 was a turning point in his life. His clowning days were now over. And it

was the English Channel that divided his youthful buf-
foonery from his more mature existence.

What was intended as a punishment turned out to be a
reward. England was Voltaire's intellectual birthplace, as
it was for Erasmus. Within a year he had acquainted himself with both the living literati and the dead. He noted
with astonishment that his newly won friends, Pope and
Swift, wrote whatever they pleased and nothing happened
to them. He wrote to a friend: "In this country it is possible
to use one's mind freely and nobly without fear and cring-
ing. If I followed my own inclinations, I should stay here,
if only to learn how to think." Here was an independent
and civilized people who had had their revolt against the
old regime. There was no Bastille, no religious persecution; the middle and lower classes compared with France
were cultured and happy.

Voltaire studied the British Constitution, which provided
tolerance and freedom for all classes. He spent much time
with Bolingbroke, Swift, Pope and Congreve. He mastered
the dramas of Shakespeare, the philosophy of Locke, and
the scientific genius of Newton. He came under the influence of Locke's *Human Understanding*, Bacon's rationalism, and Tyndale's reform. He passed into a new world, a
world of higher values. It was here that the poet become
historian and philosopher. Here his horizon was enlarged
and with it that of a continent. As Georg Brandes remarked: "England gave him the fulcrum of Archimedes
outside of France, from which he could move France and
the entire continent." [1] Through Newton he caught the
scientific attitude towards life and glimpsed the future of
physical discovery; through Everard Falkener, a com-
moner who later became Postmaster-General, he devel-

[1] *Voltaire*, Vol. I, p. 214.

oped an appreciation of the English middle-class and the dignity of the mercantile life. But most significant of all was his experience of freedom in a free, democratic and liberal country. English liberty became for him an ideal. Here no one could be deprived of his freedom by any authority; no one could be punished without trial; here was complete freedom of speech and press, complete toleration in religion. He had now seen two different systems in action and the contrast appears in his *Letters on the English*. These letters have been called the beginning of the French Revolution. Adopting the humorous or burlesque style in order to avoid direct opposition, Voltaire drew a comparison between the political and religious liberty of England with the tyranny of France. He admired the Quakers for their pacifism and the Unitarians for their intellectual integrity in religion, and both for their consistent avoidance of the sacerdotalism and dogmatism which have accrued to most religious sects. He praises the religious toleration of the English: "An Englishman, being a free man, goes to heaven by the road of his choice." Referring to political liberty he writes: "The English nation is the only one on this earth that has contrived to regulate the power of kings by resisting them. By one effort after another it finally established this wise system of government which leaves the prince all-powerful to do good, but ties his hands, if he be minded to do ill."

These letters constituted for the French and all Europe for that matter a Preface to Rationalism and Empiricism. But what appeared to the British as obvious was blasphemy to the clergy and nobility of France. It contained more political heresy, however, than theological, since the author said little about English Deism and the Reformation. But it had enough dynamite of both kinds to guarantee a public burning in Paris which took place promptly after its publication.

Cirey

The English exile lasted three years. Returning to France, Voltaire discovered that a *lettre de cachet* had been issued ordering his arrest. Smelling the rats of the Bastille again, he fled Paris and took refuge with the Marquise du Chatelet, with whom he had fallen deeply in love. The Marquise was a remarkable woman of extraordinary talents, combining a brilliant mind with passionate emotion. She translated Newton's *Principia*, knew Latin, and was an apt student of science.

At Cirey, hidden away in the hills between Champagne and Lorraine, was comparative safety. Voltaire and "the divine Emilie" had much in common. They lived in close intimacy for sixteen years. These were years of achievement and pleasure: scientific research during the day, and gay times after supper. The château became a favorite haunt of Parisians. Mathematicians came to consult these amateur physicists, others came to talk and were drafted into acting at their theatre. At Cirey Voltaire wrote two tragedies: *Merope* and *Mahomed* and two histories: *The Century of Louis XIV* and *Essay on Manners*.

The "new" history did not start with H. G. Wells and J. H. Robinson but with the hermit of Cirey. It was he who first humanized the historical process, saw it as an intense drama, a dynamic sequence rather than a static series of facts. He saw history as cause and effect and saw it whole, not a revelation or something superimposed. He wrote history from the standpoint of cultural growth and human progress, not mere political events. Indeed he may be called the first historian of modern times. While objective and accurate in his fact-finding, he was nevertheless a moralist; he had his thesis. Who, for that matter, does not? His thesis was that history is concerned with the achievements of men and the "progress of the human mind"; not with wars, intrigues, campaigns and ecclesiastical legends. For Voltaire the importance of the age of Louis XIV lay not in the pomp and circumstance of the court or military adventures but in the achievements of artists, scholars, and scientists. His economic history, to be sure, is inadequately treated due to his lack of technical training. His religious history is characterized by a total absence of sympathetic understanding, being content, as he was, to stand aloof and point to the pettiness of men who fanatically call their religion the only way of life. Being purely an intellectual, he failed to make room for the emotional and ritualistic forms which satisfied others.

The *Essay on Manners* (or Morals) is a plea for tolerance. This panoramic study of human history is heavily loaded with religion, science and the arts to the neglect of the economic and social factors but the socio-economic interpretation is a comparatively recent method and he can be pardoned for this lack of balance. What H. G. Wells and H. E. Barnes have been doing, Voltaire did amazingly well, but few people have ever been permitted to know it. He anticipated our present study of the Babylonian and Egyptian civilizations, opened up the field of comparative religions, pioneered in the recognition of the Arabic culture, introduced students to the Far East, and was the first to suggest a theory for the history of civilization. He sets forth no system but does see the history of mankind as a conflict between the prophet and the priest, the creative urge of rationalism and the reactionary influence of legalism.

The *Essay on Manners* was primarily a critique of the theory of revelation. As a deist Voltaire naturally denied the deityship of Jesus but respected him as a teacher, prophet, and religious genius. Organized religion, he said, had substituted theology for social morality. He refutes the miracles of Scripture by citing extra-biblical parallels. He traces the growth of the sacraments, reveals the scandalous conduct of the Councils, exposes the intrigues of the popes, recalls the horrors of the Spanish Inquisition and the wars of religion. He believes that progress is made possible only through human genius and rejects the environmental or climatic theory as fatalism. Such a view, while remedial for our day of economic obsessions, fails to recognize that religious and philosophical growths often occur as a result of changes in the economic sub-structure and in political life.

With all its limitations, this essay pointed the way to the liberal view of life and influenced all progressive thought in the West for two centuries. It called attention to the criterion of relative values. It demanded religious toleration, freedom of thought, constitutional government, and international peace.

Potsdam

As the chapters of his two histories came from his pen, they were eagerly read by Voltaire's admirers, one of whom was Frederick the Great. He wrote: "They are treasures of the mind. I feel that I have discovered in them the character of their ingenious author, who does honor to our age and to the human mind." This was the beginning of a famous correspondence and a long friendship. Frederick prided himself on being somewhat of a free thinker and poet, and reflected that he could become still more proficient in both capacities if Voltaire were attached to his court. The invitation to Potsdam was not accepted. Voltaire had other plans for the time. With new friends at the French court, he went to Paris and contrived in an obsequious manner to be elected to the Academy. He wrote plays, mingled with society, won titles, became again the favorite of the salons. The Marquise du Chatelet meanwhile fell in love with a M. de Saint-Lambert. This triangular situation soon terminated with du Chatelet's death. Voltaire held Saint-Lambert responsible for her death and he was probably not far from wrong since she died six days after the birth of a child—not by Voltaire.

Voltaire was now ready and willing to accept the invitation to Potsdam, especially since it was accompanied by an allowance of 28,000 francs and a few titles. His reception was dazzling and his surroundings sumptuous. He tried to avoid the military pomp and attended to the social affairs where the conversation was in French. Frederick in fact knew French better than his native tongue. The guttural German was too much for Voltaire who wished that "the Germans had more wit and fewer consonants."

Voltaire's daily chore was to tutor the King in the finer phases of the French language and to polish his poems for him. All went well for a while. His wit and repartee sparkled in the brilliant conversations around the King's table. The philosophical debates with the court savants were a challenge to the French deist. But Potsdam had its difficulties, which is not at all surprising in a circle of ambitious retainers, sensitive poets, and jealous rivals.

Ill feeling started when Voltaire was reported to have said: "The King sends me his dirty linen to launder." Frederick replied that "One squeezes the orange and throws the skin away." This relationship was aggravated by the fact that Voltaire was at this time speculating in some shady transactions in Prussia which finally resulted in a litigation. Frederick refused to have anything to do with Voltaire until the suit was settled. More words followed. The situation was climaxed with his quarrel with Maupertius, a celebrated mathematician. Maupertius had been made president of the Prussian Academy of Sciences, was an ardent follower of Newton, and an enemy of the Cartesians as the followers of Descartes, Malebranche and Spinoza were called. A favorite with the King, he could only regard Voltaire as a rival who was becoming more famous than himself. Maupertius wrote a monograph on the "law of least effort," asserting that nature always uses the minimum in physical causation. A Swiss mathematician named König criticized the paper and remarked that the theory had been anticipated by Leibnitz whom he quoted. A search was made for the original letters of Leibnitz and when nothing was found, Maupertius accused König of forgery and compelled the Academy to expel him. There was little doubt of the authenticity of the letters and it appeared to be an act of injustice. Voltaire, always interested in fair play, published a satire on Maupertius. This document offended the King as well as the mathematician and Frederick asked Voltaire to leave Potsdam.

Voltaire found it wise to do so. and at Frankfurt he was arrested by overly-zealous agents of the King. Upon his release six weeks later he began a period of wandering but finally settled down in Geneva. And so at sixty he decided to stop living on other people and support a house of his own. He purchased a villa by the lake and named it "Delight." But Protestant Geneva was no more friendly to a Deist than Catholic Paris. In an article for the *Encyclo-*

pedia he credited the Protestant clergy with a higher degree of liberalism than they themselves wished to admit and incidentally referred to Calvin as having a "cruel mind." Realizing that Geneva was no place for him, he promptly bought an estate at Ferney on the Swiss side of the border. This location had the advantage of being near enough to France to escape the heresy hunters of Geneva and, being in Switzerland, was out of reach of the French.

Ferney

Ferney marked the end of Voltaire's wanderings. Here he settled down and as lord of the manor he built cottages and factories, planted some 4000 fruit trees, repaired roads, employed and housed hundreds of refugees from Geneva, developed a silk industry, and became a pioneer in scientific agriculture and forestry. Strangely enough he built a church and over the door inscribed the words *Deo Erexit Voltaire*, claiming that he was the only person who had ever dedicated a church to God. He also constructed a tomb for himself, half of which was inside the church and half outside.

He supported a large household and was visited by many notables including such British writers as Gibbon and Boswell. He became impatient with some of his visitors who imposed on good nature. To one man who announced that he had come for six weeks Voltaire is reported to have said: "What is the difference between you and Don Quixote? You don't know? Well, Don Quixote mistook inns for châteaux, but you mistake this château for an inn."

His correspondence at Ferney was incredibly voluminous. Recognized throughout Europe as the leading thinker of the day, he was kept busy writing to Catherine II of

Russia, kings of many countries, the Encyclopedists of Paris, and countless friends. Here Voltaire, the old man, was looked upon as the lovable and generous benefactor, bringing security to hundreds of people; and his estate became a veritable shrine of liberty.

Ferney was the watershed of Voltaire's career. Here he became the intellectual force of France, not just a brilliant playwright, and from his stronghold he directed the battle for religious freedom. When the smoke of that battle cleared, it appeared that Voltaire had written enough to fill seventy-five volumes.

The Lisbon earthquake, which occurred during Voltaire's residence at Ferney and which killed 30,000 people, seriously affected his thinking. The French clergy explained it as God's punishment of the people for their sins. Rousseau blamed not God but man, who, he said, had no business living in cities and in houses. "Back to nature" was his cry. This throwback to the primitive incensed Voltaire and their philosophical enmity dates from this period. Rousseau was the romanticist, the sentimentalist, who believed emotion, intuition, and instinct furnished the key to the salvation of society. Voltaire contended that the way out and up was through the life of reason rather than passion.

Partly in opposition to Rousseau's philosophy of nature, partly as a satire on Leibnitz's philosophy of optimism, and partly perhaps as a post-mortem on the Lisbon earthquake, the sage of Ferney now produced *Candide*, his most famous work. The position advanced in *Candide* is neither the fatalistic pessimism of a Schopenhauer nor the superficial optimism of a Pope; it is that of candid realism. To insist that "everything is for the best in this best of all possible worlds" is wishful thinking. The world indeed is imperfect —at least from the human and finite point of view—and the individual must learn to accommodate himself to a universe that is full of tragedy. All is *not* well—witness the Lisbon earthquake, the judicial murder of Admiral Byng, the Seven Years' War, the burning of heretics at the stake, the curse of slavery. All is not well, but we can recognize the law of cause and effect in the physical world and the law of free moral agency in the human world, and, admitting a certain limitation placed upon us by our environment we can in the final analysis "cultivate our own garden." The fantastic tale of *Candide* carries a message for honest folk who seek for something that makes sense in a mad world: the inimitable laws of nature go on regardless of man's desires and man's freedom brings cruelty and chaos, but in our limited sphere we can do our own job well and derive internal satisfaction from the strife itself. This conclusion of *Candide* is not far from Browning's philosophy of struggle, and will always catch the imagination of free souls.

Voltaire's tranquil life at Ferney received a sudden interruption with the Calas affair. A traveller informed him of the cruel execution of Jean Calas, a highly respected Huguenot of Toulouse. He had been brutally tortured to death for the supposed murder of his son. Marc-Antoine Calas, the son, had been somewhat of an introvert with a gloomy and melancholy temperament. He had planned to study law but as a Protestant was barred from that profession. In fact, no Protestant in Fascist Toulouse could be a lawyer, physician, apothecary, grocer, bookseller, printer, or even a mid-wife. Brooding over the situation one day, the boy left the family at the dinner table, went into the nearby shed, and hanged himself. The family found him dead. The neighbors promptly spread the rumor that Marc-Antoine had been murdered by his own father because he wanted to become a Catholic and that there was a rule among Protestants that a father preferred his child's death to a change of faith.

Voltaire quit Ferney and began a thorough investigation. Every one who knew Calas testified to his fondness for his son. It appeared that another son had been converted to Catholicism through the servant, and he had forgiven the boy and even retained the servant. It was inconceivable that an old man could overpower and succeed in hanging a younger and stronger man. Furthermore, there was no evidence of Marc-Antoine ever expressing the remotest desire to become a Catholic.

The watch arrived shortly after the boy had been found dead and the whole family was arrested. The case was tried before a biased court and Jean Calas was sentenced to torture and death. The Church staged a sensational ceremony and Marc-Antoine was buried as a glorious martyr. In the middle of the church was hung a skeleton holding in one hand a paper inscribed "Recantation of Heresy" and in the other a palm symbolizing martyrdom.

By a vote of eight to five the Toulouse Parliament sentenced Jean Calas to be broken on the wheel. His death was an example of medieval cruelty and barbarism at its worst. He was first tortured on the rack. This was followed by pumping water into him. Then, practically naked and with a rope around his neck, he was taken to the Cathedral and exhibited. He was next stretched on the wheel and the executioner shattered his chest with an iron bar. The main idea of the torturers was to keep him alive as long as possible in order to give the people a keener enjoyment. After two hours' exposure on the wheel, he was strangled and his body burned. Having failed either to find any evidence of Calas' guilt or to extract a confession from the dying man, the parliament acquitted the widow but exiled the rest of the family.

All this appalled Voltaire. Convinced that an innocent man had been murdered, he determined to work for the rehabilitation of the family and a reversal of the sentence. For three years he labored incessantly and thought of nothing else. He spent a great amount of his own money on the support of the Calas family and the legal proceedings. He roused all his friends and interested the King of Prussia and the Empress of Russia. The London press took up the case and all Europe became agitated. With the utmost tact he conducted his campaign, allowing no exaggeration and squelching all demonstrations. Finally the case was retried by the King's court, the defense was heard for the first time, the decision was reversed, and Jean Calas was acquitted.

The vindication of Calas plunged Voltaire into another case, that of Pierre Paul Sirven, a Protestant of some social standing in Castres. The Sirven family was accused of the same crime and was equally blameless. The somewhat subnormal younger daughter had been abducted and forced to enter a monastery where brutal treatment and morbid surroundings brought on complete mental derangement with the result that she drowned herself in a well. In spite of the obvious innocence of the family, the Jesuit authorities at Castres were not to be outdone by the Toulouse fanatics. Sirven, knowing what would take place, fled to the Alps, but was finally caught and hanged. The rehabilitation of this family required several years and only led in turn to another case, more diabolic than ever.

A crucifix was found damaged at an old bridge in Abbéville and three young men were under suspicion. There was no evidence of their guilt but they were known to be free thinkers, had neglected on one occasion to uncover when a religious procession passed, were readers of heretical books, and that sufficed. The crucifix had probably been knocked down by a storm or a passing vehicle but it was easy to construe the incident as premeditated mutilation. One of the youths was condemned to have his right hand cut off and to be burned at the stake on a slow fire. Luckily he escaped but a second young man, de la Barre, was not so fortunate. He failed to confess under torture. The Parliament of Paris ratified the local decision and de la Barre's head came off. He had the satisfaction of resisting the executioner who tried to cut out his tongue at the root. Accompanying his head into the flames was a copy of Voltaire's dictionary.

Voltaire was by this time a changed man: the idol of the Paris salons gave way to the apostle of freedom. Wit and pleasantry were consumed by a passion for justice. Taking as his motto the words, *Écrasez l'infâme*, he declared total war on fanaticism. Ecclesiastical power had enslaved Europe long enough. There had been enough of burning of books, beheading of philosophers, execution of innocent people because they were of the wrong faith. The infamy must be crushed. Man must be emancipated from medieval superstitions, frocked fanaticism, authoritarian theocracy, and the rule of unreason. Just as he was about to launch his war against the tyranny of the Catholic Church, appeasement came his way in the form of a red hat. But instead of accepting a cardinalship, Voltaire plunged into an orgy of writing that aroused all Europe.

A Treatise on Tolerance was the first shot fired. Using the Calas affair as a point of departure, he argued for toleration of all religious faiths side by side and insisted on the right of every individual to hold and express his own opinion. God is the father of all and all men are brothers.

"Yes, I shall go even farther," he says, "and tell you that one should regard all human beings as one's brothers. —What! A Turk my brother? A Chinaman my brother? A Jew? A Siamese?—Yes, of course.—Are we not all children of the same father and creatures of the same God?" He relegated dogma to an unimportant position and made ethics the acid test of religion. Voltaire the "atheist" closes the essay with this prayer: "I turn, therefore, no longer to my fellowmen, but to you, O God of all creatures, all worlds, all times. Do not let the trifling differences in the clothing with which we envelop our puny bodies, in our poor languages, in our ridiculous customs, in our imperfect laws, our foolish opinions, our stations in society, which seem so far apart to us, yet so equal to you—let not all these petty differences be signals for hatred and persecution among the puny atoms called mankind. May all remember that they are brothers! May they all abhor the oppression of souls as they abhor the robbery which snatches away the fruits of their toil and peaceful industry. Should the misfortune of war be unavoidable, let us at least not hate and tear each other to pieces in the midst of peace, and let us make use of the brief moment we have to live, to bless equally in a thousand languages your goodness which has given us this moment."

The *Treatise on Tolerance* and the *Philosophical Dictionary* probably had more to do with the making of French liberalism than any other documents of the eighteenth century. The *Dictionary* was the means of liberalizing the middle class and also anticipated the findings of nineteenth-century biblical criticism. In both works Voltaire argued for the separation of Church and State, condemned ecclesiastical exemption from taxation, and demanded that the Church should not interfere with loans at interest. These two tracts were followed by a veritable flood of pamphlets, tales, novelettes, commentaries, histories, dialogues, letters, and essays—all aimed at the tyranny of injustice, bigotry and superstition.

Philosophy

Voltaire cannot be considered the creator of any new school of philosophy but he undoubtedly clarified and gave great impetus to religious naturalism and became the leading exponent of French Deism. Technically speaking, he was not a philosopher, yet he is France's greatest philosopher, chiefly because he *was* the eighteenth century. Like Paine, he was clearly opposed to atheism and went so far as to say that "if God did not exist it would be necessary to invent him." This indicated the utilitarian character of his deism. Following the argument of design, he reasoned that the unity and order of nature demanded a first cause, an initial impetus, and even, at times, extended the necessitarian argument to the future state, claiming that immortality presupposed a benevolent deity; although, on the whole, he was agnostic on the subject of the future life. The source of Voltaire's deism can be traced to his English visit and the writings of John Locke, but his deistic thinking might never have been expressed, at least not so aggressively, had it not been for the Calas affair, the persecution of the Huguenots, and the political power and abuses of the Jesuits. He would have been willing to put up with the creeds and ceremonies of the Church if the clergy had been tolerant, but the time came when he had to assert himself. In common with some of the English Deists, he saw in God a divine causality but not immanent in the world and rejected revelation in favor of reason. These were the essential features of Deism.

Militant deism in France, as Morais shows, led straight

to atheism, although that was not the case with Voltaire, who refused to take what Diderot considered the next logical step.[2] The atheistic implications of deism were followed also by Baron d'Holbach, who contended that nature itself held the answers to all questions including First Cause. Voltaire, holding to the necessitarian view, declared that common sense demanded the existence of an intelligent Being as Creator. Later, confronted with the dilemma of free will and the problem of evil, he found it necessary to divest God of most of the attributes that made him God. But the "genius of mockery" was never willing to accept the purely naturalistic and atheistic position. His belief in God is attested in his "Poem on the Lisbon Earthquake," and in hundreds of his letters. His attack was not on religion but on the crust of institutionalism that adhered to religion. Voltaire was, in other words, the French Reformation. His liberalism is seen not only in his opposition to miracles, clericalism, revelation, and theology *per se*, but also in his positive teaching. He was discriminating in his approach to the Bible, emphasizing the teaching of the Hebrew prophets and the Sermon on the Mount. His exaltation of Jesus, the ethical teacher, is second to none. He proposed an ethical relativity as over against the Kantian absolutism. There is no infallible, prior authority in morals; circumstance and the issue at stake are the determining factors. To worship God and live an honorable life —that is pure religion.

Recognition

The only weapon that could be used effectively in an age of clerical authoritarianism was wit, and this intellectual Mephistopheles of the eighteenth century made good use

[2] Herbert M. Morais: *Deism in Eighteenth-Century America*, p. 27.

of it. His ironic smile was enough to change the thinking of the Western world, and for one period in history at least the pen was really mightier than the sword. One of the first modern critics to recognize his true greatness was Georg Brandes who wrote: "Voltaire had more strength in the three fingers which held his pen than all the Parliaments of France in their clenched fists." [3] To this can be added the testimony of a more recent biographer: "He mocked and he destroyed; but he was probably as necessary to the well-being of Christendom as the Reformation." [4]

To describe a writer's style today as "French" is to say that he writes in the tradition of Voltaire, a style characterized by restraint, clarity, and precision. This was the spirit carried on by such representative writers as Stendhal, Flaubert, Sainte-Beuve, Renan, Anatole France and André Maurois—the Gallic tradition. When Voltaire died the throne of European letters, as Horace Walpole said, was "quite empty."

Because of the antipathy between the two men, Diderot's tribute is significant: "Were I to call him the greatest man nature has produced, I might find people to agree with me; but if I say she has never yet produced and is never likely to produce again a man so extraordinary, only his enemies will contradict me." Paine and Voltaire both suffer from the time-lag and they still bear the labels affixed in other days. But Voltaire lived long enough for many of his countrymen to catch up with him and thank him. Such was not the case with Paine.

Voltaire spent his last few years at Ferney, helping others and writing. At eighty-four he resolved to see Paris once again. He was warned by the doctors not to try it but he

---

[3] *Voltaire:* Vol. II, p. 269.
[4] Alfred Noyes: *Voltaire,* p. 634.

insisted on the trip, which was a continuous march of triumph. Reaching the outskirts of the city, the police asked whether the coach contained anything prohibited by the crown. "Gentlemen," Voltaire answered, "I do not believe there is any other contraband than myself."

In Paris he was deluged with visitors, including numerous priests who came to convert him. Benjamin Franklin came with his nephew. Placing his hand on the boy's head, Voltaire dedicated him to "God and Liberty."

When he was taken ill, a priest came to talk to him. The priest refused absolution unless Voltaire signed a full profession of faith in the Roman Catholic doctrine. He refused and promptly dictated a statement to his secretary: "I die adoring God, loving my friends, not hating my enemies, and detesting superstition."

He recovered temporarily and was driven to the theatre to see his play *Irene*. The city turned out to greet him. So for several weeks he enjoyed his triumph, renewed old friendships, and continued to wield the pen. But the strain proved too much. The end came May 30, 1778. He was denied Christian burial, but his friends secretly buried the body in Scellières. Thirteen years later, in 1791, with the Revolution at its height, the National Assembly decreed that the remains of Voltaire be brought back to the city and buried in the Panthéon. Six hundred thousand people watched the procession. On the funeral car was the following inscription: "He avenged Calas, La Barre, Sirven, and Montbailly. Poet, philosopher, and historian, he gave a mighty impetus to the human mind; he prepared us for freedom."

His body was laid next to that of Jean Jacques Rousseau, from whom he differed so much. But in 1814, at the time of the Restoration, the remains of both were seized by reactionary churchmen and mutilated. *L'infâme* had raised its ugly head again and conquered. But Voltaire's spirit lived on. That spirit is nowhere better expressed than in his message to the persecuted Rousseau—the most pregnant sentence of the eighteenth century: "I do not agree with a word that you say but I will defend to the death your right to say it."

French Rationalism

Natural Rights

Prior to the eighteenth century, liberalism was merely an intellectual attitude held by individual thinkers—Erasmus, Huss, Spinoza, and a score of others—but with the Age of Enlightenment in France, liberalism became an articulate and unified movement, a social organization. As a revolt against feudalism, the *Ancien Régime*, and the authoritarian Church, French liberalism made its attack on several fronts at once. Politically, it stood for representative government and popular sovereignty. Economically, it proposed freedom of contract and the laissez-faire principle in industry. In the realm of religion, it fought for toleration, equality, freedom of conscience, and the separation of Church and State. As a philosophy, it asserted the principle of individual freedom and civil liberty, popular education and free inquiry. Conspicuous among the contributions of the Enlightenment was the idea of progress. A reaction to the Augustinian pattern of thought was to be expected in the light of the Renaissance and the seventeenth-century scientific advance. Experience, reason, and knowledge of natural law, confronting absolutism, pointed to the error of thinking that the Golden Age lay in the past and that man had fallen from a perfect state of purity and wisdom. Without benefit of evolution the philosophers of the eighteenth century saw that social and intellectual progress had been made and that further improvement of man's status was in store. Future progress lay in the province of human intelligence and not in the belief that God would some time interfere in the downward trend of the human race and bring it back to the "City of God." The rejection of Augustinian quiescence and transcendentalism marks the beginning of modern thought. The eighteenth-century philosophers questioned both the doctrine that man had fallen from grace and the assumption that there was nothing he could do about it. They measured the common knowledge and morals of their time with antiquity and were convinced that progress had been made. They were equally certain that reason and knowledge would insure a better society in the future. This progress would ensue not from God's grace but from man's intelligence.

What made this intellectual revolution a politically and socially effective movement was the rise of the *Philosophes*. As Professor Schapiro has pointed out, these men affected the body politic because they were not "closet philosophers" but professional men of letters.[1] They were integrally related to the social, religious, and economic situation and managed to create a climate of opinion among the literate population. They themselves were recognized as belonging to the middle class and therefore had a "public." This middle-class reading public was intellectually alert and ready for a change. Consequently when the *Philosophes* began to preach against the moribund State and Church, they were given strong support; and the clash resulted in a second Renaissance.

The obscurantism of the Catholic Church in France, untempered by a Reformation, precluded any theological compromise. A Frenchman in the era of the Encyclopedists

[1] J. Salwyn Schapiro: *Condorcet and the Rise of Liberalism*, pp. 25 ff.

was either hot or cold, fanatical believer or free thinker. In England the Reformation had made possible a synthesis of religious faith and rational outlook, but when the revolt came in France, there were no half-way measures. The extent to which the Church had gone to the Right determined the extent to which the intellectuals swung to the Left. Rationalism and unbelief were the result. The *Philosophes* were opposed to revealed religion, asceticism, and the otherworldly character of the Church. They fought all vested interests and privileged classes, especially the Church, which held a vast amount of property and was exempt from taxation. They shifted the attention of thinking people from the theological to the logical and from the metaphysical to the physical. As the first thinkers to see the importance of earlier scientific research, they popularized Bacon, Copernicus, Galileo, and Newton.

The underlying political philosophy of the Age of Enlightenment was the theory of natural rights, according to which every human being, because he is a human being, has certain sacred and inviolable rights of person and property. This equalitarian doctrine, guaranteeing life, liberty, and the pursuit of happiness to all, became the central thesis of the founding fathers of the American colonies and found its way into the Bill of Rights and the Constitution of the United States.

Locke and Newton—Sources

When Jefferson penned the famous words that "all men are created equal, that they are endowed by their creator with certain inalienable rights," he was voicing a principle that was born in the French Enlightenment, to which he stood in an intimate relation. The source of the theory of natural rights was the philosophy of John Locke (1632–1704) whose political writings have been identified with the English revolution in 1688. It was Locke's belief that the function of the State is to guarantee the individual's rights, which to him were basic. Also prior to the State was the right to private property. The State, by virtue of "social contract," protects property and makes laws for the common good. Locke's influence in France was powerful and came through Voltaire and Rousseau whose opposition to absolutism brought on the French Revolution.

On the epistemological side, Locke was the author of modern empiricism. The mind, said he, contains no innate ideas. It is a clean slate upon which are registered ideas derived from objective experience. There are no general principles, moral or otherwise, which can be considered innate or universal. The mind knows nothing except through sense experience. Memory and reflection, acting upon the original experience, form mental material or complex ideas. Locke's empiricism had important theological implications in that doctrines formerly universally accepted need not now be held if they did not square with present human experience. Thus, Locke's Empiricism at once reversed medieval thought with its *a priori* universals and laid the foundations for nineteenth-century Pragmatism, which opposed transcendental sanctions and tested morality solely by its results in action.

The other great forerunner of the Enlightenment was Isaac Newton (1642–1727). Discovering the law of gravitation, the principles of calculus, and the theory of light before he was twenty-four years of age, professor at Cambridge at twenty-seven, and author of the *Mathematical Principles of Natural Philosophy*—perhaps the most important scientific work ever produced—Newton not only laid the physical foundations for the Enlightenment but made every scientist for 200 years his debtor. He was hailed by contemporaries as the Messiah and the resources of the language were exhausted in his praise. Of all the eulogies and encomiums of the time Pope's conveys best the awe in which the great mathematician was held:

> "Nature and Nature's laws lay hid in night:
> God said, Let Newton be; and all was light."

Newton's interpretation of nature, the answer to the dreams of Galileo and Descartes, defined the world as a cosmic machine, running according to perpetual mathematical principles. The universe, said he, is a uniform harmonious system, and it is the business of science to ascertain and tabulate its laws. This physico-mathematical method was applied to every field, including philosophy, ethics, and social science. The worship of the Newtonian world-machine became in fact a new religion. Man is the work of nature; he is an integral part of it and is subject to its laws. Nature is the handiwork of God and its laws are God's laws, eternally fixed, but discernible by man. Knowledge of those laws through the pursuit of science became the *summum bonum* of the eighteenth century. "What enthusiasm is nobler," exclaimed Buffon, "than believing man capable of knowing all the forces and discovering by his labors all the secrets of nature."

Locke and Newton were the two luminaries of the age of modernism, one, "the prophet of the science of nature" and the other, "the prophet of the science of human nature," as John Herman Randall, Jr., puts it. "Isaac Newton," continues Professor Randall, "effected so successful a synthesis of the mathematical principles of nature that he stamped the mathematical ideal of science, and the identification of the natural with the rational, upon the entire field of thought. Under the inspiration of Locke, the attempt was made to discover and formulate a science of human nature and human society, and to criticise existing religious and social traditions in the light of what seemed rational and reasonable." [2] Locke's Empiricism became nineteenth-century Positivism and Newton's world view evolved into twentieth-century Naturalism.

The liberalism of the Enlightenment is further seen in the substitution of reason for revelation. The *Philosophes* worshiped reason as the sole criterion in all things and the court of final appeal. Much has been made of the place of reason in the Thomistic system, but with Aquinas reason was used as a support or confirmation of the traditional Christian revelation, just as the Hellenistic Jews looked upon the Greek wisdom as an instrumentality of the Law. In other words, reason with Aquinas was secondary. So was it with the Protestant reformers, who insisted on a greater degree of reason and private judgment than the Catholic Church permitted, to be sure, but the sole authority with the Reformation leaders was the Bible. The same may be said to a certain extent of the Renaissance Humanists, where reason was present but was not the only criterion.

The first man to systematize the rational method philosophically was Descartes (1596–1650), whose *Discourse on Method* prescribed the discarding of all authorities and the acceptance of only those propositions which could be reasonably understood and demonstrated. While Descartes was ultimately eclipsed by Newton, the contribution of the Cartesian method to modern empirical thought was of prime importance.

The radical rationalism of the eighteenth century be-

[2] *The Making of the Modern Mind*, p. 255.

came more mellow in the nineteenth and was considered less inimical to religious faith, but the negative character of the Age of Reason was inevitable and served as a timely antidote to the superstitious beliefs of medieval Christendom. Following the Cartesian postulate that only those things are valid which are clearly conceived by the mind, the *Philosophes* claimed that all revealed religions were false and all forms of mysticism primitive.

Deism and Rationalism were subjected to a severe criticism by David Hume (1711–1776), the father of skepticism. Hume was more consistently empirical than Locke and followed the experiental criterion to its logical conclusion. Not only are there no innate ideas, he said, but it is unreasonable to believe anything (regardless of source) which has not been experienced and which cannot be corroborated by disinterested and complete testimony from independent witnesses. Uniform experience is the test as against isolated and improbable reports. The deistic proof of God on necessitarian grounds and the belief in immortality on the basis of rewards and punishments were also denied by Hume as lying outside of the field of experience.

Hume's criticism of physics led to a new position not unlike the most advanced scientific theory of the present day. He claimed that a scientific formulation does not stand for a cause-and-effect relationship in the objective world; it merely describes the impression made on the mind of the scientist that certain events follow in logical sequence. It cannot be inferred that such a series of events constitutes a universal law.

In other words, Hume's skepticism pushed Locke's empiricism one step farther. Even in the moral and political realms, universal principles are mere concoctions of the mind. Applied to religion, this extreme empiricism denied the miraculous element and, while not entirely opposed to the ideas of God and immortality, it laid open to question the validity of the necessitarian argument. Experience, not intellectual debate, was the criterion.

It must be said that in their worship of reason and in their infallible view of progress the leaders of the Enlightenment were guilty of oversimplification, and ignored or were ignorant of human emotion, human motive, and human nature. They failed to take into account the immortality of power and the sincerity of the devout. In rejecting blind faith and embracing cold reason, they left no place for emotion (Rousseau excepted) and, in repudiating the dogmas of the Church, they themselves became dogmatic and shortsighted. But iconoclasm here has its place; revision and compromise come with a later generation.

The *Philosophes*

The *Philosophes* were prophets but had no desire to be martyrs. Some of them were thrown into the Bastille but most of them escaped severe persecution by sugar-coating or disguising their revolutionary doctrines in fable, allegory, imaginary letters, and anonymity. Otherwise, they engaged in open warfare and fled when necessary.

Condorcet was doomed to the realm of the second-rate because he happened to live in an age that produced Voltaire, Rousseau, and Diderot. Although outshone by the more polished writers of his day, Condorcet was the perfect representative of the age. His *Sketch of the Intellectual Progress of Mankind* might well be called the Magna Charta of modern democracy. He was a pioneer of political liberalism and devoted himself to the principles of freedom of speech, constitutional government, religious toleration, freedom of labor and industry, abolition of slavery, and universal peace. He suggested the idea of a world court vested with power to judge international disputes. A world court "would destroy the seeds of war by establishing strong bonds among the nations in times of peace." He advocated the abolition of capital punishment and proposed a program of prison reform comparable to the best criminology of our day. Religion, according to Condorcet, should be divorced from the specific intellectual beliefs of the various faiths and should be concerned with right moral action. As a pioneer in the emancipation of women he was the forerunner of Mary Wollstonecraft. He was a champion of popular education. As for history, it should be so written that it can be "taught in England, in Russia, in Virginia, as well as in Berne or in Venice." The *Esquisse* was the first systematic treatment of the idea of progress, a theory which came to play a leading rôle in the later ideology of the nineteenth century. Like Voltaire's *Essay on Manners*, this sketch is a philosophy of civilization, an interpretation of history in terms of cultural progress. Conspicuous also is the doctrine of the perfectability of man, another potent influence in nineteenth-century scientific thought. Thus Condorcet is seen as a true humanist and, as a maker of the modern mind, he has never been accorded the place in history that he merits.[3]

Diderot, the founder of the *Encyclopedia*, propagandized through the volumes of that great work the cause of natural religion, scientific knowledge and industry. With him rationalism took the form of outright atheism, in which he was supported by d'Holbach and d'Alembert.

[3] J. Salwyn Schapiro (*Condorcet and the Rise of Liberalism*) is perhaps the first critic in America to do justice to Condorcet.

Rousseau, like Voltaire, was a deist, although a prudent and sentimental one. With him the heart was more reliable than the head. His deism was of a milder and more reverent type than that of Voltaire. He said God was to be felt, not mathematically proved. The term natural religion in Rousseau's case meant the experience of God through nature and the conscience and did not imply the rejection of mysticism and supernaturalism, as with all the other deists of the period. Passion and emotion were Rousseau's weapons for revolution but in these lay also the seeds of reaction and unreason. Instinct and feeling are the tools of the dictator and his "back to nature" philosophy is echoed today in the noticeable revolt against civilization, but his *Social Contract* and *Emile* led both to eighteenth-century revolution and nineteenth-century romanticism.

Turgot in political economy, Montesquieu in political and social science, and Voltaire in every field, complete the roll of the eighteenth-century libertarians. It is insufficient to say that their liberalism is dated and therefore useless; our course rather is to retain their principles in a revised social order, for their first affirmation was that institutions must change to insure progress.

The Enlightenment can be considered the beginning of the modern world because most of the thought forms of the present day had their origin in that period—democracy, reason, experience, natural rights, scientific outlook, secular education, liberty, and progress. The incipient liberalism of the Renaissance found fulfillment in the Age of Reason. The change in the intellectual climate from medievalism to modernism, begun by Renaissance Humanism, was completed by eighteenth-century Rationalism. This change has been fittingly characterized by Professor McGiffert: "The

humility, the self-distrust, the dependence upon supernatural powers, the submission to external authority, the
subordination of time to eternity and of fact to symbol, the
conviction of the insignificance and meanness of the present
life, the somber sense of the sin of man and the evil of the
world, the static interpretation of reality, the passive acceptance of existing conditions and the belief that amelioration can come only in another world beyond the grave, the
dualism between God and man, heaven and earth, spirit
and flesh, the ascetic renunciation of the world and its pleasures—all of which characterized the Middle Ages—were
widely overcome, and men faced life with a new confidence
in themselves, with a new recognition of human power and
achievement, with a new appreciation of present values,
and with a new conviction of the onward progress of the
race in past and future." [4]

Against the background of Newtonian science and the
Lockian theory of natural rights, the French Enlightenment developed the idea of natural religion. Considering
the current deification of nature and the paramount place
given to human reason, this sequence was logical enough,
as H. B. Jefferson points out: "If magic could be banished
from the physical world and all material motions be explained in a rational science of mechanics, if the myth of
the divine right of kings could be destroyed and replaced
by rational political principles, so also religion might be
freed from superstitions and made completely rational." [5]

In line also with Locke's empiricism and Newton's natural
law, the leaders of the Enlightenment looked at religion
solely from the utilitarian point of view. Its purpose was

[4] Arthur Cushman McGiffert: *The Rise of Modern Religious Ideas*, pp.
11–12.
[5] Eugene G. Bewkes, H. B. Jefferson et al: *Experience, Reason, and
Faith*, pp. 404–05.

purely to promote moral action. Mysticism and sacramentalism, doctrine and ceremony are of no consequence unless they stimulate righteous living. This is not far from the prophetic liberalism of Amos and Jesus and definitely underlies modern pragmatism.

Typical eighteenth-century religious thought differed from all previous schools in that it rejected revelation as supra-rational and supra-natural. Locke had not completely excluded revelation but in ruling out "all revelation that conflicts with reason" he left little that could be recognized. The Deists were more thorough-going in their rejection of revelation on the grounds that historic revelations have differed and are therefore fallible, and that they imply an arbitrary and unfair deity who reveals himself to some and not to others.[6] The Deists went still further in repudiating the sacramental and dogmatic accretions of Christianity as pagan and denouncing the clergy for their immorality, desire for power, and authoritarian methods.

The Enlightenment aimed to destroy the idea of the divine right of kings and gave birth to constitutionalism, dealt a staggering blow to clericalism and gave intellectual leadership to the laity, subordinated institutionalism to individualism, displaced ecclesiasticism with humanitarianism, revelation with reason, and tradition with experience. From the conservative standpoint the Age of Reason reduced religion to its lowest terms but it might well be said that in its representative form with its emphasis on God, virtue, and immortality, the Enlightenment saved Christianity for people outside the orthodox fold. Between traditional Christianity with its doctrine of human depravity and the Enlightenment with its humanitarianism, the latter held out more hope and more help to mankind.

[6] See Chapter 6.

While the Enlightenment can be viewed as an extension of the Renaissance in its shift from the transcendental to the secular and of the Reformation in its appeal to private judgment as over against authority, it differed in some respects from these and all previous revolutions in its location of authority. Whereas the Humanists had substituted the authority of the Greek and Roman classics for that of the Church, the philosophers of the Enlightenment subordinated all authority—Church, classics, and Bible—to Reason. In replacing ecclesiastical authority with private judgment, the Reformers succeeded only in shifting the basis of absolutism from the Church to the Bible. The leaders of the Enlightenment, on the other hand, rested their case on natural law and science.

Later intellectual revolutions, however, went even farther and questioned the idea of authority itself. Thus the Enlightenment, as Preserved Smith observes, did not break with the past as completely as nineteenth-century thought. Medieval Scholastics, Humanists, Reformers, and Deists alike regarded the world as "a comprehensible unit, to be fitted into a rational scheme." [7] Modern thinkers tend to view the world experientially or pragmatically and not rationally. But the pragmatic naturalism of the twentieth century would have been impossible without the rationalism of the eighteenth.

The rationalism of the eighteenth century became articulate because of the rise of the intellectuals to an influential position in politics and society. Their appeal to reason coincided with the improved condition of the upper middle class which was able both to purchase and to read intelligently the books written by the intellectual leaders. Influenced by natural science the *Philosophes* introduced a new

[7] *A History of Modern Culture*, Vol. 2, *The Enlightenment*, p. 18.

world-view or intellectual atmosphere. The Enlightenment resembled a new religion, as one modern historian says, "of which Reason was God, Newton's *Principia* the Bible, and Voltaire the prophet." [8] Science furnished new standards of truth, and Reason supplanted all traditional authorities. Under this banner the vanguard of modernism marched with optimism and enthusiasm towards a new social order. In the wake of Reason came war on intolerance, ecclesiastical tyranny, superstition, and witchcraft. Politics and morals were secularized. Freedom of thought became the new watchword.

[8] *Ibid.,* p. 21.

VII

Thomas Paine

Man Without a Country

JOHN ADAMS is reported to have said to Tom Paine: "Where liberty is, there is my country," to which Paine replied: "Where liberty is not, there is mine." That was the answer of a man without a country, whose fight for liberty was carried on in three countries, and who had much to do with the making of one of them.

Thomas Paine, British subject with a price on his head, French citizen condemned to the guillotine, and American patriot, ostracized and persecuted by high and low, was the one man in the world best fitted to give the colonies their name—the United States of America, but so complete was the ignominy heaped upon the author of *The Age of Reason* that history books have neglected to credit him with that or any other of his many contributions to humanity.

Ethan Allen and Tom Paine were both born in 1737 and they had other similarities. They were both unschooled in the formal sense, yet both succeeded more than any other Americans of the Revolutionary period in epitomizing the thoughts of the Enlightenment and the Age of Reason. They held the same deistic views in religion and fought the same fight for political liberty. Both wrote in the language of the people. If Paine had couched his *Rights of Man* and *Age of Reason* in academic terms and had used the subtleties of the scholars, the defenders of the faith would have smiled outwardly and the common people would never have been the wiser; but Paine's mistake was that he wrote in plain, unadulterated Anglo-Saxon so that he who ran could read.

Tom Paine was a pioneer in the cause of democracy and an advocate of international arbitration, emancipation of the negro, the rights of women, world patriotism, and religious freedom. "Independence is my happiness, and I view things as they are without regard to place or person; my country is the world and my religion is to do good." That was Tom Paine.

"Go west" was the advice that Franklin gave to Paine when they met in London in 1774. Tom had left school at thirteen; had worked in his father's corset factory; had run away to sea at nineteen; had tried teaching school; had begun again as a stay-maker; had lost two wives, one by death and the other by separation; had been employed twice in the excise service and had been twice dismissed; had preached without orders and was now penniless. He had also acquired some reputation as a reformer, and at a time when most young men were concerned with their own security he had given himself to the cause of humanity. While in London trying to get before Parliament a bill for the relief of excisemen, Paine met Franklin. Perhaps the American saw in Paine just the man who would be of service to the colonies; at any rate he gave him letters of introduction to influential men. Paine's arrival in the new world on November 13, 1774, was also the beginning of a new life for him.

America: *The Crisis* and *Common Sense*

Soon after settling in Philadelphia, Paine wrote some anti-slavery articles for the *Pennsylvania Magazine*. His contributions increased the circulation so noticeably that he was promptly engaged as an assistant and later became editor. As editor, he turned the magazine into a lively organ of reform, advocating abolition of war, exposing poverty, arguing for international copyright laws, describing monarchies as anachronisms, and ridiculing the practice of duelling.

In an article on war written in July 1775 one can see both his father's Quakerism and a foreshadowing of his revolutionary writings: "I am thus far a Quaker, that I would gladly agree with all the world to lay aside the use of arms, and settle matters by negotiations; but unless the whole world wills, the matter ends, and I take up my musket. . . . We live not in a world of angels."

Paine saw even before Washington and Jefferson that reconciliation with England was out of the question. Six months before the memorable Fourth of July, Paine published a pamphlet entitled *Common Sense* which made him the spokesman of a nation and led directly to the Declaration of Independence. *Common Sense* sold 120,000 copies in three months, the income from which was given to Washington for the equipment of his army. Paine never accepted any money for his writings but turned the royalties over to the American cause. *Common Sense* was the literary "shot heard round the world." It was the first clear call for separation from England and within a few months after its publication George Washington reported that it "was working a wonderful change in the lives of many men." Joel Barlow, a distinguished political writer, went so far as to say that "the great American cause owed as much to the pen of Paine as to the sword of Washington." The statement has more than once been made that "whoever may have written the Declaration of Independence, Paine was its real author." This is partially true, at least, for, as a recent biographer points out, "The principles he had laid down [in *Common Sense*] were embodied in that famous Manifesto and he was hand-in-glove with Thomas Jefferson while it was being drawn up."[1] Paine prevailed upon Jefferson to write into the Declaration of Independence an anti-slavery clause, but it was ruled out because of the objection of Georgia and South Carolina.

Paine's next move was to join Washington's army under General Greene. The days preceding Trenton were the darkest of the War and as Paine witnessed the despair of Washington and his starved and ill-clad soldiers, he knew the critical hour had come. But bad as the situation was, physically, the thing that was needed most was a spiritual reinforcement, and this Paine provided in his first *Crisis*. If *Common Sense* had aroused the country to action, this pamphlet gave the people faith to continue when all seemed lost. "These are the times that try men's souls. The summer soldier and the sunshine patriot will, in this crisis, shrink from the service of his country; but he that stands it now deserves the love and thanks of man and woman. Tyranny, like Hell, is not easily conquered; yet we have this consolation with us, that the harder the conflict the more glorious the triumph. What we obtain too cheap we estimate too lightly; 'tis dearness only that gives everything its value. Heaven knows how to put a proper price upon its goods; and it would be strange indeed, if so celestial an article as Freedom should not be highly rated."

When these words were read to the army there was a turning point in America's fortunes. Washington's men arose new creatures, electrified and filled with new hope. On they went to Trenton and victory.

Hardly had the ink dried on that potent document than

[1] Hesketh Pearson: *Tom Paine: Friend of Mankind,* p. 30.

another *Crisis* appeared as an answer to Lord Howe's proc-lamation granting mercy to the American troops if they would renounce their rebellion and acknowledge George III as King. In this *Crisis*, January 13, 1777, appeared for the first time anywhere the phrase, "the United States of America." "The United States of America," wrote Paine, "will sound as pompously in the world or in history as the Kingdom of Great Britain." During the Revolution thirteen editions of the *Crisis* were issued. The income from these amounted to some 300,000 pounds, all of which was given to Washington's army.

Meanwhile Paine was made Secretary to the Committee on Foreign Affairs. His correspondence with Washington, other military leaders, and members of Congress through-out this period contained expert advice which, if followed, would have resulted in a more efficient conduct of the war. Then came the Deane controversy which proved so disas-trous to Paine. Silas Deane was sent to France to secure financial aid and was exposed by Paine in an attempted fraud and also a plot to supplant Washington by a German. Congress, impelled by diplomatic motives, ignored the evidence, supported Deane and disowned Paine.[2] Paine's reward for this service was dismissal from office, political ostracism, and public scorn. He became ill through lack of nourishment and was too poverty-stricken to take care of his physical needs; yet he continued with his writing and giving himself to public welfare. After repeated appeals for financial help, he succeeded in being appointed clerk of the Pennsylvania Assembly, in which office he penned the first proclamation of emancipation in America, in connection with a bill for the abolition of slavery in Pennsylvania.

[2] See Moncure Conway: *Life of Thomas Paine*, for details. (Vol. I: pp. 116 ff.)

In 1781 Paine, having somewhat recovered physically and financially, accompanied Colonel John Laurens to France to negotiate a loan. Through Paine's influence with the King of France they were able to return with over two million livres of silver and a shipload of clothing and military stores. This made possible Washington's prosecution of the campaign which ended with the surrender of Cornwallis. Again Congress failed to acknowledge an historic service. As Moncure Conway has shown, it was Paine who conceived the plan to obtain French aid and it was he who successfully executed it. He had given up his projected book on the Revolution and had risked his life in making the trip (capture by the British would have meant death), but it was Laurens who received both the pay and the glory, and Paine, who had paid his own expenses, received neither. In desperation Paine wrote to Washington, who secured for him an annuity of $800 as a subsidy for his writing.

The end of the war found Paine in Bordentown, again without salary. Washington urged his friends to come to the aid of the author of the *Crisis* and this time Congress made Paine a grant of $3000. In 1787 he decided to visit Europe in order to see his parents and to complete his work on his bridge model. In France his plans were approved by the French Academy and he himself was cordially received by Condorcet, Danton and other French radicals who shared his views. He went almost immediately to England where he visited his former home, wrote pamphlets and letters, and busied himself with various ideas for inventions. He finished the bridge model and plans were under way for construction when Paine's attention was redirected to political events. On July 14, 1789, the Bastille fell and Lafayette gave Paine the key to that famous prison to present to George Washington as an evidence of "the first ripe fruit of American principles transplanted into Europe."

England: *The Rights of Man*

Recrossing the Channel, Paine, once again caught up in the radical movement which was sweeping the western world, envisaged a British democracy along American lines. Edmund Burke, who had written so enthusiastically about the American cause, now reversed his position and placed himself among the great conservatives of history as he renounced the French Revolution and apotheosized the monarchy. Burke's *Reflections* was a challenge and Tom Paine was not long in replying. *The Rights of Man* completely demolished Burke and outlined for England a democratic constitution. Few books have had such an immediate and widespread effect. Over a million copies were sold. The publishers were prosecuted, the author was tried for treason and the book was banned. But it became the Bible of the common people who went about the streets singing:

"He comes—the great Reformer comes!
Cease, cease your trumpets, cease your drums!
Those warlike sounds offend the ear,
Peace and friendship now appear;
Welcome, welcome, welcome, welcome.
Welcome, thou Reformer, here!
Prepare, prepare, your songs prepare,
Freedom cheers the brow of care;
The joyful tidings spread around,
Monarchs tremble at the sound!
Freedom, freedom, freedom, freedom—
Rights of Man, and Paine resound!"

The Rights of Man was dedicated to Washington with these words: "I present you a small treatise in defense of

those principles of freedom which your exemplary virtue
hath so eminently contributed to establish." Washington,
being President, refused to commit himself, but Jefferson,
Madison, and Edmund Randolph hailed the work as prophetic and urged that Paine be appointed to the cabinet.

The Rights of Man lacks the idea of evolutionary
achievement, but the theory of natural rights (that men
were originally endowed with natural rights but were later
deprived of them) served well the eighteenth-century radicals in their battle against privilege. The two forces which
had deprived men of their rights were the Church and the
State. The French and American Revolutions were seen as
the recovery of man's natural rights. Legalism in religion
was an enemy of freedom. "Persecution is not an original
feature in any religion; but it is always the strongly marked
feature of all law-religions, or religions established by law.
Take away the law establishment, and every religion assumes its original benignity." Divine right and hereditary
kingship are ridiculed as "a burlesque on monarchy, pre-
senting it as an office which any idiot may fill."

War was unmasked as an artificial system of government
which should be outlawed. "The animosity which nations
reciprocally entertain is nothing more than what the policy
of their government excites to keep up the spirit of the system. Each government accuses the other of perfidy, intrigue, and ambition as a means of heating the imagination
of their respective nations, and incensing them to hostilities.
Man is not the enemy of man but through the medium of a
fake system of government." In this epochal work Paine
also proposed a graduated income tax, labor unions, the
education of children at public expense, old-age pensions,
and measures to counteract unemployment.

His picture of the American experiment in democracy

(where "the poor are not oppressed, the rich are not privileged, taxes are few, because their government is just") requires some retouching in the light of later times; and we have found that the problems of society are decidedly more complex than the eighteenth-century pioneers of democracy realized. But the important lesson from *The Rights of Man* is that new conditions demand new forms; constitutions and institutions must change. Democracy and liberalism cannot be identified with any passing or historical phase, but must be revised periodically. It is the wine that is valuable; not the wineskin. "No generation possesses the right to determine the form of government to the end of time. Every age and generation must be free to act for itself. The circumstances of the world are continually changing. . . . That which may be found right and convenient in one age, may be thought wrong and found inconvenient in another. The best constitution that could now be devised, consistent with the tradition of the present moment, may be far short of that excellence which a few years may afford."

The Rights of Man was labelled seditious writing and court action was taken against Paine, who immediately revealed his whereabouts and actually appeared in an English court of his own accord. It may well be that by this time Paine's success had gone to his head and he was becoming somewhat bumptious. He began to see himself as a martyr to the cause of freedom. He probably irritated others with his high opinion of himself and his uncompromising aggressiveness. The trial, however, was postponed and when the case was reopened Paine was on the way to France.

Meanwhile great honors had come to the author of *The Rights of Man* from across the Channel. France made him a citizen and a month later he was elected to the National

Convention. Paine saw in this turn of affairs a chance to
help in the making of French history. At a dinner with
some friends he announced his decision to leave England.
William Blake, the well-known poet and mystic, advised
him to go at once. "You must go home," he said, "or you
are a dead man." The government had pressed the charges
and secured conviction. Paine left for Dover by a secret
route in order to escape the officers who had been dis-
patched to his house. Just as his packet sailed away, the
officials with the warrant for his arrest drove down the
cobble-stoned streets of Dover and pulled up at the wharf
to gaze at the departing ship.

France: *The Age of Reason*

While outlawed in England, Paine received a welcome
in France usually accorded royalty. Batteries boomed, thousands cheered, and bands played. "The birds are flown,"
cried Lafayette when the royal family fled Paris; and Paine
replied, "It is well; I hope there will be no attempt to
recall them." Paine was appointed to a committee of nine
to draft a constitution. Working with him on this historic
document was Condorcet, who stood closer to Paine in principle and in person than any other Frenchman. The onrush
of events, however, precipitated an unlooked-for terrorism
which displeased the Quaker Paine. In the uprising of the
Jacobins against the King, Paine was the only leader who
dared to oppose execution. He was against the monarchy
but not against the King; "it is the kingly office rather than
the officer" that must be destroyed. His vigorous protest
against the death penalty aroused the wrath of Marat and
other radicals and placed Paine in grave danger.

Louis, the King, was sent to the guillotine and when, in

July 1793, Robespierre rose to power, the butchery began. The purge included practically all the republican leaders but Paine; Robespierre apparently lacked the courage to give the word which would send the author of *The Rights of Man* to death. But the terrorists would soon find some pretext to take him. The statement had been uttered more than once that "Frenchmen are mad to allow foreigners to live among them" (much less write their Constitution!). Retiring to his rooms in a house once inhabited, ironically enough, by Madame Pompadour, he conferred with those republican sympathizers who were still alive. And here he began *The Age of Reason*.

The blow was not long in coming. Paine was arrested on the charge that he was an Englishman. His American friends in Paris drew up a petition for his release, but one important signature was conspicuous by its absence, that of Gouverneur Morris, the American Minister to France. Papers found later substantiate Paine's surmise that Morris was his greatest enemy in France, not the terrorists. He wrote to Monroe: "However discordant the late American minister Gouverneur Morris and the late French Committee of Public Safety were, it suited the purposes of both that I should be continued in arrestation. The former wished to prevent my return to America, that I should not expose his misconduct; and the latter lest I should publish to the world the history of its wickedness."

The details of the Morris conspiracy remained secret for a hundred years and were brought to light in 1892 by Moncure Conway in his excellent life of Paine. Differences between Paine and Morris began in America over the Silas Deane controversy, in which Morris had supported Deane. What little good feeling was left in 1792, when Morris was appointed minister, was dissipated by the fact that one was royalist and pro-British and the other, republican and pro-French. Paine's prestige in diplomatic circles and superior knowledge of French affairs of state was a source of annoyance to Morris, and in the Anglo-French War, which broke out at this time, he was further humiliated by the fact that the Convention's favorable attitude towards America was the result of Paine's influence, not his. Overruling the action of the American minister, Paine secured the return of ninety-two American ships to their owners and then asked Morris "if he did not feel ashamed to take the money of his country and do nothing for it."

Morris was a lewd dandy, an aristocratic snob, and an enemy of democracy and freedom. His hatred and fear of Paine now prompted him to plot for Paine's arrest. Genet, the French minister to America, had been recalled because of Washington's complaints. Morris accused Paine of being hand in glove with Genet in his trickery in America, adding that, as an Englishman, he was dangerous to France and was even now plotting against the country. A law was passed requiring the imprisonment of nationals from countries at war with France. Paine was promptly arrested along with all the Girondists that could be found. On December 28, 1793, the doors of the Luxembourg prison closed behind him. As he entered the cell he handed the manuscript of *The Age of Reason* to his friend, Joel Barlow.

What were the diabolical contents of this work which ruined the remainder of Paine's life and anathematized his name for all posterity? What makes this dastardly volume the Bible of infidelity and the most defamed book in history?

Paine had intended for many years "to publish (his) thoughts upon religion." He had defined for himself political freedom in *The Rights of Man*; he wanted now to define freedom in religion. Essentially there was no difference in his mind; in religion as in politics, everything depended on the basis of authority; in both man must be free. He had undermined the idea of the divine right of the State and monarchy; he proposed now to do the same with the idea of Biblical infallibility and the divine right of the Church. Bible and Church were external superimposed authorities, and should be subordinated to the ethical criterion. He would prove that the Scripture was fallible and that the Church was at best a man-made instrument, not an end in itself. Religious authority should be internal; religion should be an individual experience, not a blind faith in mysteries. Religion, above all, should be reasonable and free of superstition. To separate essential religion from theology and magic was his aim in writing *The Age of Reason*, "lest," as he says "in the general wreck of superstition, of false systems of government and false theologies, we lose sight of morality, of humanity, and of the theology that is true."

A letter to Samuel Adams sheds further light on Paine's purpose in writing. "The people of France were running head-long into atheism and I had the work translated and published in their own language to stop them in that career, and fix them to the first article of every man's creed—I believe in God." Plainly he took the same deistic position as Voltaire as over against the atheistic tendency of some of the Encyclopedists. This fanatical atheism of the Leftists went hand in hand with the political terrorism. It was Paine's purpose to strike a balance between the superstitious, priest-ridden religion of the French Church and the faithless radicalism of the revolutionaries. He dreamed of a religion of reason, morality, and humanity, the kind of religion lived by Jesus. "I believe in one God, and no more," he wrote, "and I hope for happiness beyond this life. I believe that religious duties consist in doing justice, loving mercy, and endeavoring to make our fellow-creatures happy."

These opening words rather than being the argument of an atheist are the epitome of the teaching of Amos, Micah, and Jesus, and could have come only from a deeply religious person. The test of a person's religion lies in his conduct and by that test Paine was truly a saint. He was generous and unselfish, consistently sacrificing all royalties in order to help some cause. In 1780, when Washington announced that his soldiers would mutiny if they were not relieved, Paine headed the subscription list with his total salary of $500. But generosity of mind is a greater virtue than the generosity of a more visible sort and Paine was not lacking in that respect. One of his enemies, a conceited and bombastic individual, had struck him in public, yet when he gained permission to leave the country Paine gave him travelling expenses from his own funds. With Tom Paine religion was not a theological formula, divorced from life, but a way of living. His whole life was an application of Christian idealism but the people of the world forgot his humanity, love of fellowmen, his kindness and gentleness, in their eagerness to crucify him.

In setting forth the human reason as authority in religion rather than the Scripture, Paine first attacked the idea of inspiration by showing the errors, anachronisms, immoralities, and inconsistencies of the Old and New Testaments. With Voltaire he was one of the first to prove biblical dependence on earlier myths and to point to pagan-Christian analogies. Seeing the Bible as a "history of the grossest vices and a collection of the most paltry and contemptible tales," Paine could not bring himself to call it the Word of God. "It is the duty of every true Deist," he said, "that he vindicate the moral justice of God against the calumnies of the Bible."

Paine's biblical criticism is crude and his language is blunt, but however expressed, *The Age of Reason* was an epoch-making book. One hundred years later the same observations could be made with much more safety. Paine knew his Bible more thoroughly than most of his critics, and his style, while unnecessarily belligerent, was more scholarly and technical than is usually supposed. In disproving the Mosaic authorship of the Pentateuch he used the evidence ordinarily considered original with the higher criticism of a century later; in fact, modern studies of the Pentateuch have added nothing to Paine's thoroughgoing treatment. His argument is based solely on the internal evidence of the Scripture, is transparently lucid and is utterly devoid of all pedantry; but Paine was simply ahead of his time and, as he himself later wrote, "to argue with a man who has renounced his reason is like giving medicine to the dead."

It was not Paine's motive merely to raise a laugh or to scoff; he was in deadly earnest. His method of reasoning was never casuistical but factual and intelligible. He finds in the fable of Jonah a lesson in universalism and tolerance, a satire of Gentile origin. He sees importance in the philosophical inquiries of Job and admires the deistical nineteenth Psalm. He distinguishes between the historical Jesus and the mythical Christ. In these observations and also those on biblical chronology and comparative mythology Paine anticipated Baur, Strauss, Wellhausen, and Renan.

Sectarianism, parochialism, and ecclesiasticism receive their share of the attack in *The Age of Reason*. "The adulterous connection of church and state," he writes, "wherever it had taken place, whether Jewish, Christian, or Turkish, had so effectually prohibited by pains and penalties every discussion upon established creeds, and upon first principles of religion, that until the system of government should be changed those subjects could not be brought fairly and openly before the world. . . . All national institutions of churches, whether Jewish, Christian, or Turkish, appear to me no other than human inventions set up to terrify and enslave mankind, and monopolize power and profit. . . . It is certain that in one point all nations of the earth and all religions agree. All believe in a God. The things in which they disagree are the redundancies annexed to that belief; and therefore if a universal religion should prevail, it will not be by believing anything new, but in getting rid of redundancies, and believing as man believed at first. Adam, if ever there was such a man, was created a Deist; but in the meantime, let every man follow, as he has a right to do, the religion and worship he prefers."

Paine's deistic principles underlie the entire work. "The creation we behold is the real and ever existing word of God, in which we cannot be deceived. It proclaims his power, it demonstrates his wisdom, it manifests his goodness and beneficence. The moral duty of man consists in imitating the moral goodness and beneficence of God. . . . The only idea man can affix to the name of God is that of first cause, the cause of all things."

This type of Deism relieves the deity of blame for evil, but in accrediting the beauty and beneficence of the natural world to God, it produces an unreasonable dualism. There can be only one world ground and primal cause in nature whether it be beautiful (according to our notions) or ugly. The only consistent solution of the problem of evil is to divorce completely the arbitrary activity of deity in the natural world, to regard nature as morally neutral, immutable, and to see in every evidence of adversity one of two things: man's free moral agency or the physical law of cause and effect. Considered from these two standpoints, there is no great mystery about suffering or about a flood or about an automobile accident, but some theologians still prefer mystery to realism. Paine, in going half way, at least freed the deity from the barbaric cruelty of traditional belief.

A dispassionate reading of *The Age of Reason* gives the lie to Paine's calumniators. Rather than being a book to destroy religious faith, it is a militant polemic *against* infidelity. Paine was not against God but against those who claimed a monopoly on God's revelation. It is a further misrepresentation to speak of Paine as an enemy of Christianity—unless by Christianity is meant the organized Church with its dogmas and sacraments. The unorthodox statements of Tom Paine are today the considered beliefs of most informed people.

Robespierre signed the death sentence and the "news" of Paine's execution was enthusiastically received in England. The doomed were marched past Paine's cell each day until it seemed as if he and his three companions were the only prisoners left. In six weeks 1400 were guillotined. Betrayed by Morris, who wrote nothing but lies to Washington throughout this period, and deserted by France and America, Paine waited to be dragged away. When at last his turn came he was stricken with fever and for several days was delirious. When he regained consciousness he learned that Robespierre had been guillotined and that he himself had been saved by a miracle. It was the custom to make a chalk mark on the cell door of those who were to be guillotined the next morning and this sign was made on Paine's door.

It happened that the door was open, flat against the wall, and the chalk mark was made on the inside of the door. In the morning the "destroying angel," as Paine later wrote, "passed by it." Biographers, following Paine's own surmise, are inclined to think that this was not an accident but the work of a friendly keeper.

As long as Morris was minister, no effort was made to free Paine, but when Monroe was appointed to the post measures were taken to secure Paine's release. On November 4, 1794, Thomas Paine was again a free soul after ten months' imprisonment, the physical and mental effects of which made it seem like ten years. He resumed work in the Convention, helped Monroe in his duties, and added some material to *The Age of Reason*. Washington's silence throughout Paine's imprisonment can be explained only on the grounds that his mind had been poisoned by Gouverneur Morris. Paine now wrote to Washington but received no answer. Perhaps his letters were never laid before the President. Paine bitterly renounced the man he had loved above all men.

One of his callers at this time was Napoleon, who tried through flattery to persuade Paine to help in an attack on England, stir up a revolution, and establish a sister republic. Paine was interested in the idea of a republic but he suspected Napoleon's motive and turned him down.

Ingratitude

When Jefferson became President, he invited Paine to America, and the temptation to revisit the scenes of his former labors was too strong to resist. Paine's remaining years would have been happier ones if he had stayed in Paris, for he came to America as the author of *The Age of*

Reason and not as the apostle of freedom who had done more for the United States during the Revolution than any other man except Washington.

Already the moral idealism of Revolutionary America had given way to class consciousness, religious obscurantism, commercial prestige, and political reaction. His return to America was like an attempt to invade an enemy's territory. The only wedge in this solid block of opposition was made by President Jefferson, who gave him a warm welcome and aroused the ire of press and public by walking arm in arm with Paine along the streets of Washington. Democracy-hating Federalists flayed Jefferson for receiving into the country a "lying, drunken, brutal infidel, who rejoices in the opportunity of basking and wallowing in the confusion, bloodshed, rapine, and murder in which his soul delights," and cried, "Let Jefferson and his blasphemous crony dangle from the same gallows." Religionists, pro-slavery forces, the public in general, and the press in particular heaped up abuse and villification, the quantity or quality of which has never been excelled in the history of the country. That Thomas Paine, "a drunken atheist and the scavenger of faction" should be invited to return to the country was "an insult to the moral sense of the nation," wrote one prominent editor. Finally, the pressure from all sources was so overwhelming that Jefferson himself began to avoid Paine. The latter, sensing the situation, moved to Philadelphia where he resumed work on his bridge models.

From Philadelphia he went to Bordentown, his old home, where he was again deserted by former friends, jeered and hissed. Desiring to see Monroe before he sailed to Europe to complete arrangements for the Louisiana Purchase, Paine journeyed to New York. At Trenton he was unable to hire a coach: no driver would risk his life with a cursed man. Wherever he went, doors were closed, people spat on him, and mothers picked up their children and ran to cover. Finally he moved to the farm at New Rochelle where he found some comfort in writing letters and pamphlets. Even here he was not safe. One night as he sat in his study, several bullets crashed through the window, just missing him, and lodged in the wall. The would-be assassin was his hired-man who was a religious fanatic and considered the murder a command from on high. He was arrested but Paine refused to press the charges.

Paine was spared only to receive further blows. Once more the Tory Morris was heard from. Again striking below the belt, he raised the question of Paine's citizenship. The Federalist politicians of New Rochelle called Paine a foreigner: "You may be an Englishman or a Frenchman but you are not an American, for both President Washington and Minister Morris refused to claim you as a citizen of the United States during your imprisonment in France." Jefferson wrote letters affirming his American citizenship but they were ignored by the local officials. Paine was a man without a country, unable to vote in the land he had named.

Paine had not been well since his incarceration in the Luxembourg, and now his infirmities racked both mind and body as he lay a victim of vertigo and paralysis. On June 8, 1809, after making the request that he be buried in the Quaker graveyard and that his headstone bear only the words "Author of Common Sense," he breathed his last. A great American went to his death unnoticed and unsung. The only person to follow the body to its resting place was the man upon whose shoulders Paine's mantle fell, Elias Hicks, the liberal Quaker. It was fitting, therefore, that the founder of the "Religion of Humanity" desired to be buried in a Quaker cemetery—even though the request was denied.

During the last hours preachers vied with each other in the attempt to enter his chamber and extract from the dying "atheist" a recantation, but they were refused that distinction. The religionists were not long in inventing the proper death-bed scene. It was "authoritatively" reported that Paine had died in agony and fear, calling on God to forgive his infidelity, having renounced *The Age of Reason* as the work of the devil.

The American Inquisition, as Moncure Conway called it, continued even after death as historians, deliberately ignoring the facts, omitted the name of Thomas Paine from the honored list of the founding fathers of America and sent that man down through history as "an infidel, a moral leper, and a drunkard." Excoriation and invective have come on apace, one of the most ignoble examples being the following statement of Theodore Roosevelt: "So the filthy little atheist had to stay in prison, 'where he amused himself with publishing a pamphlet against Jesus Christ.' There are infidels and infidels; Paine belonged to the variety—whereof America possesses at present one or two shining examples—that apparently esteems a bladder of dirty water as the proper weapon with which to assail Christianity. It is not a type that appeals to the sympathy of an onlooker, be said onlooker religious or otherwise." [3] There was no excuse for so scurrilous and ill-informed a tirade, the gross inaccuracy of which has been pointed out by recent American writers. [4]

And now with vandals destroying the grave and leaders

[3] Theodore Roosevelt: *Gouverneur Morris* (in *American Statesmen Series*, 1891) p. 289.
[4] See Charles A. Beard and Mary R. Beard: *The Rise of American Civilization*, Vol. I, p. 261.

in public life slandering his good name, one sympathetic
hand was held out to Tom Paine. William Cobbett, former
Tory and life-long enemy of Paine, had taken the pains to
read *The Age of Reason* and was converted. He decided to
atone for his sins by taking Paine's remains to England that
they might be buried in honor in the soil of his homeland.
He reached Liverpool but there the plan was blocked by
politicians; Cobbett was imprisoned and the bones of Tom
Paine were lost. Ingratitude and ignorance hounded his
trail even to another land.

The Polish Government in 1938 issued a commemora-
tive stamp bearing the pictures of three men: Washington,
Koskiusko, and Paine. America has still her tribute to make.
Thomas Paine's portrait has yet to be hung in that Hall of
Independence which he made sacred.

American Deism

Sources of American Deism

THE REVOLUTIONARY PERIOD shows a strikingly dispro-
portionate liberalism among political leaders of the
country. Jefferson, Franklin, Paine, Hopkins, Ethan Allen,
John Adams, Wythe, Robert Paine, Bartlett, Rush, Thornton, Jones, Randolph, Washington, Madison, and Mason
were either deists, free thinkers, or religious liberals with
deistic tendencies.[1] For them political liberalism and religious liberalism went hand in hand, freedom not only from
an autocratic government but also from ecclesiastical tyranny. For the authors of American constitutional government Deism and democracy were inseparable. Their political theories were derived from Locke, Rousseau, and the
Encyclopedists, who had written freedom, natural rights,
and equality into both the deistic and revolutionary plat-
forms. Democracy, in fact, was a religio-philosophical concept before it was a political term.

The neglect of the philosophical backgrounds of American democracy in popular discussion today is lamentable
enough but information on the exact religious views of the
founding fathers seems to have been totally suppressed.

---

[1] Washington was a nominal member of the Episcopal Church but
actually a Deist and free thinker. He commonly abstained from mentioning
Church matters and avoided taking holy communion. The clergy in fact
demanded his withdrawal from the Presidency.

As Gustav Koch observes, "it can be said of our intellectual and religious heritage, as of the Dark Ages, that it seems so dark because we know so little about it." [2] The record of eighteenth-century religious thought in America was uniformly colored by pious and unobjective historians. Free thought and rationalism were damned with or without faint praise. It is only in the last decade that historians have given proper attention to American Deism, which was really the intellectual climate of the colonies during the last half of the eighteenth century. The degree to which the Revolutionary leaders and the signers of the Declaration of Independence were religiously and philosophically informed furnishes an impressive contrast to that of later statesmen. Some of the present-day Jeffersonians, moreover, would be given a revelation if they knew the precise character of religious beliefs held by early American leaders. Then, as now, liberals like Washington and Jefferson felt it necessary to dissemble their beliefs in order to escape complete social ostracism, a fact which accounts for their avoidance of much explicit expression of free thought. A brief study of eighteenth-century Deism in the colonies will perhaps throw some light on what the American Way really is.

The sources of American Deism can be traced to the rationalism of Shaftesbury, the empiricism of Locke, the anti-clericalism of Voltaire, the cosmic science of Newton, and the naturalism of Rousseau. Other influential factors were the Latitudinarian movement within the Anglican Church and the radical movements on the Continent—the Socinians, the Gallicans and Jensenists, and the Encyclopedists. The English brand of Deism, always less radical than the French, gave to colonial thought a more cautious

[2] *Republican Religion*, Preface, p. xi, Henry Holt & Co., quoted by permission.

character. Lord Herbert of Shaftesbury in the seventeenth century had foreshadowed the deistic movement by shifting the basis of religious authority from the Bible to reason and a contemporay, Charles Blount, in his *Oracles of Reason* had subordinated dogma to ethics. They were followed by Tindal, Wollaston, and Chubb, who maintained that Jesus was a deist and advocated a return to the simple, ethical Gospel. Shaftesbury, Pope, and Bolingbroke continued the deistic emphasis on reason, natural religion, and the moral life. Professor Morais attributes the decline of English Deism to the fact that it was caught between the emotionalism of the Wesleyan revival and the radical skepticism of Hume.[3] It was too vague and luke-warm to appeal to the middle class. French Deism became more radical because of the abuses of the Church. There it took a more militant and tendentious form, as we have elsewhere observed.

The writings of Shaftesbury, Tillotson, Herbert, Blount, and Bolingbroke were widely read in the colonies as well as those of Voltaire and Rousseau. The *Principia Mathematica* of Newton circulated among preachers and professors. The Newtonian cosmology espousing the heliocentric theory of Copernicus had far-reaching implications for theology. The earth was no longer thought to be the center of the universe but a negligible speck of dust in a world of universes and its inhabitants were not the special creation of God and the objects of his favor but only part and parcel of the natural world.

One of the first Americans to revolt from Calvinism was Professor Samuel Johnson of Yale. A visit to England where he met Pope and the better-known Samuel Johnson was the cause of his conversion to liberalism. He returned

[3] Herbert M. Morais: *Deism in Eighteenth-Century America*, p. 44.

to write his *Elementa Philosophica*, an anti-Calvinistic polemic. The idea of total depravity was inconsistent, he said, with the existence of a benevolent deity and the desire to achieve happiness through the moral life was a better motive for salvation than being saved from hell by divine grace. Revelation and Scriptural infallibility were first assailed by the Reverend Ebenezer Gay of Hingham. "No pretense of revelation," he claimed, "can be sufficient for the admission of absurdities and contradictions." He was followed by Jonathan Mayhew, who applied moral self-government to politics, supplanted revelation with nature, and rejected the traditional creeds. Charles Chauncy, in his *Salvation for All Men*, argued that the benevolence of the Creator implied the natural goodness of man, and with this incipient Universalism, he campaigned against Calvinism.

Franklin and Jefferson

Deism proper appears for the first time in America with Benjamin Franklin. He tells us that at the age of fifteen he began to doubt revelation. "Some books against deism fell into my hands; they were said to be the substance of sermons preached at Boyle's lectures. It happened that they wrought an effect on me quite contrary to what was intended by them; for the arguments of the deists, which were quoted to be refuted, appeared to me much stronger than the refutation; in short, I soon became a thorough deist."

Benjamin's brother, James, was the editor of a Boston periodical, *The New England Courant*. As the chief contributor, Ben was not always supported in his articles by his brother. Shortly after the publication of Cotton Mather's *Essays to do Good*, the *Courant* ran a series of

satirical articles by a Mrs. Silence Dogood. Through Mrs.
Dogwood, the prototype of Artemus Ward and Josh Bill-
ings, the young Benjamin lampooned the class-conscious
aristocracy, the ostentatious clergy, and the stupid magis-
trates. He pleaded for intellectual and religious freedom:
"Without freedom of thought there can be no such thing
as wisdom; and no such thing as public liberty without freedom of speech; which is the right of every man as far as by
it he does not hurt or control the right of another." [4] Later
as editor of the *Courant*, he continued his jibes against
ecclesiasticism as in the following satirical paragraph on
titles:

"In old time it was no disrespect for men and women to
be called by their own names. Adam was never called
Master Adam; we never read of Noah Esquire, Lot Knight
and Baronet, nor the Right Honourable Abraham, Viscount
Mesopotamia, Baron of Canaan. No, no, they were plain
men, honest country graziers, that took care of their fami-
lies and their flocks. Moses was a great prophet and Aaron
a priest of the Lord; but we never read of the Reverend
Moses nor the Right Reverend Father in God, Aaron, by
Divine Providence Lord Archbishop of Israel. Thou never
sawest Madam Rebecca in the Bible, my Lady Rachel; nor
Mary, though a princess of the blood, after the death of
Joseph called the Princess Dowager of Nazareth. No, plain
Rebecca, Rachel, Mary, or the Widow Mary, or the like.
It was no incivility then to mention their naked names as
they were expressed" [5]

Confronted with the opposition of his brother, Benjamin
moved to Philadelphia. Already familiar with the works of
Shaftesbury, the young apprentice was further influenced
in the direction of Deism by the free-thinking governor

---

[4] *Writings* II: 25, 26.   [5] *Writings* VII: 412.

Keith of Pennsylvania. In London as a printed Franklin found himself in the midst of the deistic movement. His letters at the time reveal a strong rationalistic tendency. He repudiated the Puritan doctrines of determinism and stoutly opposed supernaturalism. He always placed conduct before creed. He was no brooding mystic or solitary scholar but strictly a man of action, a pragmatic moralist. In an essay on prayer he wrote: "The great uncertainty I found in metaphysical reasonings disgusted me, and I quit that kind of reading and study for others more satisfactory." [6] When he was eighty-four, he was challenged by President Stiles of Yale, to state his religious beliefs. Franklin's reply was unequivocally deistic, reiterating his earlier views that natural religion sufficed, that Jesus was not divine in the cosmic or metaphysical sense, and that the Sermon on the Mount was the best religion to date.

Deism found a staunch ally in Freemasonry which included in its membership, Franklin, Washington, Warren, Madison, and Lafayette. When Voltaire was initiated into the Masonic order, he entered the room on the arm of Franklin. The deistic tendency among Masons came through the French lodges, whose members attacked the established Church, and preached liberty, equality, and the "essentials of religion."

Franklin was a second Leonardo, whose many-sided genius has been admirably set forth in the two recent biographies of Fay and Van Doren [7] and whose liberalism in religion has only recently been acknowledged. He was eclectic in his philosophy, moving in the world, yet, like Leonardo, still above it; and, like Voltaire, at times, smiling at it. He seems to have been the only member of the

---

[6] *New England Courant* (1723).

[7] Bernard Fay, *Franklin, the Apostle of Modern Times* and Carl Van Doren, *Benjamin Franklin.*

Constitutional Convention to have espoused the cause of labor. With Voltaire and Rousseau, he was a powerful factor in the rise of the French Revolution. Turgot wrote of Franklin: "He snatched the lightning from the sky and the scepter from the tyrants."

More systematically deistic than Franklin was another cosmopolitan and man of the world, Thomas Jefferson, who called himself "an Epicurean" and "a naturalist," but who was commonly regarded as "the arch apostle of the cause of irreligion and free thought." He was thoroughly familiar with the writings of Voltaire, Rousseau, Bolingbroke, Shaftesbury, and the English Unitarian Priestley. As a student at William and Mary College, Jefferson came under the influence of William Small, a liberal-minded professor of natural philosophy. Before coming to America, Small had been an intimate friend of Watt and Erasmus Darwin. His profound influence on both Watt and Jefferson is indicated in a contemporary journal: "As a friend and adviser of Watt, Dr. Small ministered at the birth of invention, and as the tutor of Jefferson, he was sponsor to the birth of freedom." [8] Jefferson's idea was to reform Christianity rather than to overthrow it. He called attention to the discrepancy between the Gospel of Jesus and the organized Christian Church. Jesus, he said, was a Deist and taught reverence for nature, the love of God, and faith in the future life. In a letter to Dr. Priestley, Jefferson contemplates a treatise on Jesus. "I should then take a view of the deism and ethics of the Jews, and show in what a degraded state they were, and the necessity they presented of a reformation. I should proceed to a view of the life, character, and doctrines of Jesus, who sensible of incorrectness of their ideas of the Deity, and of morality, endeavored to

[8] L. G. Tyler in *Tyler's Quarterly*, Vol. 2, p. 287. (Quoted in Marie Kimball, *Jefferson, the Road to Glory*, p. 49.)

bring them to the principles of a pure deism, and juster notions of the attributes of God, to reform their moral doctrines to the standard of reason, justice and philanthropy, and to inculcate the belief of a future state. This view would purposely omit the question of his divinity, and even his inspiration. To do him justice it would be necessary to remark the disadvantages his doctrines have to encounter, not having been committed to writing by himself, but by the most unlettered of men, by memory, long after they had heard them from him; when much was forgotten, much misunderstood, and presented in very paradoxical shapes. Yet such are the fragments remaining as to show a master workman, and that his system of morality was the most benevolent and sublime probably that has been ever taught, and consequently more perfect than those of any of the ancient philosophers. His character and doctrines have received still greater injury from those who pretend to be his special disciples, and who have disfigured and sophisticated his actions and precepts, from views of personal interest, so as to induce the unthinking part of mankind to throw off the whole system in disgust, and to pass sentence as an impostor on the most innocent, the most benevolent, the most eloquent and sublime character that ever has been exhibited to man." [9]

Jefferson's anti-clericalism is evident in his allusion to Connecticut as "the last retreat of monkish darkness, bigotry, and abhorrence of those advances of the mind which had carried the other states a century ahead." The world will be better off, he continued, when "this den of the priesthood is at last broken up." [10]

[9] *Writings:* ed. by Ford, Vol. VIII, p. 224, footnote. See also Vol. III, p. 263 ff.
[10] *Memoirs of Jefferson,* 1829: IV: 300, 301. *Cf.* Rayner: *Sketches* (Jefferson) 1832, pp. 513–17.

In politics Jefferson was the great equalitarian who wrote the trenchant words: "All men are created equal and from that equal creation they desire rights inherent and inalienable, among which are the preservation of life and liberty and the pursuit of happiness." His motto was: "Equality for all, special privilege for none." Equality is the prerequisite for freedom, for with inequality the freedom of one class would mean bondage for another. Some historians have implied that Jefferson was not opposed to slavery and that he did not include Negroes in his idea of equality, since the Declaration of Independence does not carry any specific condemnation of slavery. The original draft is proof to the contrary: "He [George the Third] has waged cruel war against human nature itself, violating its most sacred rights of life and liberty in the persons of a distant people who never offended him, captivating and carrying them into slavery in another hemisphere, or to incur miserable death in their transportation thither. This piratical warfare, the opprobrium of infidel powers, is the warfare of the Christian king of Great Britain. Determined to keep open a market where men should be bought and sold, he has prostituted his negative for suppressing every legislative attempt to prohibit or to restrain this execrable commerce." His repeated attempts to introduce bills providing for emancipation were defeated by the conservatives in Congress.

Timothy Dwight, President of Yale and defender of the faith of New England, hailed Jefferson's election to the White House with considerable anxiety: "We have a country governed by blockheads and knaves; the ties of marriage with all its felicities are severed and destroyed; our wives and daughters are thrown into the stews; our children are cast into the world and forgotten; filial piety is extinguished, and our surnames, the only mark of distinction among families, are abolished. Can the imagination paint anything more dreadful on this side of hell?" This outburst of wrath was occasioned by the fact that Jefferson was a Deist and at this time many Jeffersonians led by Elihu Palmer of Connecticut were attempting to spread the cause of Deism among the masses. The clash of Deism and orthodoxy came to a head when Jefferson as president invited the "infidel" Tom Paine to return to America. The treatment given to Paine was an evidence of the decline of Deism, the collapse of which was accomplished by the onrush of orthodoxy and revivalism at the turn of the century.

Ethan Allen the Philosopher

The diary of Ezra Stiles, President of Yale, contains the following entry for February 13, 1789: "13th Inst. died in Vermont the profane and impious Deist, General Ethan Allen, author of *The Oracles of Reason*, a book replete with scurrilous reflections on revelation—'and in Hell he lifted up his eyes being in torments.' " This statement is practically all correct except the title of Ethan Allen's book which was *Reason, the only Oracle of God*, and the date of his death which was February 11. The Reverend Ezra Stiles was enough of a scholar, however, to know that Allen was not an Atheist but a Deist, a distinction which more recent defenders of the faith do not draw. Allen's fame as a philosopher has been eclipsed by reason of his heroic activities in the American Revolution, but his book on reason places him with Jefferson and Franklin as an important leader of early American Deism.

Allen's knowledge of John Locke came curiously enough

through Benjamin Stiles, a cousin of Ezra Stiles. More important as a deistic influence was Thomas Young, a doctor from Yale, who collaborated with Allen in writing of the *Oracle*. He was probably influenced also by Lafayette and the *Philosophes*.

The sub-title of Allen's book, "A Compenduous System of Natural Religion," reveals his intention to replace biblical cosmology by Newtonian cosmology or natural religion.[11] The *Oracle* was the first book published in America in opposition to Christianity as a revealed religion. Revelations, said Allen, are unreasonable, historically conditioned, and local rather than universal. They are inadequate because they are of no use to those who lived before them; they are applicable only to the society or culture in which they originate; and their validity is impaired because the medium of the revelation is usually a person of limited knowledge and wisdom. Furthermore, the so-called supernatural revelations have been contradictory, and therefore could not have been inspired by God.

Reason, continues Allen, has been applied to science but not to religion. Reason demands a ruling force or deity. The full nature of deity is incomprehensible to finite minds but "the knowledge of nature is the revelation of God." God represents the harmony of the universe, the creator, designer, and self-existent cause of all things. In line with Voltaire and Newton, he reasons that the orderly character of the universe necessitates a divine being and the moral nature of man requires a higher moral cause. Nature proves God's beneficence. "Every enjoyment and support of life is from God, delivered to his creatures in and by the tendency,

---

[11] It may well be, as Conway suggests, that Allen borrowed the title of his book from Blount's *Oracles of Reason*. (See Moncure Conway: *Thomas Paine*, 1892, Vol. 2, p. 192.)

aptitude, disposition and operation of those laws. Nature is the medium or immediate instrument through which God dispenses his benignity to mankind." [12] Voltaire would take exception to this optimism; this is not the best of all possible worlds; the universe is not necessarily friendly.

Allen's argument for free will is based on the fact that God's power does not extend over human choice. The problem of evil is solved by reference to free moral agency. Immortality is justified on necessitarian or intuitive grounds; the goodness of God demands it and the reasonable hope of man attests its reality. It will thus be seen that the argument of necessity, design and reasonableness, as used by Deists, survives today in the mildly liberal idealistic school rather than the naturalistic group.

In his attack on biblical infallibility the "horned devil of Vermont" exhibits a more thoroughgoing liberalism. He ridicules the idea of the special creation of the world in six days. He detects discrepancies in the "five books of Moses" such as Moses' account of his own death and burial (Deut. 34:5, 6), thus implying non-Mosaic authorship of the Pentateuch. He assigned the Garden of Eden story to the realm of pure myth. He points to the fallible or subreligious character of a score of Old Testament passages, such as God's command to Abraham to sacrifice Isaac, reference to God as a jealous deity, Joshua commanding the sun to stand still, and the sensuality of the Song of Solomon. The miraculous element in the New Testament is ruled out as conflicting with the immutable laws of nature. By the same token prayer cannot be expected to affect any change in the physical world: "To pray, intreat, or make supplication to God is neither more nor less than dictating to Eternal Reason. . . . To pray for anything which we

[12] *Oracle*, p. 81.

can obtain by the due application of our natural powers, and neglect the means of procuring it, is impertinence and laziness in the abtsract; and to pray for that which God in the course of his providence has put out of our power to obtain is only murmuring against God, and finding fault with his providence." [13]

Allen was decidedly anti-trinitarian. A trinitarian deity is a contradiction in terms, he asserted, and the divinity of Christ was denied by Jesus' own life of subordination to the Father. He dismissed the Virgin Birth theory as not worth refuting. The following paragraph illustrates his discriminating attitude and use of common sense in the religious field: "None will pretend but that the learned nations of the earth at present, are far advanced in arts, sciences and logical reasonings, above the primitive Christians: let us therefore examine, and candidly criticise for ourselves, lest the credulity of former ages obtrude their unphilosophical and inconsistent revelations upon us, as sacred and infallible truth. It is high time we were roused from our lethargy and superstition and that we demand of our spiritual teachers reason and solid argument for the ground of our faith and confidence." [14]

Professor B. T. Schantz [15] calls attention to certain lines of divergence between Allen's Deism and that of Jefferson, Franklin, and Paine: his preoccupation with immortality, his failure to stress humanitarian service as the true form of worship, his acceptance of a quasi-Calvinistic doctrine of human depravity (although holding to the idea of individual and social progress) and finally his use of intuition as well as reason. For these reasons Professor Schantz feels that Allen was not a thoroughgoing Deist and that after

[13] *Ibid.*, Sec. 270–76.   [14] *Ibid.*, Sec. 462–65.
[15] *Journal of Religion*, Vol. 18, No. 2, p. 213 ff.

the influence of Young wore off, Allen departed considerably from Deism.

Allen assuredly was not an Atheist and he can scarcely be grouped with the conventional Theists. Granting that his Deism later became diluted, he had more in common with the Deists than any other group. His emphasis on reason, the exaltation of God, and "the practise of morality," and his opposition to revelation, clericalism and dogmatic religion are clear evidences of deistic thought.

The forces and conditions making for free thought in post-Revolutionary America are well expressed by Gustav Koch.

"There was the natural disintegration or at least variation of the theocratic régime in New England, crumbling under the weight of its own worldly success. The seminaries of learning from Virginia to the North, intended for the training of pious youths for the sacred calling, were themselves insidiously corrupted with at least a mild and humanizing deism. Evangelical enthusiasm of the Great Awakening brought with it a democracy in religion disastrous to a learned and dignified clergy of whatever denomination. Association with European comrades-in-arms, first the British and then the French, impregnated the minds of American militiamen with principles sadly alien to the spiritual life. The rivalries and conflicting claims of divergent Protestant denominations made the supremacy and authority of any one of them less tenable or even impossible, as in the case of the Anglican Church. With loss of authority the enforcement of such quasi-political principles as Sabbath observance was relaxed. Diversity of sects all on an equal political footing, or striving to be so, made toleration necessary for political reasons—and toleration is at least a cousin of indifference. The idea of the equality of religions, if recognized as such, is fatal to fanaticism. With such forces as these abroad in the land, it is scarcely surprising that the starkest atheism was feared even if it did not exist." [16]

Deism appealed to eighteenth-century thinkers who rejected orthodox Calvinism and who were also repelled by the emotionalism of the Great Awakening. Such a group would have been so small as to be unheard of had it not been for the fact that it included the men who wrote the political philosophy of America. But in spite of this influential minority, Deism as a movement soon passed from the scene. Philosophically, it was both shortsighted and inconsistent. It tried to combine a naturalistic cosmology with a belief in immortality, an impersonal universe with a belief in man's innate goodness. But its virtues outweighed its defects and it was nearer the essence of religious living than some forms of organized Christianity. It transcended class, nation, and parochial interests, and subordinated sectarianism to the good of humanity. And it wrote its way into the American definition of democracy as a society of free personalities.

[16] *Republican Religion*, pp. 26–27.

Theodore Parker

Intellectual Giant

THEODORE PARKER could boast of deep Yankee roots. The first Parker came to the Bay Colony in 1635 and the Parkers lived in Lexington for almost two centuries before Theodore was born. Theodore's grandfather was Captain John Parker—*the* Captain Parker—author of the memorable challenge, "If they mean to have a war, let it begin here." The North Bridge, the Old Manse, and Wright's Tavern; Boston, Concord, and Cambridge; Emerson, Ripley, and Channing—these were his roots.

Theodore taught school in order to earn enough to enter the theological seminary and while he was teaching French and German, he picked up Syriac and Hebrew. In the Harvard Divinity School he was looked upon by his mates "as a prodigious athlete in his studies." It was a common thing to see him walking across the campus loaded with a pile of books, reading as he walked. We are told that "once he ran smack into a tree and fell unconscious, the books tumbling around him." Some claimed that he memorized all the dates in history and knew all the writings (but did not approve) of all the Church Fathers. While in seminary he tutored Hebrew, Greek, and German. He learned to read Italian, Portuguese, Dutch, Swedish, Danish, Arabic, Persian, and Coptic and dabbled in half a dozen others.

Even before divinity school days Parker had viewed

with a critical eye the whole field of theological orthodoxy. In the seminary he concluded that "the Scriptures have been interpreted in the interest of dogmatism from Christ to the present." He was there introduced to the biblical criticism of the Germans, then in its initial stage. While the findings of Eichhorn and De Wette spurred his critical faculties considerably, he stayed, on the whole, within the conventional bounds of "Unitarian orthodoxy," with an occasional jibe at the unwholesome doctrines of Augustine and Tertullian. He graduated from Harvard with much erudition and encyclopedic knowledge but without a convincing and positive philosophy.

His first parish was at Barnstable where he won a moral victory in learning how to "talk to men as if I were also a man and not merely a student." Pastoral duties were not allowed to crowd out academic pursuits and in two years he had translated De Wette's *Einleitung in das neue Testament* (*Introduction to the New Testament*) in two volumes —first fruits of his scholarly labors.

In the spring of 1837 three important things happened to Theodore Parker. He married Lydia Cabot, was ordained in the Unitarian ministry, and accepted a call to the West Roxbury parish. West Roxbury was in the country and yet, with a short drive, he could be in Boston, a situation just suited to his purposes. He had a small farm and delighted in the freedom of the open country, the soil, and his garden. Equally gratifying were his ramblings around Boston, where he could paw around in the bookshops for old volumes and keep up-to-date on the new ones. He contributed reviews to periodicals and read voraciously. His two-volume *Critical and Historical Introduction to the Canonical Scriptures of the Old Testament*, published after five years of laborious work, is proof of his intellectual industry during the early years of his pastorate. From his study came a steady stream of articles on religious, literary, and social questions. He helped Emerson, Alcott, and Margaret Fuller found *The Dial* and was himself a steady contributor with articles on German criticism and English literature, labor problems and Church history. In one of his papers he satirically distinguishes between the religion of Jesus and the organized Christian Church. "Alas for us, we see the Christianity of the Church is a very poor thing; very little better than heathenism. It makes Christianity a Belief, not a life. It takes Religion out of the world, and shuts it up in old books, whence, from time to time, it seeks to evoke the divine spirit as the witch of Endor is fabled to have called up Samuel from the dead.—Anointed dullness, arrayed in Canonicals, his lesson duly conned, presses the consecrated cushions of the pulpit and pours forth weekly his impotent drone, to be blest with bland praises so long as he disturbs not respectable iniquity slumbering in his pew, nor touches the actual sign of the time nor treads an inch beyond the beaten path of the Church." From this Voltairean paragraph one can see that Parker's liberalism was gathering momentum. He was rapidly finding his place with those souls in the past who discerned between means and end, method and content, convention and truth, form and reality.

Brook Farm and Fruitlands, reforms and utopias, Transcendentalism and aestheticism, all come in for Parker's attention but none of those things completely won him. He attended the meetings of the Hedge Club where he talked reform with Alcott, pantheism with Emerson, Catholicism with Brownson, or biblical inspiration with Channing. Another group, called the Friends, met at the Tremont House, where the young Wendell Phillips discused slavery and Alcott talked of his Temple School. Mingling constantly with these men, Parker advanced in wisdom and in stature. His philosophy was taking shape; his mind was being prepared for application; but a theory of values was first necessary. That being determined, the problem facing Parker and the rest was: through what medium shall mankind be saved from tyranny and the lower self? Can the Kingdom of God be established through the Church?

Emerson's answer to that question was Transcendentalism and he promptly left the Church. The Transcendentalists and the Left Wingers in Unitarianism said that truth itself is greater than the Church, the Bible, Christianity, or Jesus. Intuition is greater than institution. Christian truth does not depend on miraculous proof. The resulting controversy split the Unitarian Church into two factions. Parker naturally sided with the radicals but, unlike Ripley and Emerson, he did not wish to leave the Church. He wanted to believe that Unitarianism was big enough for men of diverse opinion, but in that he was wrong. He was bitterly denounced and snubbed by the Boston clergy who refused to exchange pulpits with him.

Fuel was added to the flame in an address which Parker gave at the ordination service of Charles C. Shackford in South Boston. The title of the sermon was "The Transient and the Permanent in Christianity." His thesis was the same as Emerson's, namely, that Christian truths, in so far as they are universal and eternal, derive their authority not from their connection with Christ but from their intrinsic and inherent merit. "It seems difficult to conceive of any reason," said Parker, "why moral religious truths should rest for their support on the personal authority of their revealer any more than the truths of science on that of him who makes them known first or more clearly." This principle was held by Parker not by way of minimizing Christ's place as a prophet and teacher but in order to establish the primacy of moral truth and to show that the permanent in Christianity was independent of Jesus, miracles, the New Testament, creeds, and the Church itself. This was clearly a declaration of Paine's natural religion. The sermon, which was heard by many ministers, threw Boston into a tumult. Theological pandemonium broke loose and the clergy were not long in labelling Parker's statement as heresy, one not to be countenanced by the Unitarian body. Few ministers after this incident had the courage to exchange pulpits with Parker. The West Roxbury congregation, on the other hand, saw no reason to look for another minister, so Parker continued to preach to his own flock and lecture whenever occasion offered. One by one, however, his influential friends deserted him and for a brief period he became despondent and toyed with the idea of quitting the task. It seemed as if he stood alone among strangers. The following entry appears in his Journal:

"To me it seems as if my life is a failure. Let me look at it—

1. *Domestically*—'Tis mainly so: for I have no children; and what is a house without a little mite o' teants, or 'bits o' blossoms'?

2. *Socially*—It is completely a failure. Here I am as much an outcast from society as if I were a convicted pirate: I mean from all that calls itself 'decent society', 'respectable society', in Boston.

3. *Professionally*—I stand all alone; not a minister with me. I see no young man rising up to take ground with me, or in advance of me. I think, that, with a solitary exception, my professional influence has not been felt in a single young minister's soul."

Then he reconsidered. Not all had left him. Was not his parish loyal through 'it all? Were not Ripley and one or two others still at his side?

Discourses on Religion

Theodore Parker resolved to fight and he began by delivering his famous *Discourses on Religion* in Boston. These lectures, carefully prepared, breathed not a word of controversy; they were to be a call to the deep spiritual life, the common faith. He would define religion as inherent and natural. The sanction for morality lies in human experience and reason; not in tradition or ecclesiastical authority. Christianity is not unique nor is it a divine revelation; it is a human growth and must be judged by its approximation to universal truth and reason. Transcendentalism with Parker came to mean all truth which is beyond the ephemeral and finite, the realm of the universal. The Bible did not make God; the Church did not create truth. The truth of the Bible was truth only in so far as it appealed to reason. Christ's teaching is true not because he uttered it but because it is universally true. Natural religion, then, was his answer, a religion which is both intuitive and amenable to reason. "After preaching a few months in various places," he continued, "I determined to preach nothing as religion which I had not experienced inwardly and made my own—knowing it by heart." God is a divine immanence. "Wherever a heart beats with love, where Faith and Reason utter their oracles, there also is God, as formerly in the hearts of seers and prophets. . . . So the ocean of God encircles all men. Uncover the soul of its sensuality, selfishness, sin; there is nothing between it and God, who flows into man as light into air." Nothing, he meant, except the

Church which had become the worst enemy of natural religion. The Church was the administrator of a system, not an inspiration for living the good life; a system which "degrades man."

"Man is subordinate to the apocryphal, ambiguous, imperfect, and often erroneous Scripture of the Word; the Word itself, as it comes straightway from the fountain of Truth, through Reason, Conscience, Affections, and the Soul, he must not have. It [the Church] takes the Bible for God's statutebook; combines old Hebrew notions into a code of ethics; settles questions in morals and religion by texts of Scripture. It wars to the knife against gaiety of heart; condemns amusement as sinful; sneers at Common Sense; spits upon Reason; appeals to low and selfish aims —to Fear, the most base of all passions. It does not know that goodness is its own recompense and vice its own torture; that judgment takes place daily and God's laws execute themselves. It paves Hell with children's bones; has a personal devil in the world to harry the land and lure or compel men to eternal woe. Its God is diabolical. . . . This system applies to God the language of Kings' courts, trial, sentence, judgment, pardon, satisfaction, allegiance, day of judgment. . . . The heaven of this system is a grand pay-day, where Humility is to have its coach and six, forsooth, because she has been humble; the saints and martyrs, who bore the trials of the world, are to take their vengeance by shouting 'Hallelujah, Glory to God' when they see the anguish of their old persecutors and the smoke of their torment ascending up forever and ever." [1]

Such was Parker's castigation of Calvinism. That was followed by an equally caustic disparagement of the false liberalism of the Unitarians, who were clinging to old formulas

---

[1] *Discourse on Matters Relating to Religion.*

with new interpretations. "With a philosophy too rational to go the full length of the supernatural theory, too sensual to embrace the spiritual method, and ask no person to mediate between man and God, it oscillates between the two; humanizes the Bible, yet calls it miraculous; believes in man's greatness, freedom, and spiritual nature, yet asks for a Mediator and Redeemer."

Parker's censure of the semi-liberalism of orthodox Unitarianism was accompanied by a tribute to the schismatics who, through with half-way measures, proclaimed the creedless religion of humanity. When this manifesto of natural religion, which was really a nineteenth-century edition of Deism, appeared in book form, it was received more enthusiastically abroad than at home. Such a right-about-face as this volume demanded was not calculated to fill up the ever-widening breach between Parker and his Boston colleagues. The book was roundly condemned as "vehemently deistical and subversive to Christianity."

On top of the storm produced by Parker's *Discourses* came his defense of the Reverend John Pierpont in the *Dial* of October 1842. In his sermons on "Rum-making, Rum-selling, and Rum-drinking" Pierpont had given offense to certain members of his congregation. Parker admitted that his friend spoke with "an indignant eloquence which were better let alone" but when a council was convened to investigate the case, the result of which led to Pierpont's resignation, Parker flew to his defense in a vitriolic article called "The Hollis Street Council." The work of the Council, said Parker, was "a piece of diplomacy worthy of a college of Jesuits." The controversy shifted to Parker himself, who was invited to a meeting of the Boston Unitarian Association to answer for the faith that was in him. The man who had written deistical and subversive

doctrines, who had called his colleagues Jesuits and Phari-
sees, must be asked to withdraw from the Association which
he had compromised. The statements made by the various
members of the council showed clearly the diversity of
theological opinion among Unitarians in 1842. Some entertained approximately the same heretical views as Parker,
sympathized with him and said so; others disagreed with
his biblical criticism but made room for him as a Christian;
while still others declared that Parker was not only anti-
Unitarian but anti-Christian. Mr. Parker, it seemed, had
no intention of withdrawing from the Association. Cyrus
Bartol, followed by Dr. William C. Gannett, assured the
group of Parker's sincerity and integrity. Parker was vio-
lently upset and abruptly left the room. It was painfully
disillusioning to know that some of his accusers had held
opinions quite as radical as his but lacked the courage to
stand with him. So the hearing ended without a decision.

Parker resumed his multifarious activities. He delivered
six lectures on "The Times," published *The Discourses*
and his *Critical and Miscellaneous Writings*, and finished
his work on De Wette. When the formidable task of proof-
reading his two-volume translation was completed, he
suffered a physical reaction and a rest was imperative. His
close friend, George Russell, realizing that a change of
scenery was even more important than a rest, came to the
rescue with advice and the means with which to take it.

Theodore and Lydia sailed for Europe on September 5,
1843, but neither the stormy voyage of twenty-five days nor
his tumultuous travels on the continent provided any opportunity for rest. An earlier biographer describes him as
"resting like fury." His European journey is a teeming
pell-mell of observations, statistics, rhapsodies, and interpretations. "Italy," he writes, "is the land of artistic

elegance and social deformity. She taught refinement to all Europe but kept treachery to herself." Catholicism "cultivates feelings of reverence . . . but does not affect the conscience and it does not appeal to reason." Sans-Souci in Potsdam was for him "sans everything."

The American abroad sees as much as his intellectually earned increment permits. With Parker that meant more perhaps than with any other nineteenth-century pilgrim to European shrines. He saw all the madonnas and all the stained-glass windows, all the galleries and museums, all the palaces and cathedrals. But he was interested more in people. Like Emerson, he was anxious to converse with those distinguished contemporaries whom he had never seen. In England he tracked down Carlyle and Sterling; in Germany his goal was De Wette, whose mind he already knew so intimately, and he was fortunate to meet in addition Ewald and F. C. Baur, two of the most important theologians of the nineteenth century.

Also like Emerson, he found that little was to be gained by personal contact with these intellectual giants; it sufficed to know their theories. But the trip served its purpose; Parker returned to America rejuvenated in spirit, confirmed in his scholarship, and more firmly grounded in his liberal religion. While West Roxbury welcomed him back and heard him gladly, the same could not be said for his former adversaries. Again he was drawn into controversy and perhaps it was for the best, for, as his biographer, Octavius Brooks Frothingham, remarks, if the conflict had not been renewed by his opponents, he might have remained an obscure suburban pastor the rest of his life, unknown outside of greater Boston. The exchange problem cropped up again. The Reverend John Turner Sargent, whose parish was under the Benevolent Fraternity of

Unitarian Churches asked Parker to preach for him, whereupon he was asked to resign.

Then came the "Boston Thursday Lecture" episode.
This lectureship had had a venerable history of one hundred and seventy years, but for a quarter of a century it had
lost its original popular appeal and was now an empty form
attended only by a handful of elderly women. Clearly it
was no longer a "going concern" but just a painful ordeal
week after week. Came Theodore Parker's turn. The large
church was packed long before the appointed hour and late-
comers filled gallery stairs, aisles, and choir loft. Parker's
subject was "The Relation of Jesus to His Age and the
Ages." From the homiletic standpoint it could not be called
a great sermon but in its content it was epochal. It was
an unparalleled tribute to the character of Jesus; but it
was the historical, human Jesus, not the supernatural
Christ, and the speaker made it clear that Jesus differed
from the rest of humanity only in degree. Strange that this
should excite the Association but the fact is that Unitarianism in 1844 was split in much the same way as it was to be
a century later—and on practically the same grounds. Dr.
Frothingham, who was in charge of the lectures, cancelled
the remainder of the schedule and reissued a new list,
omitting the name of Parker. His son, Parker's biographer,
concludes: "The device was ingenious, but not handsome.
The ungodly called it a trick. The divine powers did not
think it noble; for, not long after, the 'Great and Thursday
Lecture' was discontinued."

One month after Parker's famous Thursday lecture he
was asked to exchange pulpits with James Freeman Clarke,
pastor of the Church of the Disciples in Boston. Mr. Clarke
did not hold Parker's views but he believed in fair play.
The heretic's appearance in the Church of the Disciples

caused a secession with the loss of the "best families" from the church membership. And now in January 1845, with all Boston pulpits closed to him, Parker's wider influence was assured when a group of ministers met and passed a resolution "that the Reverend Theodore Parker shall have a chance to be heard in Boston."

The Music Hall

The old Melodeon on Washington Street was rented and in February Parker began his Boston ministry. At the same time he terminated his connection with the Unitarian Association by writing an open letter to the Boston Association "touching certain matters of theology." He reviewed the whole situation and then submitted a list of questions. He asked the members of the fellowship to define salvation, miracle, inspiration, and revelation. There was no agreement on these items for, as he wrote at the time, "the Unitarians have no recognized and public creed." He was not aware of transgressing any Unitarian limits and begged to know the grounds of his heresy. It appeared that there was great confusion in that also. The biblical and theological questions in this letter disclosed Parker's true position and served to widen the gulf between him and orthodoxy.

The Boston enterprise was Parker's vindication and, while he remarked that he preferred to be the pastor of sixty families in the country rather than the minister of a parish of 7000 in the city, nevertheless Boston was Boston and in 1845 was still the "hub of the solar system." The Melodeon was filled every Sunday morning with truth seekers, intelligent, sensitive people who welcomed a free and independent type of preaching. There were the inevitable fanatics and iconoclasts, but Parker's congregation also included William Lloyd Garrison, Samuel Gridley Howe, Francis Jackson, Frank B. Sanborn, John C. Holmes, Charles Ellis, Julia Ward Howe, and Caroline Thayer. His Exeter Place parsonage became a Paris salon to which came such luminaries as Wendell Phillips, Charles Sumner, Ellis Gray Loring, Horace Mann, Starr King, and Thomas Wentworth Higginson. The arrangements called for an experimental pastorate of one year but it was such a marked success that the Boston society decided on a permanent or indefinite relationship. The Melodeon ministry was organized as the Twenty-Eighth Congregational Society of Boston. As pastor of the "largest parish in America," Parker, whose personal and scholarly interests embraced the whole universe, entered upon a most strenuous life. While his parlor was a social rendezvous for Boston's intellectuals (excepting the older clergy), his study was a combined confessional, employment bureau, theological seminar, school, and public library. He carried on a steady correspondence with English and European scholars, reviewed books, lectured, and wrote critical essays. In spite of his ostracism he was happy; he was doing what he liked.

The Melodeon meanwhile had given way to the Music Hall, a more satisfactory auditorium accommodating 3000 people. What was it that attracted this heterogeneous mass of people? Parker's sermons for one thing were meaty, learned, and consistently liberal. His great themes were the glories of nature and the dignity of human nature. But it was not erudition that drew the people to Parker. The secret of his preaching was not intellect but passion. It was his prophetic genius for religion that moved this congregation. "Great as he was in intellect and in conscience," writes John White Chadwick, "he was greater in affection." It was his spirit, not his argument, in the final analysis, that won his hearers. His positive faith and moral earnestness were described by Lowell in his *Fable for Critics:*

> "And this is what makes him the crowd-drawing
>   preacher,
> There's a background of God to each hard-
>   working feature;
> Every word that he speaks has been fierly
>   furnaced
> In the blast of a life that has struggled in earnest."

But his emotional fervor would have been shallow without his deep learning, mental poise, and rationality. By the same token, mere intellectualism without human sympathy is sterile. Parker possessed both of these qualities in perfect balance.

As the years passed, his preaching at the Music Hall suffered increased interruptions occasioned by his lecture tours. Much of his itinerary was arranged so as to be back in his pulpit on Sunday but frequently his schedule took him too far away. He barnstormed Pennsylvania, Ohio, Upper New York State, and the "barbarous West" and concluded that "the superiority of New England civilization over the rest of America is quite clear." He was not a natural "trouper" and often complained of the hardships of train travel and tavern accommodations (or lack of them). In his dual rôle as popular lecturer and cultivated scholar he found himself torn between two opinions. His Boston sermons began to reflect the larger world of his itinerant life and his travels gave him a new concern—the broader application of his ethical teaching. His doctrine of human perfectability and his religion of humanity began to take a more concrete form. Parker the scholarly preacher changed to Parker the social reformer.

Not that he was a voice crying in the wilderness. The best Boston atmosphere was charged with reform. Garrison, Channing, Hale, Ripley, Phillips, Sumner, and Mann had already preached abolition, socialism, and pacifism. The greatest of them all was William Ellery Channing without whose inspiration and example Parker's career is inconceivable.

Now Parker's thoughts on social reform turned to action. He would complete what Channing had started. The Church had failed miserably. After nineteen centuries it was impotent in the face of war, crime, slavery, ignorance, poverty, vice, and injustice. Parker was through with theory; it was applied Christianity from now on. His days of theological warfare were behind; now he was to throw his tremendous energy into social reform. First there was the Anti-Sabbath Convention which had for its purpose the substitution of a sensible Sunday for the legalistic Sabbath with its Blue Laws. In his speech on "The Most Christian Use of Sunday" Parker warned against jumping from "the sour, stiff, Jewish way of keeping the Sabbath to a low, coarse, material, voluptuous, or mere money-making abuse of it." But his reform was too radical for the Church and too mild for the radicals. Then came the Temperance movement which received Parker's wholehearted support and to which he brought a scientific rather than emotional attitude. There was the Anti-Capital Punishment Convention at which Parker not only exposed the medieval methods of the prison system but laid the greater responsibility on society, the State and the Church for the milieu in which crime was nourished. He denied the right of the State to take the life of a prisoner and questioned the deterrent effect of the death penalty. "To put a criminal to death," said he, "seems to me as foolish as for the child

to beat the stool it has stumbled over, and as useless too."
Modern prison reform—the substitution of reformation
for punishment, its emphasis on early environment as a
cause of crime, indeterminate sentence, classification of
criminals, the proper attitude of society towards the criminal when released—was anticipated in full by Parker in
1845.

Parker had no illusions about war. He denounced war in
general as a false means for settling disputes and the Mexi-
can War in particular as "a war for slavery, a mean and
infamous war against the best interests of mankind." In his
attitude on labor and industry Parker was a realistic socialist. "He takes the pound of flesh," he said in his *Sermon on
Merchants*, "though that bring away all the life blood with
it. He loves private contracts, digging through walls in
secret. No interest is illegal if he can get it. He cheats the
nation with false invoices and swears lies at the Customs
House. . . . You see his character in letting his houses,
his houses for the poor. . . . He knows no right, only
power; no man but self; no God but his calf of gold."
Parker condemned the leaders of industry as a class which
ran the government and subsidized the Church. "Coöpera-
tive industry rather than antagonistic competition" was his
answer.

The Slavery Issue

These reforms were all parts of a whole. For Parker they
were inherent in his doctrine of the divine worth of human
personality, the most forceful implication of which was
the anti-slavery cause. He had preached against slavery in
1841 and again in 1843 but it was not until 1845, when
slavery became a political problem, that he made it his chief

concern. His first critical blow was dealt in a letter dated December 22, 1847, entitled "A Letter to the People of the United States touching the Matter of Slavery." This was a scientific, dispassionate statement, outlining the history of slavery, describing the condition of slaves, estimating the effects of slavery on industry and society, and defining the moral issue. Many articles followed and on the passage of the Fugitive Slave Law, as one biographer says, "the whole order of his life took on a different form and color."

As with other reforms, Parker put in a tardy appearance here also. It had been many years since Garrison had been dragged through the streets of Boston. Sumner and Palfrey had been dropped from society and spurned by former friends and Professor Follen had been dismissed from Harvard. New England, in fact, seemed to be more sensitive about the subject than the South. Slavery enjoyed the earnest support of press, pulpit, and politics. Parker's entrance into the arena may have been belated but it was an impressive one. His participation in reform up to this time had been somewhat after the manner of a dilettante. It remained for the slave question to arouse him to the full force of his energy and passion. He was always dramatic and picturesque but when it came to abolition he was fanatical. Not all his utterances were judicious or even accurate; like Tom Paine, he found difficulty in separating his opponents from their ideas, with the result that he became personal in his attacks. Slavery, in his mind, was a curse that could not be wiped out by soft words and gentle action. He has been criticized for taking the law in his hands and for using sensational methods, but the violence of a misguided John Brown and the vehemence of a "bloody Theodore Parker" were probably necessary in order to stir the imagination and emotion of the people.

Speech followed speech in the North, South, and West. Lecturing before a Garrison Society meeting in 1850 Parker said: "By and by there will be a political party with a wider basis than the Free Soil party which will declare that the nation itself must put an end to slavery in the nation; and if the Constitution of the United States will not allow it, there is another constitution that will. Then the title 'Defender and Expounder of the Constitution of the United States' will give way to this: 'Defender and Expounder of the Constitution of the Universe' and we shall reaffirm the ordinance of nature and reënact the will of God."

Parker harbored fugitive slaves in his home and boasted about it. He formed vigilance committees and made posters, warning fugitives of danger. Among the many slaves whom he befriended were William and Ellen Craft, who came to him to be married. Parker performed the wedding in a negro boarding-house. Concluding the ceremony, he told William Craft that he must defend his wife against all comers. Taking a Bible and a bowie-knife which lay on the dining room table, he placed them in the husband's hands to use "one for the body's, the other for the soul's defense." The Crafts left for England with a letter to James Martineau.

"For obstructing, resisting, and opposing the execution of the law" Parker, Phillips, Higginson and several others were indicted. The incident which precipitated this charge was the arrest of Anthony Burns, another fugitive slave whom Parker tried to have released by force but failed.[2] The date for the trial was set and he carefully prepared his defense, but Parker's counsel moved that the indictment

[2] For a dramatic account of the Anthony Burns episode see Henry Steele Commager's excellent biography, *Theodore Parker, Yankee Crusader*, pp. 231 ff.

be thrown out and it was. The unused written defense was subsequently published in a book of 125,000 words. Contemplating imprisonment, Parker wrote in his Journal: "What shall I do if I am sent to gaol? (1) Write one sermon a week and have it read at Music Hall and printed the next morning. (2) Prepare a volume of sermons from old manuscripts. (3) Write Memoirs. (4) Volume One of *Historical Development of Religion.* (5) Pursue Russian studies." But the martyrdom which he had courted did not take place and the world was deprived of a history of religion.

The months following the trial were tumultuous ones for Parker the reformer. The tide had turned. New England was changing its mind. The scene of battle shifted to Kansas which had been reopened to slavery by the passage of the Kansas-Nebraska Bill. Parker preached a memorable sermon on this "tenth victory of slavery." The "squatter sovereignty" principle was adopted, the upshot of which was an emigration of free-state men to Kansas, rifles in hand. Parker jumped to the support of John Brown and the New England Emigrant Aid Society. In 1856 his committee raised nearly $100,000 in money and arms. Parker was now convinced that emancipation could come only with war. He was for insurrection among the slaves and armed resistance wherever necessary. He justified his financial and moral support of John Brown on the grounds that only such radical action would provoke the larger conflict which was ultimately inevitable. For him the struggle now became a political one as he became adviser to Sumner, Wilson, Chase, and Seward. His correspondence with the leading statesmen of the time, as shown in the Weiss collection of letters, is ample evidence of his political influence.[3] Hern-

[3] John Weiss: *The Life and Correspondence of Theodore Parker*, 2 Vols. (Boston, 1864)

don, Lincoln's law partner, wrote to him: "May I say you are my ideal—strong, direct, energetic, charitable. If you see any expression in these pieces which are yours in essence, remember you impressed the hard steel upon the softer plate."

Going back to Springfield, Illinois, on one occasion, Herndon took with him some of Parker's sermons and addresses. "One of these," he says, "was a lecture on 'The Effect of Slavery on the American People,' which was delivered in the Music Hall, Boston, and which I gave to Lincoln, who read it and returned it. He liked especially the following expression, which he marked with a pencil, and which he in substance afterwards used in his Gettysburg address: 'Democracy is direct self-government, over all the people, by all the people, for all the people.' " The speech referred to was Parker's last great anti-slavery address. In another lecture, "The Slave Power in America," Parker used a slightly different form—"the government of all the people, by all the people, and for all the people." The Parker-Herndon correspondence, uncovering a curious but firm friendship between the New England scholar and the frontier politician, also reveals Parker's political leadership and Herndon's scholarly ambitions.

Dénouement

Parker had entered the slavery fight reluctantly, or at least tardily, but, having entered, he gave all that he had. Now he wanted to return to his writing. He published two volumes of his lectures and brought out revised editions of his *Discourses on Religion* and the De Wette translation. He contributed articles and reviews to the *Atlantic Monthly* and other periodicals. His popularity as a lecturer reached a new high because of his political reforming and the Music Hall proved to be too small for the thousands who came to hear him each Sunday morning. The orthodox world, on the other hand, did not rate him so highly; he was regarded rather as the Anti-Christ of the Apocalypse, the curse of Boston, Public Enemy Number One. "Hell never vomited forth a more blasphemous monster than Theodore Parker," said the Reverend Mr. Burnham. Parker's destruction was the theme of city-wide prayer meetings. "O Lord," one divine prayed, "send confusion and distraction into his study this afternoon, and prevent his finishing his preparation for his labors tomorrow, or if he shall attempt to desecrate the Holy Day by speaking to the people, meet him there, Lord, and confound him." Another pleaded: "O Lord, what shall be done for Boston if thou dost not take this and some other matters in hand?" But if Boston orthodoxy thought Parker was hopeless, he in turn thought the same of Boston. In one of a series of three sermons on the great revival he said: "The churches need a revival. No institution in America is more corrupt than her churches. No thirty thousand men and women are so bigoted and narrow as the thirty thousand ministers. The churches—they are astern of all other craft that keep the intellectual sea. The people mean a revival of religion, but the ministers will turn it into a revival of ecclesiastical theology—the doctrine of the dark ages, which we ought to have left behind us centuries ago."

This renewal of public activity in 1856 was his last plunge. The great reformer suddenly began to feel the effects of his earlier life: carelessness about health, overwork in his youth and early manhood, poor diet, travelling under unhygienic conditions. He had never been able to play, relax, and was never satisfied unless he was doing the work of three men. Then there was an inherited pulmonary weakness which was aggravated undoubtedly by his inordinate activity in the anti-slavery campaign. (Of his ten brothers and sisters eight had died of consumption.) Never again would he walk thirty miles a day, as he had often done. He was an old man at forty-seven, burned out. He had planned a sermon on "The Religion of Jesus and the Christianity of the Church." The Music Hall was filled to capacity and all waited expectantly for his appearance on the steps of the platform, but Parker did not come. Fear and dismay swept over the house as the deacon mounted the steps and read a note from the preacher: "Well beloved friends, I shall not speak to you today; for this morning a little after four o'clock I had a slight attack of bleeding from the lungs or throat. . . . I hope you will not forget the contribution for the poor, whom we have with us always. I don't know when I shall again look upon your welcome faces, which have so often cheered my spirit when my flesh was weak. May we do justly, love mercy, and walk humbly with our God, and his blessing will be upon us here and hereafter, for his infinite love is with us for ever and ever."

Pleurisy led to tuberculosis and he was ordered to the West Indies. Here at Santa Cruz he took care of his correspondence, put his business in shape, and prepared to depart this life; then, unexpectedly finding himself still in the land of the living, he threw himself into a last minute chore—his autobiography, which he called "Theodore Parker's Experience as a Minister," a candid, faithful account of his stewardship. This was in the form of a letter which he sent to his church in Boston.

Upon the advice of his physician he went to England, but he found the English dampness as bad as the West

Indian heat, and the fruitless quest for health sent him on. The dry air of the Swiss Alps restored his vigor temporarily but with the winter's cold he was ordered off to Rome. There was something final about the Eternal City, too final. Here he found some books that he had been trailing for many years. He mingled with many old friends, and if there were any eminent persons whom he had not met before, he met them here—the Brownings topping the list. Even so, he did not wish to die in Rome. He wrote to his friend Ripley: "O George, it is idle to run from Death. I shrank down behind the sugar canes of Santa Cruz; Death was there too; then I sneaked into a Swiss valley, there he was; and here he is at Rome. I shall come home and meet him on my own dunghill." Vowing that he would not die "on this accursed soil," he hurried away. Florence was a more fitting place in which to die, more fitting at any rate, for Theodore Parker. On a Sunday morning at the hour when he was accustomed to stand at his desk in the Music Hall, he was buried in the Protestant Cemetery, not far from the grave of Elizabeth Barrett Browning. Only a handful of people accompanied the body to the cemetery. The service consisted of the reading of the Beatitudes by a friend—that was all. "But it so happened," writes an early biographer, "that Florence held a feast that day, and the streets were all abloom with flags, as for a faithful soldier welcomed home."

The inscription later placed on the monument in Florence—"The Great American Preacher"—still serves to define his real place in the history of American life. In philosophy he was the interpreter, not the original thinker. In the academic field he was more a critic of systems than a creator of one. His scholarship lacked accuracy and he was often pedantic, always verbose. His function was that of organization rather than original design. He was a popularizer in the better sense of the word. He was too encyclopedic to be an artist. He did not know the value of omission but showed all his wares, quoted every source, talked overtime. His speeches and writings have an overstuffed quality but he was never guilty of superficial intellectualism and he never had his tongue in his cheek. He was primarily a pulpit orator, not a writer, and his appeal came solely from his personal presence. His sermons were exhortations to action rather than literary masterpieces and they were effective only in their oral form. When read today, these discourses which thrilled the Music Hall audiences of a century ago seem devitalized, crude, and fearfully redundant. His scholarship was quantitative rather than qualitative, synthetic rather than analytic. But no preacher, and few professors, had a greater familiarity with the world's best literature; few American scholars have possessed a wider linguistic knowledge; and no one could boast of a library like his with its 13,000 volumes and 5000 unbound documents—the largest private collection in America.

Yes, the word "preacher" defines Parker's greatness, for it was as a preacher at the Music Hall that he dominated the thought of New England for fourteen years. His theme was natural religion. His religious philosophy was only partially transcendental; only in its universalistic aspects could it be considered Concordian. Today he would be called a pragmatist. Mysticism without fruits held no interest for him. Dogmas were to be tested by daily deeds. He was a practical realist in all things and his roots were in the soil.

As a preacher Parker was an independent, self-reliant fighter, pandering to no denomination or machine but forever challenging injustice, sham, and obscurantism, forever differentiating the permanent in religion from the transient. He shares with Channing the honor of fathering the cause of religious liberalism in this country but actually he did more than Channing to free New England from narrow ecclesiasticism and orthodox theology. Channing, the more disciplined mind, preached liberalism in the abstract and laid the philosophical foundations for freedom; Parker went to the people.

Like his great contemporary and fellow-liberal, Emerson, he was a product of Unitarianism. He may have been a problem child and, while he lived, a disowned son, but his liberal views are inconceivable except on the background of that great movement and eventually Unitarianism gratefully embraced both the man and his ideas. At Parker's memorial services held in Boston, Emerson said: "Ah, my brave brother! It seems as if, in a frivolous age, our loss were immense, and your place cannot be supplied. But you will already be consoled in the transfer of your genius, knowing well that the nature of the world will affirm to all men, in all times, that which for twenty-five years you valiantly spoke. The breezes of Italy murmur the same truth over your grave, the winds of America over these bereaved streets, and the sea which bore your mourners home affirms it. Whilst the polished and pleasant traitors to human rights, with perverted learning and disgraced graces, die and are utterly forgotten, with their double tongue saying all that is sordid about the corruption of man, you believed in the divinity of all, and you live on."

X

New England Unitarianism

The Enlightenment in America

A MOVEMENT THAT can account for practically all the genius in the Golden Age of American letters merits recognition, more perhaps than has ever been given. The Adamses, the Alcotts, the Channings, the Danas, the Emersons, the Everetts, the Fullers, the Hales, the Lowells, the Ripleys, Bancroft, Bowditch, Bulfinch, Garrison, Hawthorne, Holmes, Longfellow, Motley, Norton, Parker, Parkman, Prescott, Sparks, Stuart, Sumner, Thoreau, Ticknor, Webster, and Whittier—all were Unitarians except Whittier and Alcott who were half-Quaker. The "flowering of New England" was a culture cycle comparable to the Age of Pericles, the Italian Renaissance and the Elizabethan Period in England—the creative expression of something universal, prophetic. There was a sense of awakening and of freed imagination, a new and elemental appreciation of nature and an authentic spirit of learning. As a recent critic of that period remarks, it was an age when "auctioneers quoted Shakespeare" and "blacksmiths argued about free-will."

Most of those Olympians were distinguished as much for their religious and philosophical thinking as for their literary accomplishments. It was their religious liberalism that turned Boston into an American Athens which "opened and kept open," according to Oliver Wendell Holmes, "more turnpikes leading to free thought and free speech and free deeds than any other city in the country." The same liberalism turned New England from joyless Calvinism to a new Enlightenment.

New England Unitarianism was a reconciliation of science with religion, an attempt to bring religion into line with the modern spirit. It should be viewed as an attitude towards life, a *Weltanschauung*, rather than a mere denomination, for when it became denominationally conscious it atrophied and ceased to create. As a collective impulse or way of thinking it became the most influential movement in the history of American thought and letters.

No movement in American history stands closer to the fundamentals of liberal democracy than Unitarianism. Most of the founding fathers of the United States were of the Unitarian conviction. Twenty of the seventy-two distinguished Americans in the Hall of Fame are Unitarians. This group claims only one-tenth of one per cent of the Protestant Church membership, yet a check of the persons listed in *Who's Who in America* shows a representation that is twenty-eight times as great as the normally expected figure. The qualitative contribution of this fellowship in science, education, and reform is recognized at the mention of such names as Susan B. Anthony, Dorothea Dix, Julia Ward Howe, Louisa L. Schuyler, Louis Agassiz, J. C. Calhoun, Peter Cooper, Charles W. Eliot, Justice O. W. Holmes, David Starr Jordan, Thomas Starr King, Horace Mann, John Marshall, Thomas Mott Osborne, C. P. Steinmetz, and William H. Taft.

Whence emerged this leaven of liberal thought that produced more illustrious thinkers in New England in thirty years than all the rest of the states could produce in two centuries? In the first place, New England Unitarianism fell heir to eighteenth-century American Deism, yet it also had its European antecedents; and it is to these early continental heresies that we first turn.

Continental Unitarianism

Incipient Unitarianism appeared in early Christianity with Origen, Arius, and Pelagius who opposed orthodox trinitarianism and the emerging doctrine of total depravity. The authoritarian system that followed Nicea and Constantine stamped out all heresy for a thousand years or more. Then in the wake of the Renaissance-Reformation came Servetus, who followed the logical implications of Luther's doctrine of "the freedom of the Christian man" and went one step further. Discarding ecclesiastical tradition and established creeds, Servetus attempted to interpret the Scripture along critical lines. He rejected the metaphysical trinity, held to a Spinozistic theism and preached freedom of the will. He might have recalled the fate of Arius who opposed the dogma of the trinity, but he was a disputatious young man and came out with a book. He was optimistic enough to try to interest Calvin in it. That was his big mistake. A book written to show that the Council of Nicea had decided wrongly about the person of Jesus was not calculated to go well, either with Catholics or Protestants. The result was that its author had to go into hiding. But he was not satisfied with an incognito existence, and, like a moth darting into a flame, he appeared suddenly in Geneva with the naïve idea that Calvin might still listen. This time he saw his blunder and disappeared as quickly as he had come. But Calvin's inquisitorial spies caught up with him and brought him back to the Protestant dictator. For contradicting Calvin, Servetus was thrown into a damp dungeon and was kept there for months with irons on hands and feet. The most primitive demands of hygiene were refused him. The "trial" was conducted by Calvin himself, and it was easy enough to get a man already driven mad with starvation and rats to utter words that the council might construe as heretical. His burning at the stake was one of the most sadistic episodes in history—a deed boasted of from the Cathedral pulpit the following Sunday morning. It must be said in all fairness to Calvin that in a moment of generosity he suggested that the prisoner be decapitated instead of burned! Servetus replied that he had done nothing worthy of death, that he, being a Spanish subject, was outside Calvin's jurisdiction, but that if doctrinal disagreement existed between them, he would be willing to debate the matter publicly. Whereupon the infuriated Calvin consigned the heretic to the flames.

A manifesto on tolerance suddenly appeared. Its author was one Castellio, a great humanist who had once before crossed blades with Calvin. This time he was out to rehabilitate the innocent but dead Servetus. In this document he said: "To burn a man alive does not defend a doctrine, but slays a man." Calvin suppressed the book and spread out his dragnet. Castellio was caught and this time Calvin refused to appear at the "trial." Happily he was denied the supreme triumph of seeing Castellio suffer the terrible fate of Servetus, because death mercifully overtook the prisoner shortly after his incarceration. Orthodoxy had again triumphed. Unitarianism was evidently not yet ripe, at least in Switzerland.

It would be a contradiction in terms to expect a reformation in Italy, but there were at least two Protestants in that country in the sixteenth century—the Sozzinis. Lelio Sozzini came from a line of judges and bankers. He himself studied for the law, but he also read some theology. Perhaps his independence of thought was a result of his travels, for he spent ten years seeing the sights in London, Vienna, Wittenberg, Zurich, Cracow, and a hundred other cities. He even visited Geneva, but not without the knowledge of the Calvinistic Ogpu. It was rumored about that this visitor, Lelio Sozzini, had Servetian leanings. Calvin had by this time pigeonholed the Servetus episode, thinking that antitrinitarianism was thoroughly and finally squelched. But the martyrdom of Servetus had only fanned the flames. Castellio and Servetus, it was said, had influenced many people in other countries. This stranger was probably one of them. So either at the suggestion of the Genevese ruler or acting on his own hunch, Lelio suddenly craved a change of scenery. As it happened, the Holy Inquisition later relieved Calvin from dealing with the Sozzini heresy.

Lelio's nephew, Faustus Sozzini, was an even more ardent antitrinitarian. He spent his early years in commercial travelling and returned to Italy in 1563. However, it occurred to him that it might be safer for a man with his views to live on the *other* side of the Alps. He settled down in Basel and wrote some books. His life of Jesus fell into the hands of a Dr. Biandrata in far-off Transylvania. Biandrata became an antitrinitarian and converted his patients to the cause. Following Biandrata's request, Sozzini went to Transylvania; there he was married. After a year he went to Poland and there spent the rest of his life. He wrote a treatise on tolerance and liberalism and this became the platform of all Socinians. It called for freedom of conscience, individual interpretation of the Scripture, and a return to first-century Christianity. But the Inquisition of the Counter-Reformation was already at work, and the light of Socinianism was soon snuffed out.

Here in Eastern Europe, then, for a brief span, liberalism had again become articulate. The Socinians shared with all humanists, like Erasmus and Colet, the belief that man was of infinite worth and could achieve his own salvation through character. They saw no reason for the atonement and disbelieved in Jesus as deity. They placed reason above revelation and individual freedom above the authority of the Church. They said that Christianity was not a belief but a practice; that conduct, not creed, was the determining factor.

During the years of persecution some of the followers of Sozzini found refuge in Holland, where they were known as Polish Brethren. The Racovian Catechism of the Polish Brethren, really the work of Faustus Sozzini, is the best statement of Socinian belief in existence and might well be called the Manifesto of Continental Unitarianism. Socinianism spread also to Hungary, Germany, and later to England, where it affected the views of many English Protestants. As a system of belief, it represented a simplified and rationalized Protestantism. It repudiated Augustinianism and Institutionalism, Catholic or Protestant. It regarded baptism as purely symbolic and without saving efficacy, and it held that the celebration of the Supper was a memorial only. It taught that Christ was a teacher of moral truth, not a divine Saviour or part of the Godhead.

The Socinians as an organized body disappeared, but their antitrinitarian views were disseminated in England in the seventeenth century by John Biddle and Thomas Firmin, who were imprisoned for their beliefs. Arianism was revived by Thomas Emlyn, a Presbyterian minister, Samuel Clarke, an Anglican rector, and others, mostly Presbyterians. Unitarianism finally became a fact when Theophilus Lindsey, a Socinian, circulated a petition asking that clergymen be relieved from subscription to the Thirty-nine Articles of Faith. Parliament refused. In 1774 Lindsey, having withdrawn from the established Church, organized a Unitarian Chapel in London.

American Backgrounds

Considered as a temper rather than a Church, Unitarianism in America goes back to Puritan days. Not all the Puritans were "puritanical," as the names of Roger Williams, Henry Vane, Richard Saltonstall, William Pynchon, and John Wise bear witness. These individualists were Puritan liberals, prophets of freedom, tolerance, and reason. With them grew the liberal movement which later became Unitarianism.

The Arian position of the American Deists and their close connection with New England Unitarianism are suggested in a letter written by Jefferson to a Unitarian correspondent. "I should as soon undertake to bring the crazy skulls of Bedlam to sound understanding," wrote Jefferson, "as to inculcate reason into that of an Athanasian." Yet in the continuation of free thought from American Deism to Unitarianism there was a polite transformation, the nature of which is typified by Priestley, who in 1794 wrote an "Answer to Mr. Paine's *Age of Reason*," in which, while assailing the doctrines of the Trinity and the Atonement, he defended revelation and miracles. His later *Discourses relating to the Evidences of Revealed Religion* (1796) gave further direction to the Unitarian movement in the formation of which Priestley was a powerful influence. The earlier radicalism undoubtedly suffered a toning down and the mantle of Deism was worn rather lightly. The liberalism of Unitarianism was modified somewhat by the mystical transcendentalism of the Concord group and the bibliocentric supernaturalism of the right wing. Even in its diluted form Unitarianism remained much more liberal than any other influence in America, an evidence of which is the exclusion until recently of Unitarians from active membership in evangelical organizations.

The advance guard of American Unitarianism was known as Arminianism. This was a left wing Reformation movement which emphasized the rational spirit, natural laws, and the application of criticism to the Bible. It was more than a sect or a set of dogmas; it was a school of thought midway between Deism and orthodox Unitarianism and may be said to have served as a transition from one to the other. It was a liberal interpretation of life, rational in temper and inclusive in spirit. The followers of Arminius distinguished between the Bible as external authority and as an inspiration to moral conduct. With them it was not a fetish or a tyranny but a source book in ethics to be used with discrimination and reason.

Arminianism made possible the latitudinarian movement in England, another source of American Unitarianism. Chillingworth, Tillotson, and Samuel Clarke were prominent latitudinarians in their outright devotion to reason, experience, and nature, to deeds rather than creeds, and to tolerance. As a milder form of Deism the Arminian movement in America stood for rationalism, democratic methods, and the pragmatic emphasis. It asserted human equality, a native spiritual capacity, and a benevolent deity rather than the sovereignty of God. Just as Calvinism with its belief in divine sovereignty bequeathed to posterity the doctrine of total depravity, so Arminianism with its belief in democracy passed on the idea of human perfectability.

The growth of Arminianism in eighteenth-century America can be traced in the lives and opinions of Ebenezer

Gay, Jonathan Mayhew, and Charles Chauncy. These three men were typical of the larger faith that was making itself felt within organized religion and are now regarded as the first outspoken Unitarians in New England. Their first principle was free inquiry and private judgment in all questions of religion. They disapproved of creed-making and ridiculed the common tendency to accept certain tenets as "mysteries" that were beyond the human mind. Christianity, they said, was "the art of living virtuously." Man was a self-determining, self-prefecting creature endowed with moral capacity. Reason was their final court of appeal in all religious matters. They rejected the doctrine of the Trinity and held to the divine Unity. The deistic character of this early Unitarian school is clearly evident, especially in the common emphasis on the benevolence of deity and the "religion of humanity."

An important event in the background of the Unitarian movement was the reorganization in 1782 of King's Chapel along liberal lines with the appointment of James Freeman as minister. He was assisted in this reorganization by the English Unitarian, the Reverend William Hazlitt, father of the English critic. During his New England visit, Hazlitt sowed much Unitarian seed and Freeman reported that after Hazlitt's return to England there "were many churches in which the worship is strictly Unitarian." Boston ministers were in correspondence with Theophilus Lindsey and Dr. Priestley, the chief British Unitarians. Yet in the organization of the first parishes of Portland, Salem, and Boston in the last decade of the eighteenth century there was no denominational consciousness; in fact, the word "Unitarian" was rarely used. Having left one sect, most of the early Unitarian leaders were not anxious to create another. Such a condition could not last long, however, and it ended with the official organization of the American Unitarian Association in 1825.[1]

Emerson, Thoreau, and Channing

Unitarianism rapidly became popular, respectable, and conservative. Channing, lamenting the drift to traditional theology, wrote: "And now we have a Unitarian orthodoxy." Emerson suddenly outgrew his Boston pulpit and so shocked the Harvard authorities in his celebrated Divinity School address that he was not invited to return for forty years. Then appeared the inevitable right and left wings between which there was a wide intellectual cleavage. The beginning of the rift in the ranks was marked by the formation of the Transcendental Club with Emerson, Parker, Channing, Ripley, and Hedge as the charter members. This "symposium," as it was called, was an evidence of the potent influence of German philosophy on New England thought in the middle decades of the nineteenth century. It might also be considered as an attempt to revitalize the Unitarian movement which had already become static and stilted. The American brand of transcendentalism issued from the rationalistic romanticism of Immanuel Kant who furnished philosophical confirmation for the Protestant principle of the primacy of faith. On the other hand, it came as an antidote to deistic rationalism which it supplemented with intuition. The mystical element came by an Oriental route. With the spices and tea from India came the doctrine of the Oversoul, passive resistance, Nirvana, and the philosophy of withdrawal. In turning eastward the Concordians became more concerned with mysticism than theology. The Emersonians were apparently unable to find a satisfactory

[1] For details see G. W. Cooke: *Unitarianism in America*, pp. 126–27.

check on their inherited rationalism at home, so they blended Hindu theosophy, Confucian wisdom, and Mohammedan poetry into a composite Transcendentalism. With Emerson it expressed itself in the doctrine of the Oversoul; with Thoreau it took the form of asceticism, and with Alcott, a consuming interest in the propagation of universal Scriptures.[2]

Transcendentalism was the Concordian answer to a narrow and prematurely orthodox Unitarianism. The Emersonians welcomed the inclusiveness and serenity of the Hindu Scriptures and saw in them an idealism which eighteenth-century rationalism lacked. But the idealistic mysticism of the Transcendentalists did not survive its enthusiastic exponents. Its rapid demise and fading influence were due to its eclectic and imported nature and its esoteric character, which made no appeal to the common man. It broke down before the persistent problem of evil, for it had no better answer than the pantheistic cults of present-day New England.

Emerson, like his twentieth-century counterpart, Santayana, defies classification; he will not "stay put." This is because of his insistence on being eclectic, at once the shrewd, practical Yankee and the devotee at the mystic shrine of Buddha. At heart his eclecticism, which combined the Hindu Oversoul and Western Humanism, was essentially liberal. Emerson was thoroughly opposed to conventionalism in all its forms, even that of Unitarianism. This same eclecticism, however, made him a loose and irresponsible thinker, always uttering fragments of truth. Consequently his reputation lies not so much in his systematic religious liberalism as in belles-lettres and the epigram-

[2] An excellent study of the Oriental influence on the Concord group has been made by Arthur Christy in *The Orient in American Transcendentalism*.

matic-poetic essay. This probably gave him a wider following among the unlettered than his less widely-known fellow-liberals who were more consistently rational. Intuition was his forte, not reason. He was a seer, not a critic.

Emerson possessed the Oriental revulsion to debate and often confessed to a non-Christian attitude in private that he refused to state publicly. Like Erasmus, he could not be drawn into open controversy, nor could any self-defense be extracted from him. "To attack him," writes Francis G. Peabody, "was like smiting a feather pillow, which yielded softly and presently took its old shape." [3] Asked on one occasion to defend his heretical stand on the Sacraments of the Church, Emerson said: "There is no scholar less willing or less able than myself to be a polemic. I could not give an account of myself if challenged." In his essay on "Self-Reliance" he said: "As man's prayers are a disease of the will, so are his creeds a disease of the intellect." Such a statement calls for explanation but Emerson would not face the philosophical implications of his own epigrams. He boasted that he cared nothing for consistency. The irritation produced in others by this spirit of tranquil detachment is noticeable in a remark made by contemporary, Father Taylor. "Mr. Emerson," said he, "is one of the sweetest creatures that God ever made. He must go to Heaven when he dies; for if he went to Hell, the devil would not know what to do with him. But he knows no more of the religion of the New Testament than Balaam's ass did of the principles of the Hebrew grammar." Emerson's fragmentariness was disparaged even by more sympathetic contemporaries such as James Martineau, who wrote: "The failure of coherent continuity of thought leaves his fine material in an unorganized and fathomless condition. Much as I

[3] *Pioneers of Religious Liberty in America*, p. 310.

love the man, I seek in vain to learn from him. The fault is probably in me." Less sympathetic was the studied observation of Matthew Arnold. "Emerson cannot be called with justice a great philosophical writer."

Emerson's eclecticism produced one doctrine which is basically liberal, and yet in its extreme form shows the weakness of the transcendental position—the principle that truth should be divorced from personality. This was a protest—and a valid one—against the exaggerated Christocentricism of the more evangelical and, surprisingly enough, even of the Unitarian churches. The particular idioms of Christ, said Emerson, have usurped the place of ethics for its own sake; the personal authority of Jesus has been made more important than the universal truths which his teachings contain. Is the principle of moral integrity true just because Jesus uttered it or is it true regardless of its source? This protest against the undue importance attached to the person of Christ or to his mystical office was a much-needed criticism of particularism, but to separate Jesus' teachings from his character is a contradiction in terms. Religious truth cannot be taught in a vacuum; it is best appreciated through the medium of a person. Truth is an expression of personality and the greater the personality the more profound the truth.

Emerson followed his own star and cultivated the life of self-reliance. Pushing aside the hair-splitting theological problems, he climbed to the stratosphere of universal mind. Just as Darwin spent twenty years accumulating evidence for his scientific theory, so Emerson spent those years in solitude communing with nature and learning the secrets of the gods. The secret which he found was the same as that found by Channing, Thoreau, and Parker; Condorcet, Rousseau, and Voltaire; Paine, Franklin, and Jefferson—

namely that the universe is friendly if men themselves can arrive at congeniality, that as part of developing nature man is equipped with self-perfectability.

Emerson's liberalism is seen not so much in his mystical transcendentalism as in his philosophy of individualism. "Whoso would be a man," he said in his essay on Self-Reliance, "must be a non-conformist." Likewise his Americanism is revealed in the Unitarian principle of freedom rather than in his Hindu metaphysics. The idea of man's freedom as a creature of nature came in turn from the earlier American Deism. Emerson rejected the rationalism of the Deists and scorned the worship of pure intellect. He preferred the evangelical dynamic to the "pale negations" of rational religion. Here then is an odd mixture of Puritanism and libertarianism, of pioneer pragmatism and Oriental abstraction, of critical insight and naïve optimism. But however abstract in his teaching on God, Emerson was crystal-clear in his belief in the divinity of man, and in that Unitarian doctrine he was a conscious liberal.

Thoreau was even more of an independent than his master, Emerson. Thoreau, the town character and eccentric philosopher, was the perfect paradox, half Hindu and half Yankee, half mystic and half scientist, a man with confused aims and a divided allegiance. He was lost in the midst of a multitude of things he wanted to do. Totally lacking in coordination and drive, he was, as Henry Seidel Canby says, "A neurotic in love, a rebel in social contacts, and a thwarted genius." [4]

In an age when democracy is on the defensive, Thoreau's doctrine of the supreme importance of the individual emerges as an integral part of the American tradition. At a time when man finds himself the victim of his own inven-

[4] *Thoreau*, p. 38.

tions, being crushed by the robot of his own creation, the Walden experiment in simplicity appears extremely pregnant. Was not the remark about the locomotive—"an improved means to an unimproved end" poignantly prophetic of a generation which would realize too late the discrepancy between technological gain and human values? Thoreau's experiment, regarded by his contemporaries as the "bravado of perverse idealism," caught the imagination of Gandhi; and the New England essay on "Civil Disobedience" became a Bible for the Hindu leader in his campaign for passive resistance. Both thinkers were arch enemies of the machine and the State. The New England Gandhi prophesied the enslavement of man by the means of life rather than the ends. Walden had no cultural lag, no surplus goods, no unnecessary labor. Walden was Thoreau's answer, but it cannot be ours. The machine must be mastered and it can be mastered only on the field of economic battle—not through intransigent passivity.

Of the three men of Concord—Emerson, Thoreau, and Channing—the last perhaps deserves the most important niche in the history of American liberalism. The first two were isolated thinkers, standing outside the stream of institutional life, whereas Channing was integrally related to a religious movement. This difference accounts for the wider reputation of the first two men; Channing's connection with Unitarianism has limited his following, a fact which does not detract but serves to enhance the quality of his liberalism.

Born in the Roger Williams state and having as a grandfather a signer of the Declaration of Independence, William Ellery Channing came by his love of liberty honestly. But his early environment was made up of "Berkshire Divinity" or "Consistent Calvinism" with its predestination and total depravity. The young Channing learned that whether one were destined to be saved or damned, it was for the glory of God and that there was "nothing good or generous in human nature."

Channing was not "willing to be damned." Travel and reading led him to the belief that man is not born in sin, but is by nature a child of God with divine capacity and in this sonship is free. Respect for man as man became his passion. He took the deistic position that "all virtue has its foundation in the moral nature of man." His sanction of morality lay not in supernaturalism but in the human conscience. This exalted view of man for Channing meant method as well as motive as he threw himself into a program of rehabilitation, relief, cultural opportunity for the underprivileged, and moral reform. His mind was focussed on economic and social problems: the effect of the factory system, the condition of the poor classes, the evil of competition, the worship of money. "Channing," writes Van Wyck Brooks, "was the father of half the reforms that characterized the Boston of his age." [5] The dignity of human nature must be restored. The human soul must be liberated as well as the body. He outlined a plan for adult education. He pleaded with the South to end slavery peacefully and avoid war. He sympathized with prohibition but warned that "men cannot be driven into temperance."

Channing's Christology was Arian but not Unitarian in the accepted sense of the word. He rejected the theory of consubstantiality and other phases of trinitarianism but followed the doctrine that Jesus was pre-existent and only short of God. The theological debate in his time, however, was not the nature of Christ but the nature of man. The

[5] *Flowering of New England,* p. 110.

underlying issue was freedom and on this point Channing's liberalism was unequivocal. His zeal for liberty applied to institutions as well as to the individual. "I have no anxiety to wear the livery of any party. I indeed take cheerfully the name of a Unitarian because unwearied efforts are used to raise against it a popular cry." He feared institutionalism and foresaw the coming of a new Calvinism in the liberal Churches. He expressed impatience with the Boston Unitarians who had complacently settled down with the conviction that no further changes were necessary.

As the leader of the intellectual and moral awakening, Channing aroused New England from the stupor and stupidity of Calvinism which had crushed man's faith in himself. New England was becoming the home of the priest rather than the prophet. Commerce was uppermost in man's mind. Making a living was more important than making a life. In the pulpit, on the lecture platform, and in the open air, Channing stirred the imagination of his listeners and kindled the spark of moral responsibility.

Channing's influence was felt not only in social reform and in the liberalizing of Calvinistic New England but in the literary and cultural Renaissance which occurred in the first half of the nineteenth century. Few scholars of that day had a more intimate acquaintance with foreign authors than he—Schiller, Shelley, Wordsworth, Goethe, Coleridge, Madame de Staël, Fichte, and Fenelon. He had been charged with the revolutionary doctrine of the French thinkers, had taken kindly to the "nature philosophy" of the Germans, and had imbibed the cosmic mysticism of the English Romanticists; nevertheless he envisaged an American independence in letters. Foreign forms, he said, must not be imitated. An American tradition must emerge but it can be nurtured only in native soil. "A country, like an individual, has dignity and power only in proportion as it is self-formed."

Because of his unclarified Christology and his belief in miracles, Channing's theological liberalism cannot be considered as consistent as that of Parker, but there can be no question on his advocacy of freedom. "I have lost no occasion," he wrote, "for expressing my deep attachment to liberty in all its forms, civil, political, religious; to liberty of thought, speech, and the press, and of giving utterance to my abhorrence of all forms of oppression." A man of fervent yet dispassionate eloquence, impeccable character, and deep learning, Channing was the true representative of essential Unitarianism.

Darwin

A Fateful Letter

FOR ONE to work assiduously for years on a book, a theory, or an invention, and then, just as he is about to reveal to the world the fruit of his labors, suddenly to see some one else independently publish the identical thesis or theory, has been the fate of more people than the world knows about. The classic example of this kind of tragedy is the experience of Charles Darwin. On June 18, 1858, Darwin, sitting in his study at Downe, received a letter postmarked Ternate, an island in the Malay Archipelago. Its sender was Alfred Russel Wallace, who enclosed a manuscript entitled, *On the Tendencies of Varieties to Part Indefinitely from the Original Type.*

The already ailing scientist was struck dumb by this bolt from the blue. What anguish and bitter disappointment must have flooded his soul—after a life-time of research, twenty years of painstaking investigation for complete support of his hypothesis, to find his young friend Wallace asking him for a final check on this, his own theory! The manuscript Darwin held in his hand that morning not only bore the same title but contained the same development and chapter headings which he had intended to use. Here, almost word for word, was the exposition of his secret, bril-

liantly explained and ready for publication. It seemed as if
his fame were blotted out in one stroke and the labor of a
life-time gone only to the confirmation of a colleague's
theory. He had been warned against deferment many times
by his friends, Hooker and Lyell, who urged him to publish the theory of natural selection before amassing any
further evidence, but Darwin was reluctant to print the
work in incomplete form. The desire to bring to bear irref-
utable and overwhelming support on the thesis, coupled
with his innate caution and modesty, resulted in tragic delay and later, as he began to realize grimly the danger of
competition, he became panic-stricken, compelled, as he
was, through sickness, to curtail his hours of work.

But Darwin rallied. He wrote to Lyell that he would
see to the immediate publication of Wallace's essay and
apologized for his first reaction of disappointment. It is an
evidence of true greatness that in his hour of seeming tragedy he should think only of the success of the unknown bird
collector. "I would far rather burn my whole book," he
wrote, "than that Wallace or any other man should think
that I behaved in a paltry spirit."

Thus would Darwin have settled the matter but fortunately he had previously taken Lyell and Hooker into his
confidence and they were not long in acquainting both
the public and the scientific world with the earlier correspondence, proving that Darwin was actually the first in
the field with the theory of natural selection. These friends
arranged for an abstract of Darwin's theory to appear in
connection with the publication of Wallace's paper. Thereafter Darwin insisted upon sharing the discovery with Wallace, constantly quoting the latter's findings along with his
own. Darwin's magnanimity, however, was matched by that
of Wallace who said: "Why should Darwin not have the

credit! He worked twenty years, while I hastily wrote mine in a week." On November 24th of the next year, the *Origin of Species* was published, the result of which was a revolution in thought equalled in its consequences only by the discoveries of Galileo.

Days of Indecision

Perhaps if Darwin had found his *forte* earlier in life he would have been spared the experience related above.[1] The indecisiveness and caution which characterized his career of research appeared also in his earlier vocational struggles. His father sent him to the University of Edinburgh to study medicine but he soon grew restive under the conservative academic system which he regarded as a waste of time. The lectures were dull and the operating clinics sickened him. He transferred to Cambridge where he was supposed to be studying for the ministry, but theology, especially the Cambridge variety, appealed to him less than medicine.

But at Edinburgh and Cambridge he met two men who awakened in him a dormant interest and shifted his attention from the macroscopic world of theology to the microscopic world of nature. The first was Dr. Robert Edmund Grant, skillful professor of Zoölogy at Edinburgh. Dr. Grant took a special interest in Darwin and together they attended the meetings of the scientific societies. Walking one day with Grant, Charles was astonished to hear the

[1] Darwin was born February 12, 1809, a year which produced a banner crop of geniuses: Lincoln (same day), Gladstone, Mendelssohn, Chopin, Tennyson, O. W. Holmes, and Elizabeth Barrett Browning. Darwin's father, Robert (six feet two inches and 350 pounds), was a physician; his mother, Susannah, was the daughter of Josiah Wedgwood of pottery fame. His grandfather, Erasmus, was a celebrated naturalist and forerunner of Charles in the theory of evolution. Sir Francis Galton, noted biologist, was Darwin's cousin.

professor "burst forth in high admiration of Lamarck and his views on evolution." While Charles had read *Zoönomia*, a book on evolution by his grandfather, Erasmus Darwin, and knew something of Lamarck's conjectures—for that is all they were—the young student, like most of his contemporaries, either ignored the idea of evolution or considered it absurd. He listened vaguely to Dr. Grant's inquiries into the nature of a species, not knowing that it was to be his fate to answer that question.

Completely bored with his medical studies, Darwin dropped out of Edinburgh at the end of the term. His father, a physician, could not appreciate this indifference and, not wanting his son to become just "an idle sportsman," he decided that the ministry would be the proper alternative. Charles, only eighteen at the time and still lacking a sense of direction, acquiesced but without conviction. If he had been intellectually more mature, his Unitarian background would have ruled out any thought of accepting the dogmas of the Church of England, but he did not allow that complication to deter him at this time.

Cambridge was a rich man's school and Charles found himself in the company of the sporting set more often than the theologues. What made Cambridge a profitable experience was J. S. Henslow, professor of botany. Bug collecting was a fad among the undergraduates and Charles with hundreds of others had become an enthusiast. He had been privileged to attend some of Henslow's field expeditions and had taken a great liking to the popular instructor. One day he ran breathlessly to Henslow with what he thought was a great botanical discovery but which was, at least to experts, a well-known phenomenon. Henslow handled the situation like a gentleman and explained the particular occurrence without humiliating him. What might have been the end of a friendship was in reality the beginning of a remarkable intimacy between the two men. Before his student days were over Darwin was known as "the man who walks with Henslow." By that time entomology had replaced theology in the mind of Darwin. Nevertheless he completed his divinity course and graduated tenth in his class.

In the Steps of Magellan

In the interval between his graduation and his entrance into the ministry, an opportunity came that settled his vocational problem once and for all. Returning from a geological trip, he found a letter offering him the position of naturalist on a scientific expedition sponsored by the British Government. The offer came from George Peacock, a tutor at Cambridge, who asked Henslow to recommend a man for the position. Peacock stated that the government ship *Beagle*, in command of Captain Fitz-Roy, was to encircle the globe, stopping at Tierra del Fuego and the South Sea Islands, and to return by way of the Indian Archipelago. Enclosed with the offer was a letter from Henslow to Darwin.

I fully expect that you will eagerly catch at the offer which is likely to be made you of a trip to Tierra del Fuego, and home by the East Indies. . . . I have stated that I consider you to be the best qualified person I know of who is likely to undertake such a situation. I state this not on the supposition of your being a finished naturalist, but as amply qualified for collecting, observing, and noting, anything worthy to be noted in Natural History. . . . Don't put on any modest doubts or fears about your disqualifications, for I assure you I think you are the very man they are in search of. So conceive yourself to be tapped on the shoulder by your bum-bailiff and affectionate friend.

J. S. Henslow.

For the first time in his life Darwin was ecstatic, unequivocally convinced that he knew what he wanted. Hesitancy and caution this time came from the family. Dr. Darwin, his father, again found himself frustrated in his plans for his son. Where was there any rhyme or reason in a minister going off to sea for five years on a crazy expedition for seaweeds and barnacles? Who recommended his son for such an escapade? There was grave doubt also as to his physical fitness for a sea voyage on a small boat like the *Beagle*. How could he settle down to clerical life after experiencing the *Wanderlust* and rough life of the sea?

Dr. Darwin felt so strongly about it that Charles decided to reject the offer. He went on a shooting expedition instead, and tried to forget his disappointment. Meanwhile, the Wedgwood side of the family had taken up his cause. Uncle Josiah argued that it would be a good experience for a minister, would broaden and enlarge his interests. In the end, the Wedgwoods won, Dr. Darwin consented, and Charles reported to Captain Fitz-Roy.

The voyage of the *Beagle* was the turning point in the life of Charles Darwin. He left Plymouth an obscure candidate for the ministry and returned a well-known naturalist, whose findings were quoted by the leading scientific authorities in England. What made this transformation? For one thing, the young Darwin was thrust from the medieval deductive system, which he had disliked intensely, into a five-year period of inductive learning. From a memory system and the practice of passively retaining the dictation of the past, he jumped into an active observation of life in all its forms. On this voyage he discovered the scientific spirit, which is characterized by intellectual curiosity, respect for facts, free inquiry, and accuracy of observation. From the established theological method of proving by syllogism an assumed generalization he took up the objective search for factual data, their analysis, classification, and, finally, their significance for life. Thomas Huxley often spoke of his "untiring search after facts, his readiness always to give up a preconceived opinion for that which was demonstrably true." The habit of concentrated attention to minute phenomena and the patient tabulation of the same under the difficult conditions aboard the *Beagle* served Darwin well when, in later years, he was forced by his long illness to utilize every minute at his disposal.

The *Beagle* was held in Plymouth Harbor for two months by gales. Time and again it got under way only to be beaten back into the harbor. Finally calm weather came and the 100-foot brig with seventy-five men aboard left Plymouth behind and headed for Teneriffe. The two months of deathly sickness experienced by Darwin in Plymouth Harbor were only the beginning. The constant rolling of the vessel kept him in a continuous state of nausea and retching, and he never managed to overcome the tendency to seasickness throughout the voyage. "In the Bay of Biscay," Darwin wrote to his father, "there was a long and continuous swell and the misery I endured from seasickness is far beyond what I ever guessed at. . . . On the fourth of January we were not many miles from Madeira. . . . I was much too sick even to get up to see the distant outline." From the time he had read Humboldt's *Travels* several years before, Teneriffe had excited his interest and now that it was sighted he was eager to climb "this long-wished-for object of my ambition," as he wrote in his diary. But to seasickness was added terrible disappointment. Rumors of cholera in England had reached the island and the British vice-consul came alongside to declare a strict quarantine of twelve days. For the expectant adventurer this announcement was calamitous. Captain Fitz-Roy gave orders to sail direct to the Cape Verde Islands. Gradually Teneriffe faded from view and with it both disappointment and sickness, for the voyage to Santiago proved to be more pleasant. Darwin occupied himself with catching and examining strange fish and reading Lyell's *Principles of Geology*. This book, more than any other, shook the young cleric loose from Babylonian cosmology and Mosaic chronology and accelerated his acceptance of the inductive method. So greatly indebted was he to the volume that he dedicated his *Journal* to Lyell "as an acknowledgment that the chief part of whatever scientific merit this *Journal* and the other works of the author may possess has been derived from studying the well-known and admirable *Principles of Geology*."

Three weeks on the Cape Verde Islands gave Darwin his first real opportunity for collecting specimens and making geological observations. Then came the three-thousand-mile voyage to Bahia, Brazil. On February 28, 1832, he beheld the coast of South America and on the next day experienced the incredible magic of the Brazilian jungle, "nothing more or less," he wrote, "than a view in the Arabian Nights, with the advantage of reality." And so the exciting ship-and-shore adventure continued, following in the steps of Magellan down the eastern coast, touching at Rio de Janeiro and Montivideo, through the Straits and "the land of storms" and up the western coast to Valparaiso.[2]

[2] For itinerary and maps see Charles Henshaw Ward: *Charles Darwin, The Man and his Warfare*, in loco.

Fitz-Roy was more than pleased with the work of his naturalist and their friendship, despite periodic quarrels, grew deeper each day. Darwin made extensive geological observations, discovered the cause of coral reefs, ascertained the cause and nature of barnacles, collected thousands of specimens of insects, birds, fossils, and plants and gathered a wealth of knowledge about the habits of all kinds of plants and animals. His *Beagle Journal* is a veritable encyclopedia of natural history and geology.

But most important of all during the trip was his discovery of an *idea*, an idea that was terrifying in its implications. His discovery was the answer to Dr. Grant's question: "What is a species?" At Cape Horn he received the second volume of Lyell's *Geology*. Lyell's interpretation of "creation" could by no stretch of the imagination be construed as hinting at evolution; but the book precipitated further questions in Darwin's mind. What is the origin of species? What is the origin of man? Was he made in his present form or did he evolve from lower forms? A second impetus towards the theory of evolution was his observation of the natives at Tierra del Fuego. His study of volcanic peaks, the distribution of fossils, and the variations in flora and fauna in South America began to lead him to the conclusion that the facts of nature were not to be explained by special creation but by transmutation, or the evolution of species by adaptation. This was his tentative answer and it called for years of confirmation.

Standing thus on the brink of "the mystery of mysteries," he continued steadily to classify and verify as the cruise took him to the Galapagos Islands and Tahiti. The remainder of the world voyage is a dramatic novel in itself and cannot be described here. Only by a perusal of Darwin's *Journal* can one begin to appreciate the amplitude of his research and the richness of the treasures which he stored up in his mind during those five years. Each day on his expeditions he encountered new birds, reptiles, insects, plants, and rock formations and each night he analyzed and recorded his findings, comparing species, and trying to solve the riddle of distribution and variety. The adventure came to an end on October 2, 1836, when the *Beagle* docked at Falmouth, and Darwin, both seasick and homesick, inquired for a coach for Shrewsbury, his home.

He had many things to do. After his homecoming, he must see Lyell, Hooker, Henslow, and Uncle Jos Wedgwood. Then he must complete his records, see to the housing of his specimens, prepare papers to be read, and, finally, settle down to the task of correlating isolated facts for purposes of generalization. Business and study did not occupy all his time, however. Love letters had been penned along with scientific reports throughout the voyage and one of his first visits upon his return was to the Wedgwood estate, where he resumed his intimacy with Emma, his cousin. During the summer, while on vacation, he became engaged to her and on January 29, 1839, they were quietly married. After three years of residence in London, they bought an estate near the village of Downe in the Kentish hills. Here Darwin lived and wrote for the forty remaining years of his life and here he became the affectionate father of ten children.

The Origin

The observer now became the writer as the fruits of the seeds sown on the world adventure began to ripen. His first books were reports of his *Beagle* investigations: *Geological Observations, Journal of the Voyage of the Beagle, The Zoölogy of the Voyage of the Beagle*, and *Cirripedia*. With these works as a background, he was ready to undertake his main objective—the answer to Dr. Grant's question. The discovery that he made while on the *Beagle* was that variation in species occurs by adaptation to environment, or natural selection. His task now was to validate that hypothesis by the accumulation of confirming data. The famous *Notebook* was begun in 1837 and for twenty years "Charles Darwin, Farmer," as the local directory had it, faithfully entered his findings, reasoned with himself, conferred with Lyell, Hooker, and Gray, and interviewed horticulturists and breeders. After reading Malthus' *Essay on the Principles of Population*, he argued that, just as the population is held back by various checks, the varieties of plant and animal life which overcome obstacles and adapt themselves will survive. This, he said, is a case of natural selection. He found that man could aid the process of change of species by selecting the plants he liked and preventing the poorer plants from reseeding. By constant selection the quality of the species improved and was strengthened. This deliberate selection was observed also in the case of horses. Now if man can breed whatever type of horse he desires, does it not follow that nature accomplishes the same process for herself? Nature indeed kills off the weak and the type is eliminated. Only the stronger and the more intelligent survive to reproduce. This must be true since it is obvious that all animals and plants produce more offspring than can survive. A fierce battle for existence is constantly being waged. This notation led him to the principle that most organisms are happily adapted to their environment and the types continue, but under different conditions a change in the organisms will occur and over a period of geological time different types will develop by adaptation. (Later, in his *Descent of Man*, he was to add to this principle of natural selection the complementary one of sexual selection.) Modification in species occurs in the endeavor to fit a changed environment and, if the adaptation is not made, the creature dies and the species becomes extinct. Darwin, in fact, had found the remains of many varieties that had perished in the battle of adjustment. Natural selection, he concluded, would account for the evolution of higher forms of life, geographical distribution, and the existence of partially vestigial organs.

In support of this principle Darwin collected examples of natural and sexual selection, improved and changed types, and the divergent evolution of plants and animals in isolated regions. He refrained from premature statements and continued his painstaking collecting and analysis. After repeated advances and retreats he cast the die and set about the actual composition of his book. Even in this he worked all too slowly, always projecting the day of publication two or three years into the future. Then came the fateful letter. Wallace's essay stung the leisurely Darwin into action and soon thereafter the *Origin of Species* made its belated appearance.

It is rather generally recognized now that the theory of evolution cannot be attributed exclusively to Darwin. As early as the fourth century B.C., Aristotle observed that there is a tendency of life to advance to higher forms in a scale of increasing complexity. The Roman poet Lucretius (60 B.C.) noticed the developmental laws of nature and intimated that man himself had evolved from a lower animal-like form. Goethe noted the mutations in plant and animal life. Buffon, an early contemporary of Darwin, in his *Histoire Naturelle*, seeing the struggle of nature, hinted at the evolutionary theory and the descent of man. Geoffroy Saint-Hilaire, another French naturalist, proposed the same theory. Darwin's immediate forerunners were his

grandfather and Lamarck, who declared that the evolutionary process was due to adaptation to environmental
changes. Erasmus Darwin propounded the idea that all
organic life descended from one common ancestor while
Lamarck felt that the descent of organic forms was a
branch-like process. Lamarck's weakness was lack of verification and proof. His method often led him to assume or to
adopt unsound notions. His main conclusions on evolution,
the most coherent up to that time, were as follows: new
conditions create new needs and from these needs animals
develop new organs; the growth of these organs is determined by their use; and the new characteristics are transmitted. Most of his ideas were valid and were later accepted by Darwin but his claim that new wants on the part
of animals created new organs was either erroneously stated
or misconstrued by other scientists. The fact remains that
by his statement of that principle he lost much prestige.

All this pre-Darwinian speculation was for the most part
guess-work and was unaccompanied by systematic proof.
Contemporaries like Huxley, Lyell, Hooker, Gray, and
Owen were either skeptical of the theory or, half-believing,
were afraid to face a hostile world with it. After the break
was made most of them rallied to its support. But Darwin's
theories were backed by incontestable evidence—that was
the difference. The *Origin of Species* was released November 24, 1859, and the whole edition of 1250 copies was sold
that day.

The Storm Breaks

In the face of the deluge of vilification that was sure to
come from the orthodox world and even from the majority
of scientists, Darwin was particularly anxious to receive ap-

proval from the men whose opinions mattered: Huxley, Lyell, Hooker, and Gray. To Huxley he wrote: "I shall be intensely curious to hear what effect the book produces on you. I know that there will be much in it which you will object to, and I do not doubt many errors. I am very far from expecting to convert you to many of my heresies; but if, on the whole, you and two or three others think I am on the right road, I shall not care what the mob of naturalists think." [3] To Louis Agassiz, the American naturalist, whose friendship was firm but whose views on evolution were shaky, if not orthodox, he wrote:

I have ventured to send you a copy of my book on the *Origin of Species*. As the conclusions at which I have arrived on several points differ so widely from yours, I have thought (should you at any time read my volume) that you might think that I had sent it to you out of a spirit of defiance or bravado; but I assure that I act under a wholly different frame of mind. I hope that you will at least give me credit, however erroneous you may think my conclusions, for having earnestly endeavored to arrive at the truth. [4]

Huxley's response after reading the book was gratifying to Darwin because his praise was given on the background of a critical approach.

Since I read von Baer's essays nine years ago, no work on Natural History Science I have met with has made so great an impression upon me, and I do most heartily thank you for the great store of new views you have given me. Nothing, I think, can be better than the tone of the book; it impresses those who know nothing about the subject. As for your doctrine, I am prepared to go to the stake, if requi-

[3] Francis Darwin: *The Life and Letters of Charles Darwin* (New York, 1896), Vol. 1, p. 527.
[4] *Ibid.*, Vol. 2, p. 11.

site, in support of Chapter IX, and most parts of Chapters X, XI, XII; and Chapter XIII contains much that is most admirable, but on one or two points I enter a *caveat* until I can see further into all sides of the question.

As to the first four chapters, I agree thoroughly and fully with all the principles laid down in them. I think you have demonstrated a true cause for the production of species, and have thrown the *onus probandi*, that species did not arise in the way you suppose, on your adversaries.

I trust you will not allow yourself to be in any way disgusted or annoyed by the considerable abuse and misrepresentation which, unless I greatly mistake, is in store for you. . . . I am sharpening up my claws and beak in readiness.[5]

With certain technical reservations, Darwin's famous colleagues—Hooker, Lyell, Gray, Huxley, Lubbock, Jenyns, Watson, Carpenter—concurred in the main theory of evolution, and with this encouragement, he plunged into a revised edition. The modest tone of his letters through this period is truly remarkable. To his opponents he wrote in the most conciliatory and humble spirit; from his sympathizers he begged for severe criticism.

Most of the newspapers and magazines, accepting the popular misconstruction of the theory of evolution, carried hostile reviews. The *Athenaeum* was first in the field with a severe castigation, and others followed, ridiculing the author as "an inhaler of mephitic gas attempting to dethrone God." A notable exception to the journalistic onslaught occurred in the *Times*. The reviewer, writing anonymously, made a careful survey of the book, and, after a few "ifs," "ands," and "buts," threw the weight of his argument on the side of evolution and finished with a tribute to its author. "Mr. Darwin," he wrote, "abhors

[5] *Ibid.*, Vol. 2, pp. 26–27.

mere speculation as nature abhors a vacuum. He is as greedy of cases and precedents as any constitutional lawyer, and all the principles he lays down are capable of being brought to the test of observation and experiment. The path he bids us follow professes to be not a mere airy track, fabricated of ideal cobwebs, but a solid and broad bridge of facts." [6]

Darwin, writing to Huxley the next day, exclaimed: "Yesterday evening when I read the *Times* of a previous day, I was amazed to find a splendid essay and review of me. Who can the author be? I am intensely curious. It included an eulogium of me which quite touched me, though I am not vain enough to think it all deserved. The author is a literary man, and German scholar." [7]

The unknown reviewer in the *Times* was none other than Huxley himself. Lucas, the staff reviewer, "was as innocent of any knowledge of science as a babe," as Francis Darwin writes, and, not knowing what to do with such a bombshell as the *Origin*, asked Huxley to review it. Huxley, in assuming the rôle of critic, began his review in a cautious, neutral vein, claiming that the book admittedly "deserved a respectful hearing." From his initial skepticism he proceeded with an objective examination and finished with an enthusiastic salute.

Meanwhile the storm of theological opposition had burst in all its fury. Led by Bishop Samuel Wilberforce, the clergy denounced the work of Darwin as an "utterly rotten fabric of guess and speculation." Theological orthodoxy was not long in perceiving that the theory of natural selection invalidated the biblical story of special creation. The mass of evidence in the *Origin* was more than sufficient to take care of any and all the attempted refutations of conservative scientists but scientific proof was lost on the re-

[6] *Ibid.*, Vol. 2, p. 49.   [7] *Ibid.*, Vol. 2, p. 47.

ligionists, who merely raved about the "monkey business"
and sanctimoniously vented their spleen on the former
clergyman who was now seeking to "remove the soul from
man." One revivalist exclaimed: "Darwin! There's a man
I have trounced a hundred times from my pulpit. Thank
God I have never read a line he has written." [8]

It must not be supposed, however, that all the churchmen were opposed to Darwin and his theories. Not a few
ministers, intellectually upset for a time by reason of the
impact of this cataclysmic idea, accepted the theory of evolution as valid and adjusted themselves to this "larger
view" of life.[9] Chief among the liberal clergymen was
Charles Kingsley who wrote to Darwin as follows:

I am so poorly (in brain) that I fear I cannot read your
book just now as I ought. All I have seen of it *awes* me;
both with the heap of facts and the prestige of your name,
and also with the clear intuition, that if you be right, I must
give up much that I have believed and written.

In that I care little. Let God be true and every man a
liar! Let us know what *is*. . . .

From two common superstitions, at least, I shall be
free while judging of your books: (1) I have long since,
from watching the crossing of domesticated animals and
plants, learned to disbelieve the dogma of the permanence
of species . . . [10]

Darwin's great champion was Huxley, who stood off
both the attacks of the churchmen under Wilberforce and
the scientists under Owen. The first monkey-trial and fore-

[8] Quoted in Fred Eastman: *Men of Power*, Vol. III, p. 190.
[9] For the testimony of numerous clergy who reacted favorably and saw
the importance of Darwin's work, see *Evolution in the Light of Modern
Knowledge; a Symposium by a Group of British Scientists, Philosophers, and
Clergymen*, pp. 477 ff.
[10] Francis Darwin: *Op. cit.*, Vol. II, p. 81.

runner of the Dayton (Tennessee) fiasco was the meeting of the British Association for the Advancement of Science. The rôle of William Jennings Bryan was played by Bishop Wilberforce and that of Clarence Darrow by Huxley. The speech-making lasted for several days and was attended by upwards of one thousand people. One of the witnesses for the opposition, curiously enough, was Fitz-Roy, now an admiral and Fellow of the Royal Society. The suspicious attitude which he had taken towards Darwin's investigations while they were together on the *Beagle* had become intensified. He now testified that he had often rebuked his old friend for advocating views contrary to the Bible and was now greatly pained by reading the *Origin*.[11]

The Bishop confined his efforts to ridiculing Huxley and finally, inquiring of the scientist whether his apish ancestry was on his grandfather's side or that of his grandmother, sat down amid the cheers of the mob. Whispering to his neighbor, "The Lord hath delivered him into my hands," Huxley arose quietly and with stern dignity replied: "I asserted—and I repeat—that a man has no reason to be ashamed of having an ape for his grandfather. If there were an ancestor whom I should feel shame in recalling, it would be a man of restless and versatile intellect, who, not content with success in his own sphere of activity, plunges into scientific questions with which he has no real acquaintance, only to obscure them by an aimless rhetoric, and distract the attention of his hearers from the point at issue by eloquent digressions and skilled appeals to religious prejudice."[12] True to tradition, the British audience, recognizing that the Bishop had hit below the belt, swung

[11] Five years later, Fitz-Roy, unbalanced by overwork, committed suicide.

[12] This report of Huxley's words (of which there is no actual record) was made by the historian J. R. Green. See Charles Henshaw Ward: *Charles Darwin, the Man and his Warfare*, pp. 313–15.

to the support of Huxley. More vociferous than Huxley was Hooker, who jumped to Darwin's defense and accused Wilberforce of never having read the *Origin* and being absolutely ignorant of biology.

Thus the battle waged and has continued to wage to the present day. But Darwin's theory slowly gained ground in England, on the Continent, and also in America, where Asa Gray of Harvard championed the cause. Its progress has always been impeded by both unintentional and deliberate misinterpretation. The term evolution has shared the fate of "socialism," "liberalism," "freedom," and "democracy" in being continually and almost universally misrepresented. The popular perversion of the anti-Darwinians of 1860 that the theory of evolution implied descent from monkeys has stuck and the essential meaning of the doctrine is seldom appreciated by the untrained citizenry.

As far as the descent of man is concerned, the theory of evolution held, and holds, that the anthropoid ape and man have apparently branched out from a common progenitor in the remote prehistoric past and from that common origin the ape and man have developed along independent lines. More essentially, evolution refers to the selective change in organic life. It relates neither to the origin of life nor to the idea of future progress, but to the one indisputable fact that every form of animal and plant life, including man, has developed from a previous, simpler form. The constant change occurring in organic life was described by Darwin as natural selection, the process of accommodation to a changed environment. The struggle for existence causes new forms and, with the preservation of the variations, new species are produced. The most important implication of the evolutionary theory is the inevitability of change and the relativity of all things. The principle of change rather

than fixity as the key to life's puzzle is the chief characteristic of modern liberalism.[13]

Darwin the Man

In the *Origin*, Darwin was extremely cautious on the
subject of human evolution. He was well aware that, because of popular prejudice, any discussion of the human
ancestry would jeopardize his main thesis. Consequently no
mention of human evolution was made and the one reference to racial differentiation was deleted in the final edition
of the book. But the concluding statement of the *Origin*—
"Much light will be thrown on the origin of man and his
history"—foreshadowed the logical continuation of the
theory of natural selection to its human application and the
Descent of Man was the result. In this volume he lost some
of his reticence and boldly pressed home the conclusions he
had reached in the intervening twelve years. Here he
demonstrated that man was subjected during primeval
times to natural selection; otherwise "he would never have
attained to his present rank." He continued:

Man is liable to numerous, slight, and diversified variations, which are induced by the same general causes, are
governed and transmitted in accordance with the same
general laws, as in the lower animals. Man has multiplied
so rapidly, that he has necessarily been exposed to struggle
for existence, and consequently to natural selection. He has
given rise to many races, some of which differ so much from
each other, that they have often been ranked by naturalists
as distinct species. His body is constructed on the same
homological plan as that of other mammals. He passes

[13] For the results of this idea in modern thought see the next chapter,
The Nineteenth-Century Age of Criticism.

through the same phases of embryological development. He retains many rudimentary and useless structures, which no doubt were once serviceable. Characters occasionally make their reappearance in him, which we have reason to believe were possessed by his early progenitors. If the origin of man had been wholly different from that of all other animals, these various appearances would be mere empty deceptions; but such an admission is incredible. These appearances, on the other hand, are intelligible, at least to a large extent, if man is the co-descendant with other mammals of some unknown and lower form.[14]

The *Descent of Man* therefore can be considered a necessary supplement to the *Origin,* as were all Darwin's subsequent writings: *On the Various Contrivances by Which Orchids are Fertilized, The Variation of Animals and Plants under Domestication, The Expression of the Emotions in Man and Animals, Insectivorous Plants, Cross and Self-Fertilization, The Different Forms of Flowers on Plants of the Same Species, The Power of Movement in Plants,* and *The Formation of Vegetable Mould through the Action of Worms.* All these were written in his study at Downe where he passed the remaining years of his life. Naturally such specialization exacted its toll at the expense of his emotional life. This loss of aesthetic taste is more than once lamented in his autobiographical notes:

My mind seems to have become a kind of machine for grinding general laws out of large collections of facts, but why this should have caused the atrophy of that part of the brain alone, on which the higher tastes depend, I cannot conceive. A man with a mind more highly organized or better constituted than mine, would not, I suppose, have thus suffered; and if I had to live my life

[14] *Descent of Man,* 2nd ed., pp. 47–48.

again, I would have made a rule to read some poetry and to listen to some music at least once every week; for perhaps the parts of my brain now atrophied would have been kept active through use. The loss of these tastes is a loss of happiness and may possibly be injurious to the intellect, and more probably to the moral character, by enfeebling the emotional part of our nature.[15]

This self-effacement is qualified by Francis Darwin in his own commentary where he speaks of his father's love of fine music, although he admits that his literary tastes and opinions were not "on a level with the rest of his mind." In view of his self-criticism, the exploitation of Darwin's deficiencies by religious fanatics has been unreasonable and vicious. Only a bigot could harp on these things after reading Darwin's own confession of weakness. His emotional atrophy can easily be explained: it was the price he paid for concentration, a lack of balance discovered in all great geniuses.

His incapacitating illness was another concomitant of his restricted life. Suffering from an inherited weakness, Darwin hardly knew a day of health during the last forty-five years of his life, as constant entries in his diary show. On many days he was allowed to work only one or two hours. The secret of his enormous production, like that of one of his modern biographers, Gamaliel Bradford, who suffered in a similar manner, was a methodical routine, strictly followed every day. Stomach disorder, vomiting, giddiness, black spots before the eyes, fainting, and complete exhaustion clutched him throughout his life but his courage never failed.

On the subject of religion, Darwin was decidedly taciturn. From the *Beagle* days to the *Descent of Man*, much

[15] Francis Darwin: *op. cit.*, Vol. 1, pp. 81–82.

theological water passed under the bridge; orthodoxy was abandoned, traditional doctrines were given up, and in his later life he labelled himself an agnostic. He confessed to complete bewilderment in the matter of metaphysics. It was not his field; so he preferred to keep quiet. As a scientist, he rejected revelation and mystical religion. Where faith without knowledge was the criterion, he refused to engage in discussion. His agnosticism on the questions of immortality, design, and theism was a reverent and open-minded one. With those who believed he had no quarrel; the future life, ultimate purpose, and the benevolence of God were not unreasonable in view of the evolutionary character of the universe; but he had no proof, and the whole question, in his mind, was "insoluble." He confesses to a modification of his views on theism:

When thus reflecting, I feel compelled to look at a First Cause having an intelligent mind analogous to that of man; and I deserve to be called a Theist. This conclusion was strong in my mind about the time, as far as I can remember, when I wrote the *Origin of Species;* and it is since that time that it has very gradually, with many fluctuations, become weaker. But then arises the doubt, can the mind of man, which has, as I fully believe, been developed from a mind as low as that possessed by the lowest animals, be trusted when it draws such grand conclusions? I cannot pretend to throw the least light on such abstruse problems. The mystery of the beginning of all things is insoluble by us; and I for one must be content to remain an agnostic.[16]

As a scientist and a liberal, Darwin was not interested in theological speculation or ecclesiasticism, but who shall say that he was not deeply religious? Religion is what a man is;

[16] *Ibid.,* Vol. 1, p. 282.

it is discovered not in his dogmatic beliefs but in his conduct; not in the observance of external forms but in the attitude of good will and generosity of mind. Judged on this basis, Charles Darwin was a saint. He was never cynical or mocking in his attitude towards those who opposed him. His greatest concern was the danger that he would offend the orthodox with the publication of his books. His feeling towards the clergy and all who differed from him was characterized by the utmost tolerance. Cant and affectation were utterly foreign to his character. Patience under misrepresentation, humility in the face of facts, kindness to his enemies—these were his characteristics. If being a Christian means having the qualities of Jesus, then Darwin was a great Christian.

What shall be said of Emma, whose whole life was devoted to his comfort and well-being, and who sacrificed travel and personal desires in order to make him the center of her existence? Of her selfless devotion Francis Darwin writes: "No one indeed except my mother knows the full amount of suffering he endured, or the full amount of his wonderful patience. For all the latter years of his life she never left him for a night; and her days were so planned that all his resting hours might be shared with her." How often a great man is eulogized by a biographer with no mention of the one person who pushed him along and without whom his achievement is inconceivable!

Fame and recognition found their way to the secluded village of Downe, as country after country and university after university honored the author of the *Origin of Species* and the *Descent of Man*. Abuse and invective also continued to pour down upon him. He accepted the one with calm and the other with a gentle tolerance. Neither could deflect him from his research and correspondence which continued to the last. Even more significant than his theories, as one surveys the man and his works, was his personal attitude towards life, which, in its tolerance, integrity, and freedom of thought, was the perfect embodiment of the liberal spirit. His particular theory has been a mixed blessing, giving birth to the Nietzschean biological ethic and other misapplications; but his personal philosophy has been an unmixed good, bequeathing to the modern world the scientific viewpoint of disinterestedness, the conception of eternal change, and devotion to the truth.

He was accused of robbing man of his divine past but if he did, he gave humanity a divine future by replacing the fatal fixity of man's existence with a glorious destiny. That was his achievement; and his own life—from the days of his directionless youth to his old age as the great benefactor of mankind—was an example of the existence in the human being of that divine spark of growth. When Darwin died, April 19, 1882, and was laid away in Westminster Abbey next to Sir Isaac Newton, the humorous magazine *Punch* paid serious tribute: "Recorder of the long descent of Man and a most living witness of his rise."

XII

The Nineteenth-Century
Age of Criticism

Toward an Empirical Theology

THE TWO GREATEST upheavals affecting modern culture were caused in each case by the discovery of a scientific theory, one in the field of astronomy and the other in biology; one gave mankind a new universe, the other, a new history. Darwin's doctrine of evolution, in fact, may well be considered more potent in its effect than the heliocentric theory of Copernicus. The intellectual temper of western civilization had been seriously modified by the Renaissance, the Enlightenment, and the Deistic movement, but in spite of Galileo, Voltaire, and Locke, Mr. John Doe had continued to follow the traditional theological pattern. According to that pattern the universe was created by an omnipotent deity and, in the universe, the earth held the pivotal position. All animal and human life on the earth was created by God in its present form. Man, the highest form of creation, was the special object of divine favor. The first man was originally free from sin but fell from grace and plunged all posterity into a state of total depravity. In time a plan of salvation was achieved in the death of Christ, which atoned for human sin, and man, by believing in that atonement could inherit eternal salvation.

The Bible was the infallible revelation of the plan of salvation and the Church was the means through which it was made available to mankind.

The theory of organic evolution completely undermined this world-view and, what is more, demanded a new formulation of theology, philosophy, ethics, anthropology, and psychology. The idea that produced this tremendous upheaval and the most important implication of the evolutionary theory was *the inevitability of change*. It became evident by the middle of the nineteenth century that the world is not fixed; nature in all its forms changes constantly. Even morals change. Man's ideas of God, the Bible, truth, and the nature of reality are forever undergoing changes. The mind itself is a product of organic growth and is only an instrument for man's adaptation to environment. Absolutism was surrendered in favor of relativism; revelation gave way to the pragmatic method. Instrumentalism became the proper means of inquiry. Men came to doubt the existence of "fixed forms," "anterior truth." New levels of truth emerge; fresh forms arise. There is no "Absolute Truth"—only one generation's verified approximation of truth. Certainty is only tentative. "Degree" became the typical phrase of a scientifically-minded age—"degree of truth," "degree of probability." Knowledge is only that which can be verified and then it is only the knowledge of today. Today's truth is tomorrow's untruth. For ideas, theories, truths, there is no such thing as tenure but only probation.

The revolution of evolution was experienced most critically in the field of religious thought. To recognize the fact of change meant the surrender of the belief in revelation, the idea of the Absolute, the infallibility of the Scripture, and all previous ideas of God and man. Once again there was a shift in the basis of authority as the new scientific emphasis turned religious thinking along empirical lines. Religious authority from primitive times had been in the form of a supernatural revelation, externally imposed— the Jewish Torah, the Catholic Church, or the Protestant Bible. Religion was thoroughly theocentric, a revealed quantum to be accepted in toto. It followed that right belief was the prime prerequisite for salvation. For Catholics the Church held the keys to eternal life and through its infallible hierarchy made known the will of God to its adherents. With the Protestant schism, the principle of assurance was transferred to the Scripture, which was invested with inerrancy and which became the supreme authority in religion. But the authority of the Bible in orthodox Protestantism became just as external and legalistic as that of the Church. The canon was closed; revelation was finished. A static Protestantism was the result.

The breakdown of Scriptural authority, prefigured by eighteenth-century rationalism which substituted reason for revelation, was completed by the higher criticism of the nineteenth century. Progressive Protestant theology, accepting the central significance of change and relativity introduced by evolution, defined the ultimate reality as the individual and social experience of the divine. Thus the first step in the direction of religious humanism was taken by the early "modernists." The character of Jesus became the authoritative norm rather than the Bible itself. Dogmatic belief was relegated to a secondary place along with sacrament.

While the shift within the Christian Church was only semi-liberal, often resolving itself into a matter of reinterpretation rather than a clean-cut break with traditional dogma, it did result in a degree of flexibility, which in itself is a guarantee of unlimited progress. Absolutism was never to regain complete sway. Hand in hand with this nineteenth-century growth of religious relativity was the expansion of the democratic method in politics, education, institutional, and family life.

Another effect of evolution was the encouragement it gave to the doctrine of divine immanence. The pre-revolutionary theology with its static universe demanded a transcendental God, above and apart from the world. Nineteenth-century theologians now saw the world as a process rather than a machine set in motion by an independent creator. God was the soul of the world, or to use Spinoza's expression, the world was the body of God. They saw God as an immanent force, not at rest, but always at work, an "infinite and eternal energy, intelligent and beneficent, an infinitely wise and holy spirit dwelling within the universe and shaping it from within," as Lyman Abbott wrote.[1] From the Enlightenment on, the more science ascertained about the natural world, the less imperative was the belief in the activity of a transcendent God. While immanence is a more modern and more liberal doctrine than transcendence, it served at this time as a conservative influence in making the belief in God intelligible in the face of the scientific upheaval. Bruno, Lessing, Spinoza, Herder, Schleiermacher, Schelling, Fichte, and Goethe had given partial expression to the idea of divine immanence but with the acceptance of emergent evolution in the nineteenth century it became the dominant or typical ideology. It lent itself easily to the Romanticism and Pantheism of Wordsworth, Coleridge, Tennyson and Emerson. The literary construction of immanence was equivalent to outright pantheism, a reaction to eighteenth-century

[1] *Theology of an Evolutionist*, p. 13.

"natural religion." God, according to Coleridge, was "Nature's vast everlasting Energy." For Tennyson God was an all-pervading spirit, closer than breathing "and nearer than hands and feet." Wordsworth saw God as

> An active Principle: however removed
> From sense and observation, it subsists
> In all things, in all natures; in the stars
> Of azure heaven, the unenduring clouds,
> In flower and tree, in every pebbly stone
> That paves the brooks, the stationary rocks,
> The moving waters and the invisible air.
>
> .   .   .   .
>
> Spirit that knows no insulated spot,
> No chasm, no solitiude; from link to link
> It circulates, the soul of all the worlds.

Evolution joined Immanence to define the Universe as unity of process and substance, embracing an infinite consciousness or divine energy. Man was conceived as part of this divine energy and therefore did not require any supernatural, miraculous, or magical regeneration but only an awakening to his divine potentialities. According to the romantic liberals, Jesus' higher consciousness of this union with the divine was the key to his moral excellence and his differentiation from the rest of mankind was one of degree, not kind.

Thus the doctrine of immanence is to be seen on the whole as a liberalizing influence in theology and as such is rejected by present-day Barthians and Neo-Supernaturalists who anachronistically revert to the earlier transcendentalism.

The drift towards an empirical theology was accentuated by John Stuart Mill and Herbert Spencer, who were influenced in turn by the positivism of Comte and Hume in their denial of the Absolute. Spencer (1820–1903) was the philosopher of evolution and the most important representative of nineteenth-century agnosticism. He held that knowledge is limited to phenomena or appearances. "Deep down in the very nature of life the relativity of our knowledge is discernible. The analysis of vital actions in general leads not only to the conclusion that things in themselves cannot be known to us; but also to the conclusion that knowledge of them, were it possible, would be useless." [2] The Absolute is assumed but cannot be verified. Dean Mansell and Sir William Hamilton, sources of Spencer's agnosticism, claimed that the Infinite or Absolute is inconceivable. According to Spencer, all is in a state of flux or evolution and the equilibrium established in this motion gives the appearance of stability. What we call truth is only a functional or instrumental datum to be tested by adaptation to environment and usage.

It can now be seen that the most important theological change in the nineteenth century was the breakdown of absolutism. If evolution implied anything, it was relativity. It implied that there was no such thing as finality or infallibility. All was change, growth, development. The force of this implication permeated every branch of learning and was to continue its ramifications down to the middle of the twentieth century. Authoritarianism was given its first real set-back. Dogmatism ceased to dominate the minds of the people. The belief in an *a priori*, pre-existent, revealed norm of truth, to which man must conform, no longer appeared valid. God himself was not omnipotent but limited. The Bible was not a supernatural revelation, infallible and equally inspired from cover to cover, but a human

[2] *First Principles* (1877), p. 86.

document, recording the history of one people's search for reality, containing much that was transient and much also that was inspiring. Fixity surrendered to flexibility. In the place of religious security came struggle, but with struggle came the hope of individual and social progress. The Golden Age was in the future, not the past. Man had risen from a lower state, not fallen from perfection. The purpose of life is the achievement of moral values on this earth rather than the hope of a return to a former paradisaical state. Life is an educative process, good in itself, rather than a mere vestibule to Heaven. Religion is not an independent section of life, to be segregated from the so-called secular. Nor is man the scene of a constant warfare—spirit against flesh, righteousness against sin, the supernatural against the natural; but a unified personality, bearing the marks of his long descent and holding within himself divine potentialities.

Evolution and Ethics

The relativism of evolution, with its terms "survival," "adaptation" and "struggle," led in the next place to an experiential or pragmatic ethics. The founder of pragmatism as a philosophical method was William James (1842–1910), who came to philosophy by way of medicine, comparative anatomy, physiology, and psychology. The word pragmatism was first used by James in 1898 in a lecture at the University of California. He had seen the term in an article by Charles S. Peirce on "How to Make Our Ideas Clear." "To find the meaning of an idea," wrote Pierce, "we must examine the consequences to which it leads in action." [3] James' "radical empiricism" is simply a philo-

[3] *Popular Science Monthly* (1878) pp. 286 ff. (See Peirce's *Collected Papers*, edited by Hartshorne and Weiss, pp. 248–71.)

sophical expansion of that sentence. His pragmatic rule in philosophy, arising as a violent reaction to German metaphysics with its abstractions, is a continuation of the Baconian criterion of verification. By "radical" James meant fundamental, root, thoroughgoing, and with the term "empiricism" he reasserted the claims of Locke and Hume that all knowledge is derived through the senses. The value of an idea lies in the difference it will make in human experience.

This empirical emphasis gave a practical and realistic turn to American thought. The pragmatism of James denied monism and all forms of absolutism. Creation, he said, is not finished and man has a part in it. God is not omnipotent but finite. The universe is not a *fait accompli* but an experiment, a laboratory. Everything depends upon man's actions. With James free will and progress were real. It is no wonder, then, that the pragmatic philosophy of William James became the bible of pioneering, industrial America. Applied to religion, it said that life is a moral struggle; goodness is ethical conduct, not metaphysical belief. Morality is that which serves humanitarian purposes and enhances society as a whole.

To this interpretation of ethics the empirical tendency of Ritschl and Schleiermacher was admirably fitted. They shifted the sanctions for morality from metaphysics to religious experience and made the character of Jesus central. All this was a confirmation of Jesus' own words: "Not every one that sayeth unto me, 'Lord, Lord,' shall enter into the Kingdom of Heaven; but he that doeth the will of my Father who is in heaven. . . . Therefore by their fruits ye shall know them." This philosophy of moral struggle received articulate expression in the poetry of Robert Browning. Life with him was all potentiality. "Man is not man as yet . . . Man partly is and wholly hopes to be . . . Man must burn his way through the world." The failures of life are the raw materials for the building of manhood. Life is a probation and conflict is the key to character.

> Then welcome each rebuff
> That turns earth's smoothness rough,
> Each sting that bids nor sit nor stand but go!
> Be our joys three parts pain!
> Strive and hold cheap the strain;
> Learn nor account the pang; dare, never grudge the
>   throe! [4]

Browning was the poet of aspiration and courage. His ideal character was

> One who marched breast forward
> Never doubted clouds would break, never dreamed,
> Though right were worsted, wrong would triumph;
>   held
> We fall to rise, are baffled to fight better, sleep to
>   wake.[5]

The application of the law of adaptation to religion was a salutary outgrowth of the new science. If religion does not produce better character in the individual and make for social amelioration it does not deserve to survive. The modernist movement of the late nineteenth century asserted that conduct could be the criterion in religion and it is this pragmatic tendency that has characterized liberal religious teaching of the last fifty years.

And yet in the mind of Friedrich W. Nietzsche (1844–1900) the criterion of utility meant something quite dif-

---

[4] *Rabbi Ben Ezra.*   [5] *Epilogue to Asolando.*

ferent from Browning's teleological ethic. Schopenhauer
had called attention to the compelling urge that drives men
on and he called it the "will to exist." The will is never
satisfied, he said, because the wants of life always exceed
the gratifications. In a world of will and struggle, therefore, life is essentially evil. In a world where one's reach
forever exceeds his grasp, the only solution is resignation
or *Nirvana*.

Nietzsche agreed that there is an elemental force or
drive but he took a different attitude towards it. He reasoned thus: if the nature of the world is struggle for survival and all living organisms are compelled to fight for
their existence, why not accept this fact and become strong
so as to overcome? To overpower others must be a biological law and therefore natural and right. The "will to
power" is the solution of life's struggle. The best will
survive; survival depends upon strength; therefore the
strongest is the best. Power, not weakness, is life's morality;
domination, not cooperation. The superman must be
evolved. "Live dangerously; live in a continual state of
war." The Roman way of pride, power, and aggression is
"the wave of the future"; the Christian way is weak because it breeds conscience, humility, and democracy. Instinct, not reason; obedience to authority, not freedom; war
not peace—this is the salvation of society.

With this *tour-de-force* application of Darwinism,
Nietzsche furnished philosophical affirmation to Bis-
marck's imperialism and laid the groundwork for Hitler's
Nazism. All of which has led modern interpreters to call
Nietzsche the "child of Darwin and the brother of Bis-
marck." In the case of Darwin the relationship is too close
to be accurate. A scientist discovering the laws of the
natural world cannot be held responsible for a perverted

interpretation of the words "fittest" and "good" in the ethical world. Darwin's corrective for a biological ethic of blind force would be an insistence on the "ought," the values at stake, the end in view. The ethical "ought," according to Darwin, has its origin deep in human ancestry and therefore cannot be ruled out of the struggle of life. The evolutionary process produced an ethical will from earlier blind instincts. "Darwin himself," writes Höffding, "has shown how the consciousness of duty can arise as a natural result of evolution. Moreover there are lines of evolution which have their end in ethical idealism, in a kingdom of values, which must struggle for life as all things in the world must do, but a kingdom which has its firm foundation in reality." [6] Moral factors cannot consistently be equated with biological factors. Evolution is on the side of the Hebrew-Christian tradition of humility, fidelity, integrity, unselfishness, and cooperation, not the biological ethic of Nietzsche.

To interpret Darwinism as materialistic is another false construction. In the present betrayal of liberalism the apostles of defeatism, frantically searching for supernatural straps upon which to hang, hold Darwin responsible for the materialism which, they say, has brought the "end of an era." Typical of the recent attempt to rehabilitate the older idealism is Jacques Barzun in his attack on Darwin, Marx and Wagner as the shapers of twentieth-century materialism. Darwin's theory of accidental variation, it is held, destroyed purpose and introduced materialism which in turn destroyed ethics. This together with Marx's idea of the evolution of society, where the individual counts for nothing, is responsible for *Realpolitik*, Machiavellianism, and atheism. Darwin is pictured as the ruthless sower of all that the world is now reaping and his theory is described as

[6] A. C. Seward (ed.): *Darwin and Modern Science*, p. 464.

"a dish of rank materialism cleverly cooked and served up merely to make us independent of a Creator," as the conservative Sedgwick put it in Darwin's day.

Since in every European country between 1870 and 1914 there was a war party demanding armaments, an individualist party demanding ruthless competition, an imperialist party demanding a free hand over backward peoples, a socialist party demanding the conquest of power, and a racialist party demanding internal purges against aliens— all of them, when appeals to greed and glory failed, or even before, invoked Spencer and Darwin, that is to say, science.[7]

Such charges against science in general and Darwin in particular are obviously false. His principle of accidental variation and survival through struggle remains to this day a verified fact. He himself was not opposed to purpose, and is not to be held responsible for an unwarranted application of his biological theories to social life. Pessimists presumably must accuse somebody, but evolution cannot be blamed for materialism any more than science can be blamed because young people have used the automobile for immoral purposes. Evolution produced a vitalistic ethic, not materialism.

The effect of evolution on ethics finally was to show that the moral system was not fixed for all time by Moses on top of Mount Sinai. There was a long growth of moral consciousness over the centuries from lower levels to higher. What was considered good in the days of Abraham was not accepted as good four thousand years later. Moreover, space as well as time made a difference in ethics: what was considered moral in one place was looked upon as immoral in another. The nineteenth century, in short, dis-

---

[7] *Darwin, Marx, Wagner—Critique of a Heritage*, pp. 102–03.

covered ethical relativity, a principle which has elements of danger as well as great benefit. Relativistic ethics, unscrupulously applied, results in the vicious doctrine that the end justifies the means, but the same principle is found in absolutist Jesuitism. Relativism, like democracy or any other vital force, has its risks. Pragmatism in morals means that whatever serves the social good should be retained. Because men differ in what is considered good is no valid reason for reverting to a theological basis for morals. Mistakes in value-judgment are inevitable in the evolutionary scheme. Stability is achieved in the process, for there are certain ethical values, deposits of the social conscience, which have merited undisputed acceptance. Stability and change must move in perfect balance, but the priestly office must never be allowed to override the prophetic. Automatic regeneration is just as false a doctrine as automatic degeneration. Man must make his own moral progress.

Historical Criticism

Another direct result of the biological age was the introduction of the genetic study of religious history. History as a whole was now observed as an evolutionary process, a series of continuous changes, each state emerging causally out of a previous state. In England and on the Continent scholars began to speak of "the evolution of religious ideas," "the evolution of Christianity," "the evolution of conscience." The genetic method when applied to the field of religion opened up the scientific studies of comparative religion, the history of religions, archaeology, biblical criticism, philology, and the psychology of religion.

Progressive scholarship came to see that it was unscientific to limit religious knowledge to the contents of the canonical books of the Bible, that historical inquiry must be concerned with an organic process, not a book. It was now clear that no religion can be properly understood without a knowledge of its sources and early growth. The Hebrew-Christian religion must be studied in the light of archaeological backgrounds in the Near East and beyond those backgrounds in primitive religion. The historico-genetic principle replaced (in liberal circles) the purely biblical and dogmatic method. The older *modus operandi* ended only in the blind alley of proof-texting and allegory. The Bible must be seen as a cultural deposit in the course of history, an expression of the religious life of a people, not an end in itself, complete and self-sufficient. The proper object of study is not the Bible in a vacuum but the organic evolution of the Hebrew-Christian civilization. The genesis of Genesis, not Genesis itself, became the prime consideration, not the books of the Bible per se but the sources of the ideas found there. Heredity and environment became the watch words. To pursue a mechanical exegesis of the New Testament without a knowledge of antecedent Jewish sources and contemporary Græco-Roman influences was to spend one's energy on an intellectual treadmill. The Sermon on the Mount has significance only on the background of Jewish law and history. To read Paul's letters without an acquaintance with the Mystery-religions or the Fourth Gospel without reference to Philo is a futile game of shadow-boxing. Christianity, it was now seen, is no *sui generis* movement, but is to be studied, like any other stratum of civilization, in connection with antecedent conditions and environmental influences. The organic view of history revealed the interdependent and derivative character of all religions. The terms "variation," "adaptation," and "development" were now applied to nascent Christianity as that religion assumed in the minds of scholars the likeness of a vital, growing tree with roots, branches, and leaves, affected by the soil, the sunshine, and the rain, needing transplanting and even pruning.

The developmental view was entertained only by the more liberal critics and churchmen. Probably no name is more important in this connection than that of Adolf Harnack who set the pace for liberal theology and historiography in America for half a century. Such a radical departure from tradition would logically suffer the same fate at the hands of orthodoxy as the scientific theory which gave it birth. Not many were willing to consider that the inception of the revealed religion of Christianity had been accompanied by any birth pangs or that it had experienced any growing pains. The established Church insisted that the Christian religion was a static, quantitative entity, a revealed body of truth. It was apparent to a few conservative ecclesiastics perhaps that change and variation would have to be admitted sooner or later if only to square with the facts of Church history.

The genetic point of view ushered in the scientific study of Scripture known as historical or higher criticism. Biblical research of a historical nature had been carried on by isolated investigators such as ben Ezra, Erasmus, Spinoza, Goethe, Voltaire, Simon, LeClerc, Astruc, Herder, Ilgen, Geddes, Michaelis, and Reimarus, most of whom had applied the principles of criticism to the Pentateuch and the Gospels. But it remained for the evolutionary upheaval of the mid-nineteenth century to generate the systematic science of biblical criticism, the result of which was to invalidate completely the traditional conception of the Scripture as an infallible and unique revelation. But freedom to pursue the truth in biblical matters has been slowly achieved in England, France, and especially in America. At the end of the century the Presbyterian Church deposed two of its best Old Testament scholars: Charles A. Briggs and Henry Preserved Smith; and the Methodist church dismissed from his teaching post Hinckley G. Mitchell. In England the fight against scientific criticism was bitterly contested by the conservatives Cardinal Newman and William E. Gladstone. The irony of history is that unwarranted hostility and insult have always been directed towards men whose only ambition is to find the truth. The attack upon Wellhausen by an American theologian is typical of the abuse showered upon these scholars: "The Old Testament is to him a corpse, the corpse of a criminal laid on his dissecting table for the skill of his hand with knife and pincers, and the joy he derives from it is in discovering a new ganglion of contradiction."[8] The classical illustration of heresy-hunting in England was the case of Bishop John W. Colenso. For hinting at the non-Mosaic authorship of the Pentateuch he was excommunicated and ostracized by the Church of England.

The struggle within Christendom arising from the introduction of the higher criticism has continued to the present day with the Roman Church universally opposed to the scientific temper and the Protestant Church split into two groups: the Fundamentalists who still refuse to accept the results of historical analysis and the liberals who follow, more or less strictly according to their particular shade, the implications of the critical method in matters of doctrine, Scripture, and history.[9]

[8] Quoted in Ernest R. Trattner: *Unravelling the Book of Books*, p. 59.

[9] Loisy, Duschesne, and Tyrrell are examples of Roman Catholic scholars whose adherence to the critical method led to their excommunication. The intransigent reaction of official Catholicism to nineteenth-century liberalism is seen to best advantage in the famous Syllabus of Errors in 1864, which commences with the pointed statement that "it is an error to believe that the Roman Pontiff can and ought to reconcile himself to, and agree with, progress, liberalism, and contemporary civilization."

The function of criticism as applied to the Bible is to determine the origin, authorship, unity, purpose, and meaning of a book. Its first law is that every book must be read in the light of its historical background and interpreted in its own setting. Biblical literature must be subjected to the same unprejudiced analysis as any other literature. It needs no arguing that great literature possessing unusual moral inspiration or historical value will emerge from the critical process enhanced rather than depreciated, a point not recognized by conservatives who throughout history have insisted on biting the hand that feeds them. Critical scholarship has saved the Bible for mankind by translating it into the modern languages, discovering through manuscript study the most accurate text, and clarifying the meaning of the text. The Bible has nothing to lose and everything to gain by criticism, for, as it has often been said, "If we study the Bible like any other book, we shall find that it is not like any other book."

Biblical criticism is of two kinds: the lower or textual criticism and the higher or literary criticism. Textual criticism attempts to approximate the original Hebrew and Greek text of the Bible from a comparative study of manuscripts which in the case of the Old Testament go back only to the ninth century A.D. and in the New Testament to the fourth. Among the thousands of manuscripts in existence, countless textual variations occur, depending on the age of the manuscript and the scribe who copied it. The critic examines the various schools of manuscripts, determines their age, relates them to each other, and estimates their value for the discovery of the original text. In his comparative study he consults in addition early versions and patristic citations. The result of his work is the Hebrew and Greek text which is printed in acceptable form for translating into a modern language.

The function of the higher or literary criticism is to determine the meaning of the content, the kind of literature represented, the identity, character, purpose, and locale of the author, and the sources of his ideas. The literary critic must also engage in a comparative analysis, investigating possible dependence of the book upon earlier or contemporary documents, and its relation to the literature of older civilizations and to the other books in the Bible.

Professional criticism took its rise, not in England where the scientific temper was most in evidence, but in Germany. Here, commencing with Strauss, Baur, Wellhausen, De Wette, Ewald, Graf, Hupfeld, and Delitzsch, biblical research became more precise and systematic. Hupfeld, following the lead of Ilgen and Eichhorn, continued the documentary study of Genesis and proved the presence of three authors, two, using the term *Elohim* for God, and the third, *Jahweh*. Wellhausen and De Wette (and Kuenen in Holland) found that these three strands ran through Genesis, Exodus, Leviticus, and Numbers, and that Deuteronomy represented a fourth and independent authorship. Their historical study showed that the first five books of the Old Testament contain many parallel but contradictory accounts. They concluded, for instance, that one author could not have written two different stories of the creation and the flood, each with different details. Laws and customs from different periods in history stood side by side, clearly revealing different strata of composition, later combined. These strands or documents differed in style, internal evidence, and teaching, and therefore could not represent a unified authorship. Again, it did not take long to perceive that the contents of Deuteronomy reflected a seventh-century situation and that, since the death and burial of Moses are described in Deuteronomy in detail and post-Mosaic events are related throughout, the book could hardly have been written by Moses. De Wette's investigations showed that Deuteronomy was written in the seventh century B.C. and was to be identified with the "Book of the Law," discovered by Hilkiah during repairs in the temple of Jerusalem and that this law-book became the first Bible of the Jews.

So continued the pioneers of criticism and from their labors emerged the Graf-Wellhausen theory, which holds that the Pentateuch is non-Mosaic in authorship and consists of four independent strands: the J or Jahwistic document from 850 B.C., the E or Elohistic document from 750, the D or Deuteronomistic document from 621, and the P or Priestly document from 500. The J, E, and P documents by reason of their differences in style and contents were identified and traced throughout the Pentateuch. It was finally observed that the four documents were combined in the fifth century B.C. to make the Pentateuch or "Law."

As the historical method was extended to other sections of the Old Testament it was found that the book of Isaiah was composite in authorship, the first thirty-nine chapters being from the eighth-century prophet and chapters 40 to 66 coming from the period of the Exile (586–538 B.C.). The traditional assumption that the Psalms were written by David was undermined by calling attention to their internal references to post-Davidic times. Books commonly assigned to ancient times were placed in a later setting. English, French, and American scholars joined in the study of chronology and canon, the Hebrew language, and the development of Hebrew history.

New Testament criticism also received its initial impetus in Germany with the Tübingen School of F. C. Baur, to be followed by the first great lives of Jesus by David Friedrich Strauss in Germany and Ernest Renan in France. Baur and Strauss were strongly influenced by the Hegelian *Tendenz* philosophy, which interpreted New Testament literature in terms of tendency or bias. Like all special theories, the *Tendenz* interpretation of the Jewish-Gentile problem was overworked but it laid the foundation for the scientific study of the New Testament.

The cardinal interest of New Testament criticism was the Gospels. In the face of obvious duplication and disagreement among the Gospels the question of origin and authorship demanded immediate attention. The attempt to account for the double and triple traditions (material duplicated two or three times) in the first three Gospels led to the "Synoptic Problem." The result of this investigation of the Synoptic Gospels became known as the Documentary Hypothesis or Two-Source Theory, which may be summarized as follows: Mark was the first Gospel to be written (about 70 A.D.) and served as a written source for Matthew (80 A.D.) and Luke (80 A.D.) in the narrative material of the life of Jesus. Matthew and Luke in their final edited form were dependent upon a second written source (now lost) called the Logia or "Q," which was a collection of the sayings of Jesus dating from the middle of the first century. Matthew and Luke combined Mark and "Q," with some slight additional material unique to each, to make their complete Gospels. This solution of the Synoptic Problem received almost universal support among reputable critics of the late nineteenth century, but, along with other areas of investigation, was modified by the introduction in more recent years of Form Criticism. (Applied to the Gospels, Form Criticism aims to separate the various layers of tradition or "mixed forms" which accumulated around the historical figure of Jesus. Form Criticism, a product of German scholarship, received its initial impetus in the

writings of Martin Dibelius, K. L. Schmidt, and Rudolf
Bultmann. R. H. Lightfoot, F. C. Grant, V. Taylor, and
B. S. Easton have been instrumental in developing the
theory in England and America.)

The Fourth Gospel presented a second puzzle known as
the Johannine Problem. Before the era of scientific criticism this book was considered the work of John the disciple
of Jesus, but the historical method has always thrown doubt
upon that assumption. Critics differ in their conclusions, but
a consensus of scholarly opinion places its date of composition not earlier than 100 A.D. and assigns it to an unknown
author or authors who, under the influence of Philonic and
Greek ideology, wrote a philosophical interpretation of
Jesus as supernatural Lord and Saviour. Other New Testament problems of a literary nature were the Pauline
authorship of the Pastoral and other epistles, the sources of
Acts, the interpretation of Revelation, and the authorship
of the Epistle to the Hebrews. Questions of canon, backgrounds and beginnings of Christianity, Messianism, and
Apocalyptic presented themselves and have continued to
occupy western scholarship down to the present moment.

What, then, has been the net result of historical criticism? While the term higher criticism is purely a technical
one, referring to a method of study, its appearance in the
nineteenth century indicated a liberal tendency and its findings resulted in what is known as "modernism." In the first
place, criticism had the effect of re-defining inspiration as
referring to the author rather than to the book. According
to the traditional doctrine, the Bible was true because it was
inspired; the scientific view held that the Bible is inspired
because it is true and only in so far as it is true. The old idea
was that the authors of the Bible were passive instruments
in the hands of God who mechanically dictated to them

every word of the Scripture. The critics, calling attention to the differences in degree of inspiration within the covers of the Bible, regarded as inspired only those writers who were so superior to other men in religious insight as to be able to inspire others. "We never acknowledge authority," wrote Martineau, "till that which speaks to us from another and higher strikes home and wakes the echoes in ourselves." [10] Relativity as applied to the Bible differentiated the genuine from the spurious, distinguished between fact and fiction, secondary forms and primary content. Scientific study gave to the Bible a tested and verified security rather than the security of dogmatic and arbitrary authority. In returning the Bible to its proper setting and analyzing its growth, the critics humanized it, made it vital and real, something to be used rather than a fetish to be worshiped. Biblical criticism, finally, recovered the historical Jesus. From the accumulation of magic and miracle surrounding the traditional figure of Jesus, criticism has succeeded in setting forth in bold relief the character of Jesus and the ethical import of his teaching.

The handmaid of biblical criticism was the science of archaeology, which grew simultaneously with the historical studies and, with the spade, rewrote religious history. Early in the century the doors of ancient Egypt had been unlocked by Champollion who deciphered the Rosetta Stone and thereby made possible the modern knowledge of the hieroglyph. The key to Babylonia was found by Rawlinson who mastered the Behistun Rock inscriptions and subsequently wrote the first grammar of the cuneiform language. During the middle of the century Mesopotamia literally arose with the Old Testament in her hand. Clay tablets

[10] *The Seat of Authority in Religion* (Preface), quoted in George Holley Gilbert: *Interpretation of the Bible*, p. 270.

found by Hormuzd Rassam in the palace of Ashurbanipal in Nineveh contained an ancient Babylonian flood story, resembling so closely the later biblical account as to point to the Hebrew dependence on the earlier tradition. The spade likewise unearthed Babylonian creation accounts of 2000 B.C. which served as probable sources for the authors of Genesis. Primitive Babylonian laws, Jonah and Job stories, and Psalms suggested the evolution of Hebrew forms out of the earlier Chaldean traditions.

The sands of Egypt gave up lost gospels, missing links in the chain of Hebrew history, prototypes of the Wisdom literature, and the sources of monotheism. The Holy Land, carefully combed by the archaeologist, revealed successive strata of civilizations, proving, in the high places of Gezer, Canaanite influences in the Hebrew religion, and furnishing through Winckler's discovery of the Boghaz-Keui tablets the clue to the forgotten empire of the Hittites. Sir Arthur Evans found in Crete the cultural bridge between Egypt and Greece and Schliemann proved Trojan myth a fact. Under Sayce, George Smith, Rawlinson, Sarzec, Breasted, Maspero, Petrie, Macalister and others the sciences of Assyriology and Egyptology confirmed the findings of criticism and recreated a world that had its being and ceased to be before Greece and Rome were thought of. Comparative religion made its appearance as an aid to historical criticism, showing the interdependence of religions and scriptures. Manuscripts discovered at Athos and Sinai made possible a new and better text of the book of books.

Marx and Socialism

Traditional Christianity had been highly individualistic. Medieval Christendom, knowing nothing about social amelioration, acquiesced in its poverty and found its only remedy for the ills of society in the negative virtue of charity. Even the liberalizing tendencies of the Renaissance, Reformation, and Enlightenment, protesting against regimentation, accentuated the trend towards individualism. But individualistic capitalism, originally a corrective of feudalism, bred the inevitable evils of industrialism and by the nineteenth century a humanitarian reaction was overdue. The conviction grew that society as a vital organism could change, that social reconstruction was possible.

The principle of cooperation was first championed in England by Robert Owen (1771–1858) whose crusade to organize industry on a democratic basis led to the first use of the word socialism. Owing to his advocacy of free thought, he became, like Paine before him, the most hated man of his time. His program of reform—model homes for workmen, popular education, and cooperatives—fell by the wayside but he succeeded in awakening his country to the cause of labor. The social emphasis of the early nineteenth century found expression also in the utopias of Charles Fourier, Saint Simon, Frederic Maurice, Thomas Cooper, Charles Kingsley, Thomas Hughes and the unsuccessful Chartist movement.[11] The idea of cooperative societies, begun by these early prophets, has since become successful even in communities otherwise hostile to socialism as a whole. The humanitarian reaction was felt also in America where Washington Gladden, Graham Taylor, Josiah Strong, and Walter Rauschenbusch pioneered in social ethics.

The early social reformers believed that the capitalistic

[11] For a recent and scholarly account of the Chartist movement and especially of the work of Thomas Cooper see Robert J. Conklin: *Thomas Cooper, the Chartist.*

class would see the necessity of social change and lead the way. Class warfare was farthest from their thoughts. But gradually the popular disillusionment over the failure of the upper classes to cooperate led to a new class-consciousness, the appearance of which was one of the important phenomena of the mid-nineteenth century. Marx and international socialism were the result.

Before making a systematic statement of Marx's socialism, it is necessary to trace the sources of his method. The clue to the Marxian philosophy is the Hegelian dialectic. The doctrine of evolution in Hegel's mind became a new definition of history. With him however the idea of change implied absolute purpose and progress. History is a process of growth, rejection of the outworn, and recombination. This formula of thesis, antithesis, and synthesis was given the name dialectic. Every department of life is in process of transition: for every *status quo* there is a reaction, and out of this conflict emerges a new, harmonious form. The history of civilization is one grand triadic movement in which action and reaction are continually opposing each other to create in turn a resultant state.

The Hegelian dialectic profoundly impressed Karl Marx (1818–1883), who applied it to the evolution of society; but where Hegel had posited an "Absolute Force" behind his dialectic process, Marx inserted the economic factor. Hence, the Marxian economic interpretation of history which asserts that the changes in social institutions are rung not by Deity moving towards a goal but by social and economic situations. It is well to bear in mind, however, that the economic determinism of present-day radicals is not traceable to Marx, for, unlike many of his followers, he did not make the error of thinking that the socio-economic factor is the only one in history and that "environmental circumstance determines everything." Fortunately, he was able to take into account the will of the individual. "The materialistic doctrine," wrote Marx in criticizing Feuerbach, "that men are products of conditions and education, different men therefore products of other conditions and a different kind of education, forgets that *circumstances may be altered by man* and that the educator has himself to be educated." [12] By the same token the current mechanical and materialistic interpretation of Marxism is unjustified. As Ernest Trattner points out, Marx struck a balance between Hegel's absolute idealism and Feuerbach's materialism. [13]

The Hegelian trilogy for Marx, then, meant that there is no fixity in the social process. Man's primary consideration, he reasoned, is material needs. Everything is conditioned upon securing food, clothing, shelter, and security. All human institutions are determined in turn by the method of meeting those needs. But the means of supplying the wants of society have changed as civilization has progressed through the nomadic, agricultural, handicraft, and machine ages. The institutions that have arisen upon these shifting methods have a tendency to remain fixed, but they must change to fit the new means of production and distribution. Capitalism is one means of supplying the material needs of mankind. Other economic methods preceded and other methods will supplant capitalism. Its function was valid in a pioneer world of expanding markets, but the *laissez faire* policy in industry is foredoomed to wreck itself on the rocks of surplusage. State controlled production and distribution for the use of the people rather than

[12] Quoted in Ernest R. Trattner: *Architects of Ideas*, p. 245 (Italics mine).

[13] *Ibid.*, p. 245.

the excessive profit of a few men will characterize the new system of society. This, in brief, is the burden of Marx's epoch-making book, *Das Kapital*.

Marx's hands were tied in Germany where his radical ideas prevented him from securing a position. Taking up residence in Paris, he came into contact with various intellectual forces, historic and contemporary. In the realistic naturalism of Voltaire, Diderot, and Holback he found a philosophical background, but the idealistic socialism of Owen, Fourier, and Saint-Simon, then having its inning in France, was, in his mind, unscientific and impractical. He wanted a workable economic system based on the facts of production, not a utopian dream. The turning point in his career came when he met Friedrich Engels. Entertaining the same radical views, they joined forces. Fortunately for Marx, his colleague was the son of a wealthy industrialist and was more than willing to keep the wolf away from the door of the Marx family. The two men moved about considerably, not always from their own desires, and finally settled in London. Here, with Marx's wife and family almost starving to death in two small rooms, Engels came to the rescue time after time.

Together the two reformers worked out the theory and practice of international socialism and finally drafted the "Communist Manifesto." This document, more emotional and less scientific than *Das Kapital*, is a call to arms, an organ of propaganda. It describes the class struggle as a conflict between oppressor and oppressed, exploiter and exploited, the capitalists and the workers. The institutions of capitalism must be overthrown by the workers, who are destined to rule through the State, which, in turn, will control the instruments of industry. Under this régime there will be equality and freedom. "Economic crises" will be forever avoided. From the conflict of thesis (capitalists or bourgeoisie) and antithesis (proletarians) there will emerge the synthesis of a classless society.

It remains only to place Marx and socialism in the framework of the nineteenth century. Marx's philosophy of revolution and class struggle may justly be criticized as emotional and based on rationalizations and wishful thinking. Dialectic, to be sure, is not always scientific and at times is a fallacious method. But it must be conceded that his economic interpretation of history, if not regarded as the only factor, has become one of the basal doctrines of modernism and his ideal of socialism as a cooperative enterprise is the only hope for a bankrupt world. Scientific socialism is an integral phase of nineteenth-century democracy, a fact recognized by Max Kohn: "Without democracy there would have been no socialism, so that in its modern form it is a product of democracy, of the faith that a new order can be created by man to correspond better to the ideal of the equality of men and of their right to happiness."

Various forms of Christian socialism sprang up here and there in America in the closing decades of the century. Most of these programs of reform were proposed by Protestant liberals seeking an antidote for individualistic Calvinism on the one hand and materialistic Marxism on the other. Their inspiration was Henry George whose method was gradualism rather than revolution and whose philosophy was theistic rather than materialistic. Such a brand of socialism, being based on human brotherhood and social justice, was entirely consistent with the Sermon on the Mount. It stood for political reform, the annihilation of "bossism," woman suffrage, "eight-hour day," better housing, and government ownership of utilities. Its motto was cooperation rather than competition. This was the Social Gospel of Walter Rauschenbusch, Thornton Munger,

William D. P. Bliss, Washington Gladden, and George D. Herron, and, while it did not sweep the country, it bore fruit in the social platform of the Federal Council of Churches of Christ in America and other progressive programs of industrial democracy. Liberal theologians now saw the connection between the doctrine of immanence and the Social Gospel. They perceived that virtue and vice are both social things, that the community as well as the individual must be redeemed, that the way to save the world is to be a part of the world, not apart from it.

The Great Century

We have seen how the evolutionary concept of change, relativity, and development gave birth to the modern spirit as seen in the appearance of an empirical theology, a pragmatic ethics, the historico-genetic method, biblical criticism, and the social emphasis. The nineteenth century may well be called "the great century," bringing to a head and utilizing, as it did, all the emancipating forces of the seventeenth and eighteenth centuries. The time was ripe in the exciting years of the fifties for new voices. Consider the year 1859 which saw the publication of the three most important works of the modern age: Mill's *On Liberty*, Marx's *Critique of Political Economy*, and Darwin's *Origin of Species*. These three books, setting forth the new spirit in terms of constitutional government, socialism, and evolution, were the forces which shaped our time.

The nineteenth century was primarily an age of criticism, made so by the new science which rendered the older orthodoxy untenable, discredited former infallibilities, and compelled scholars to view everything critically, inductively, and with thoroughgoing discrimination. Contemporaneously with Darwin and equally significant for the introduction of the new scientific temper was Louis Pasteur (1822–1895). In the face of violent opposition from intolerant and reactionary medical circles, Pasteur experimented his way through to the germ theory of contagious disease and the method of producing immunity. The story of his hard-won victory is one of the most moving dramas in human history, a story of faith in self, of courage and relentless search for the facts. But Pasteur did more than discover and prove a theory; he gave the world a new attitude, a new technique, and inspired a generation of students with a profound love of truth.

Another new world was opened before the eyes of the complacent medical profession when Sigmund Freud, recognizing the centrality of the sexual factor in mental disorders, provided a new approach to the problems of personality and through his discovery of psychiatry and psycho-analysis joined hands with William James in turning psychology from pure theory to practical function.

Jeremy Bentham, champion of the middle class, established the utilitarian method in a program of economic and political reform which aimed to serve the interests and promote the happiness of the whole community rather than a few individuals. His disciple, John Stuart Mill, in his *Political Economy* penned the Magna Charta of modern economic liberalism with the famous statement that the problem of society is "how to unite the greatest individual liberty of action with a common ownership in the raw material of the globe and an equal participation of all in the benefits of combined labor." Mill's *System of Logic* formulated as a scientific axiom the law of causation, asserting a basal postulate of liberal thought that for every phenomenon in nature there is a cause. Rejecting theology and metaphysics and following the law of scientific induction, Auguste Comte formulated the religion of Positivism based on social and ethical needs. Lyell's *Antiquity of Man*, Buckle's *History of Civilization in England*, and Tyler's *Primitive Culture* provided a new anthropology later to be made more scientific by Franz Boaz in *The Mind of Primitive Man*. Herbert Spencer's *Principles of Psychology*, connecting structure and function, was the first statement of the unified biological view of personality.

Harriet Beecher Stowe's *Uncle Tom's Cabin* stabbed a nation awake to the evils of slavery. Edward Bellamy's *Looking Backward* prophesied a new industrial order. Walt Whitman's *Leaves of Grass* preached the gospel of rebellion for a new age of naturalism. Edwin Markham's *Man With the Hoe*, the "battle-cry of the next thousand years" and a revolution in itself, epitomized the awakening social conscience of America. Tolstoi's *War and Peace* wrote into the platform of modernism the plank of pacificism. Dickens' novels cried for a much-needed social, educational, and industrial reform. Ibsen's plays pricked the balloon of social convention and prepared the modern world to face realistically the problems of family and community life. Heine's *History of Religion and Philosophy in Germany*, combining the Greek and Hebrew traditions, vindicated the rights of the spirit and helped to mould political and social institutions along liberal lines. The writings of George Eliot, Tyndall, Huxley, Lecky, Matthew Arnold, Morley, Lange, Theodore Parker, Martineau, Robertson Smith, Haeckel, and Taine all served to buttress the growing structure of free thought, rationalism, and enlightenment. These were the new voices in the struggle of reason against authority, freedom against oppression, critical thought against dogma. That was the nineteenth century—the great age of liberalism.

XIII

Dewey

Philosopher of a Continent

THE EVENTFUL YEAR of 1859, which brought forth the epoch-making works of Mill, Darwin, and Marx, prophetically enough gave birth also to John Dewey. Born and educated in New England, coming to intellectual maturity in the Middle West, and spending his productive years in the East, Dewey was well prepared to become the philosopher of a continent. The honest, democratic life of his Vermont boyhood, the progressive, pioneering spirit of Michigan and Illinois, and the cosmopolitan atmosphere of New York City all had their part in shaping his character and thoughts. But more important than his geographical connections in his relation to history. In him are consummated the empirical tendencies of former times. As a recent interpreter remarks, "he has carried to completion a movement of ideas which marks the final break with the ancient and medieval outlook upon the world. In his doctrines the experimental temper comes to self-consciousness." [1] In him are focused all the findings of modern science and criticism. More consistently than many of his twentieth-century contemporaries who have betrayed the legacy of liberalism, he has extended the

[1] Sidney Hook: *John Dewey, An Intellectual Portrait*, p. 3. (Quoted by permission of the John Day Co.)

257

principles of empiricism to humanistic naturalism. As the representative philosopher of twentieth-century America, Dewey has applied his system of thought to every realm of modern life—politics, education, religion, morals, art, and industry.

Dewey's contribution to the history of thought lies in the simple fact that he has taken the irrelevance out of philosophy. Most philosophical systems have emerged as an extension or modification of previous systems with an apparatus of terms and concepts applicable to a former age but out of tune with the present world. Dewey's philosophy of instrumentalism, starting from scratch, frees his philosophic connotations from a dependence on former cultures. He connects things and values, tests the validity of ideas by their usefulness in society, settles all social problems by the application of the scientific method.

The key to Dewey's general philosophical principles is the radical empiricism of William James. All knowledge, according to James, is derived from experience through the senses. His was the philosophy of practical experience by which every theory, idea, or concept is subjected to the pragmatic test of utility. This anti-metaphysical method was derived in turn from Mill, Spencer, and Locke. Also back of Dewey's thought is the Darwin-Huxley worldview which gave a biological or naturalistic turn to the empirical school. Dewey, as John Herman Randall, Jr. observes, "more than any other man has caught the vision of what the scientific method and the idea of evolution really means." [2] With Dewey the human being is an organ affected by environment and under the influence of environment can change its nature. Process, growth, change are all-important. Society can be understood and controlled

[2] *The Making of the Modern Mind*, p. 480.

by the social sciences just as nature is understood and controlled by natural science.

Applied to morals and religion, Dewey's relativity means that there is no absolute good; all is relative. Faith is "a tendency towards action" and "experience is the sole ultimate authority." Social amelioration must come through education but education must be functional, not a detached dialectic. Environment, not supernatural intrusion explains all phenomena. The only divinity is within. The path to social and cultural progress is that of organized intelligence, not faith in theological mysteries. Reasoning should begin with problems, not premises. Applied politically, Dewey's experimental method demands democracy as "the wave of the future," a democracy which helps every one to help himself. The problems of the State must be met with "specific experiments, not magnificent generalizations." His philosophy, in short, is concerned with the scientific method of control and the intelligent direction of social life.

Dewey's boyhood in Yankee Vermont gave him a democratic start and, if his own environmental theory has any truth in it, his present leadership in a score of organizations devoted to civil liberties, equal rights, democratic institutions, and religious tolerance is the natural resurgence of early influences. His youth was spent in an atmosphere of rustic simplicity, common respect for individual rights, and love of the soil, characteristics deeply ingrained in the retired teacher of eighty-odd years. His theological background, while intuitive and mystical rather than rationalistic, was fairly liberal so that he did not experience the struggle of adjustment so common in the middle of the last century. He had no difficulty rejecting the creedal formulas and supernatural concepts of traditional Christianity.

His graduation from the University of Vermont in 1879 was followed by two years of high-school teaching in Oil City, Pennsylvania, and one year in Charlotte, Vermont. His increased interest in philosophy, as evidenced in articles already published, induced him to take graduate work at Johns Hopkins University, where he matriculated in 1882. At Johns Hopkins he heard Charles Peirce, although it is doubtful that his attention was directed at this time to experimentation as a philosophy. His major work was done under the direction of Professor George S. Morris. His doctoral work was devoted to the study of Immanuel Kant. From that he went to the historical approach of Hegel, being attracted to the scheme of continuity in the Hegelian synthesis of history and the unity of man and nature. Under the influence of Hegel he lost all vestiges of orthodox dualism—heaven and hell, God and the devil, body and spirit, the natural and the supernatural,—and came to see the human personality as a unified, integrated whole with positive potentialities.

Moving to the prairie lands of Minnesota and Michigan, Dewey experienced still further intellectual changes. The hand-to-mouth existence of the pioneer West produced in him a more flexible view of things. Life in the Middle West was always problematic; social customs were not fixed as in New England; and adaptation to existing problems continually occupied one's mind. Here Hegelian idealism lost its hold on Dewey's mind. Intuition and *a priori* reasoning did not seem to fit the concrete biological world. Finality and the absolute could not be pre-supposed; experimental action was the test of validity.

The experimental trend of Dewey's thought began to manifest itself in his teaching at the University of Chicago to which he was called by its first president, William

Rainey Harper, and where he taught from 1894 to 1904. (He had taught at the Universities of Minnesota and Michigan from 1884 to 1894.) Here he applied James' pragmatism to educational philosophy and began the process which rightly and wrongly was to change the entire system of American public school education. The basic principles of the "new education" were worked out in the Experimental School of Chicago of which Dewey was the director. In this educational laboratory the method of scientific inquiry was extended to all aspects of human experience and from it dates Dewey's reputation as the source of the new spirit in education not only in America but in Russia and the Orient. *School and Society*, published in 1899, carrying the story of his experimental High School, created a pedagogic revolution and has since become a classic. The beginnings of social work and psychiatry on a professional plane are also to be traced to the Chicago Experimental School. The first psychiatric clinic to be connected with a court was in Chicago, as was the first institute of juvenile research. Because of his practical philosophy Dewey was made a trustee of Jane Addams' Hull House, where he had charge of a Sunday afternoon forum.

Coming to New York in 1904 as a member of the department of philosophy in Columbia University, Dewey was challenged by the social, political and cultural problems of the machine age with the result that his empirical philosophy took a more concrete form. Known internationally as the leader of the new educational movement, he was invited to counsel and direct the program of educational reform in China, Japan, Mexico, Russia, Turkey, and South Africa. At Tokyo he gave a course of lectures on philosophy. In China Professor and Mrs. Dewey were so well received that they were given an additional leave of absence from Columbia. Dewey lectured at the University of Nanking and Mrs. Dewey demonstrated coëducation and established the deanship of women. In 1929 the University of Edinburgh invited him to deliver the Gifford Lectures, a distinction given previously to William James and Josiah Royce. Mainly because of Dewey's visit, Russia made public schools for all a part of its new social order, schools in which education was creatively connected with life. Wherever he went Dewey was recognized as a great democrat and to this day remains to all who know him just the plain man from Vermont.

Probably no public figure has indulged in so little that is autobiographical as has John Dewey. His oral and written deliverances are always concerned with the problems of the outside world and other people. His personality is aptly described by Sidney Hook:

In his relationship with people he is unassuming, sometimes almost to the point of effacement. His simplicity, directness, and complete lack of self-consciousness puts even the shyest person at his ease, and yet leads him to do more things and to do them better than he ordinarily would. His intellectual humility is so profound that it might seem to be a pose affected by a great man were it not so obviously sincere. Whether it is a farmer or teacher, storekeeper or factory worker, public official or student, he exchanges ideas with him as if he were the learner, or both were learners in a common enterprise. . . . Despite his gentleness there is a deep vein of Vermont marble in his character. None have been so shocked as those who have mistaken this gentleness for softness. In controversy he does not give ground easily and hesitates not at all in getting rough with opponents whose good faith he has reason to challenge whether they are ambassadors or newspaper columnists.[3]

[3] *Op. cit.*, pp. 18, 19.

Dewey's philosophy of relativity and experimentalism pervades even his method of writing. At the advanced age of eighty-four he is not ready to utter any *ex cathedra* conclusions for posterity. His philosophical writing is that of a person thinking on paper. Where he is reasoning his way to a new theory his style is extremely abstruse and he does not seem to "come out anywhere." Where he revises or reworks an older theme, the reading is much more facile if not rich in prose style.

Dewey appears to lead a dual existence, for no man in the world of public affairs is more belligerently active in the promotion of progressive movements than he. Whenever there is a battle to fight, a cause to uphold, an underdog to defend, the absent-minded professor and author of some twenty-five books turns into an aggressive campaigner and one to be reckoned with. He represents the rare combination of speculative thinker and public spirited citizen. One does not normally expect the author of books on logic and aesthetics to be the Vice-Chairman of the City Affairs Committee of New York. His liberalism, in other words, is not always in the abstract. As co-founder of the Teachers' Guild and the Farmer-Labor Party; as chairman of the League of Independent Political Action and the Peoples' Lobby; as organizer of the American Civil Liberties Union and the American Association of University Professors, as head of the Commission of Inquiry into the Moscow Trials which exonerated Trotsky; and as chief defender of the allegedly innocent Sacco and Vanzetti, Dewey has for many years led the liberal minority in this country in its crusade for justice and fair play. Democracy with him is not just a word in a Fourth-of-July oration but a social condition that must be fought for here and now. The fact remains that wherever obscurantism and privilege flourish in the United States, Dewey's name is anathema.

Re-defining Religion

The most persistent problem in the history of thought is that which concerns the basis for intellectual authority. The question philosophically stated is this: Is reason or perception the ultimate test of knowledge; is intuitive conception or sense experience the criterion for ultimate reality? The history of liberal thought, the critical periods of which have been described in this volume, is the record of the continued expression of the second of these two views. John Dewey, heir to this tradition, applies the experimental method to the problem of authority in the field of religion and ethics where he is led to deny the idea of the absolute and the need of a perfect reality.

Previous philosophers for the most part have concentrated their efforts on the quest for security. In his Gifford Lectures [4] Dewey takes a purely naturalistic position and assigns the demand for a metaphysical sanction of morality to the failure of modern thinkers to face frankly the risks of the human struggle. In the economic warfare we find security in the practical effort to understand and then control nature. The act of experimenting, building, earning a living, tilling the soil, and manufacturing brings assurance and provides satisfactions. But in the religious and philosophical world we seek a supra-natural, supra-mundane, unchanging reality, upon which we are dependent. Above and beyond the changing phenomena of life, this infallible Absolute remains the unchanged, immutable authority. "When men began to reflect philosophically," writes Dewey, "it seemed to them altogether too risky to leave the place of values at the mercy of acts the results of which are

[4] From *The Quest for Certainty*, by John Dewey. (Courtesy of G. P. Putnam's Sons)

never sure. This precariousness might hold as far as empirical existence, existence in the sensible and phenomenal world, is concerned; but this very uncertainty seemed to render it the more needful that ideal goods should be shown to have, by means of knowledge of the most assured type, an indefeasible and inexpugnable position in the realm of the ultimately real." [5] Belief in such a security, according to Dewey, is unnecessary, is, in fact, a sign of weakness. Authority in religion should arise not from cosmic sources but from within; the sanction for morals should come not from supernatural revelation but from human experience. This is not to say that Dewey's naturalism precludes a reverent attitude towards the universe. Man is not left alone. There is a cosmic force before which man must bow in the spirit of humility. There is, of course, little comfort to be had here and it is not to be wondered at that both orthodox and radical camps find Dewey's naturalism inadequate. If he sees a cosmic force it is spelled with small letters. To this Dewey would answer that if he believes in a cosmic order it is not the immutable supernaturalism of the Church, but an identification of man with nature. If he is an atheist, his atheism is neither ignorant self-sufficiency nor philosophical nihilism but the substitution of natural forces for an arbitrary personal deity who rules over and overrules the destinies of mankind. The imperfections of nature as they impinge upon man's existence are not to be regarded as foreordained impediments or inexplicable evils from which to escape but situations to be understood, mastered, and acted upon as part of man's natural life.

This substitution of experience for immutability, the "naturalization of intelligence," is now seen to be the ap-

[5] *Ibid.*, p. 33.

plication of the scientific method in religion. Its acceptance by the philosophical world of the nineteenth century would have facilitated greatly the rapprochement between science and religion, as Dewey points out: "If men had associated their ideas about values with practical activity instead of with cognition of antecedent Being, they would not have been troubled by the findings of science. They would have welcomed the latter. For anything ascertained about the structure of actually existing conditions would be a definite aid in making judgment about things to be prized and striven for more adequate, and would instruct us as to the means to be employed in realizing them. But according to the religious and philosophic tradition of Europe, the valid status of all the highest values, the good, true, and beautiful, was bound up with their being properties of ultimate and supreme Being, namely, God. All went well as long as what passed for natural science gave no offense to this conception. Trouble began when science ceased to disclose in the objects of knowledge the possession of any such properties. Then some roundabout method had to be devised for substantiating them." [6]

Religion for Dewey refers to the process by which ideal values are actualized. God is the activistic relation between the present actuality and the future potentiality, the means through which the ideal is transmuted into action. The Kingdom of God is the process through which human intelligence cooperates with the divine order in consummating these ideal ends. Defining God as a social process and the "divine" as nature obviously leads to misunderstanding and Dewey may well be criticized by radical religious Humanists and conservative theologians alike for reading private meanings into traditional terms.

[6] *Ibid.*, p. 42.

Dewey sees religion as an active attitude towards life rather than an adherence to rules and forms. In his *Common Faith* he draws the distinction between religion as a segregated compartment of life, a quantitative set of observances and beliefs, and religion conceived as the integrating core of life, a qualitative interpenetration. It is the difference between *being religious* and *having a religion*. The distinction between "religious" and "secular" is false. Religion cannot be held as a definite kind of experience as differentiated from activities, called scientific, aesthetic, or political. Considered as a specific or quantitative thing, religion becomes an innocuous and ineffective formula, an elective in the curriculum of life, merely chosen for the purpose of making life complete and "well rounded." But put at the center and identified with life itself, religion becomes the motivating principle, the determining factor in all of life's activities. Religious faith then becomes the act of harmonizing the self around life's highest values, or, as Dewey, puts it, "the unification of the self through allegiance to inclusive ideal ends, which imagination presents to us and to which the human will responds as worthy of controlling our desires and choices." [7]

The specifics of religion—the Mass, the Bible, prayer, the Koran, conversion, the creed, beliefs, dogmas, and ceremonies—are purely incidental to the culture into which any one person happens to be born. The devotee of any given religion describes his adjustment to life or religious experience in terms of the cultural deposits of his own civilization. The particular experience described is authentic with him and proves his faith. These deposits are important as means or instrumentalities but they are not the end of religion. All religions have specific beliefs

[7] *Common Faith*, p. 33.

to which their adherents attach intellectual importance and which are incumbent on all believers. Each religion has its own channel to truth, its revelation from on high. These claims are not the primary element in religion. When once freed from the specific beliefs and practices, religion would be found to be a common faith. Religion, then, is not a matter of times and seasons, prohibitions and command-ments, feastings and fastings; it is an active faith in the possibility of achieving individual and social ideal ends. "Any activity," continues Dewey, "pursued in behalf of an ideal end against obstacles and in spite of threats of per-sonal loss because of conviction of its general and enduring value is religious in quality." [8]

Valuable and timely as this practical emphasis is, a word of qualification must be added. Just as Dewey's accent on *method* in education, when applied rigorously, has to be tempered with a more systematic attention to "content knowledge," in the same way, his functionalism in religious philosophy lacks proper regard for generalization and end results. Logically enough, in supplying neglected emphases in education and religion he finds himself at the other end of the pendulum swing. "Concrete situations," "social con-sequences," "techniques," "experiment," do not tell the whole philosophical story. Room must be left in the mod-ern reconstruction of philosophy and ethical theory for abstract reason, intuition and first principles. Empiricism must always be accompanied by critical reasoning in any estimate of what is "good." Subjective judgment as to the rightness of an ideal end is inevitable. [9]

[8] *Ibid.*, p. 27.
[9] For a sound philosophical criticism of Dewey's instrumentalism see Julius Seelye Bixler: *Religion for Free Minds*, pp. 117 ff.

The New Education

Diametrically opposed to scholasticism and even the "liberal education" of the older universities, Dewey teaches that learning can be achieved only by doing. (Curiously enough, Dewey himself prefers to lecture to classes in the traditional "classical" style and undoubtedly has a large personal library upon which he is forever dependent.) "Fellowship in occupation" rather than a snobbish, leisure-class, classical education is his slogan. "Education should be for life rather than for literacy," say his followers. The school should teach through the trial-and-error method. "How" is more important than "what." Education should not be regarded as an accumulation of knowledge, a process which ceases at a certain time, but a life-long continuous growth. The school furnishes only the tools; real education comes after school. Education is for experience's sake, not for its own sake. Dewey defines education as "that reconstruction or reorganization of experience which adds to the meaning of experience, and which increases ability to direct the course of subsequent experience." [10]

This educational theory can be recognized as the point of departure for "progressive education," adult education, vocational guidance, and the recent emphasis on the applied social sciences as over against the conventional classical training. According to Dewey, the function of the school is to develop social attitudes useful in "life-situations" rather than to stuff the child with predigested facts and figures. It follows that the educated person is the one who can take care of himself in any environment. The degree or quality of education attained is measured by the growth in capacity and character of an individual over a given period rather

[10] Joseph Ratner: *The Philosophy of John Dewey*, p. 382.

than the amount of knowledge memorized or the meeting of arbitrary standards for graduation. The materials of education should be relevant to the present need; the child should be personally motivated; the subjects taught should be purely functional; and the educational process should be cooperative,—not superimposed, but "shared."

Such a democratic and practical theory of education strikes any fair-minded person as a much-needed corrective for the effete and aimless programs of education frequently found. The influence of Dewey's ideas brought about radical changes in the direction of "vocationalism" and social studies even in the more conservative universities. It had a vitalizing effect on the whole process of education in America in revealing the ineffectiveness of the stereotyped curricula and mechanical drill. But Dewey's followers among professional educators have perverted his philosophy by making extreme applications of method without due regard for his basic principles or for the local situation, which in many instances is the last place in the world upon which to impose the informality of progressivism. All of which has led Dewey in recent years if not to disown his child at least to write a book pointing out the defects of progressive education and cautioning against the shortsightedness of the "either-or" school. He writes:

Yet I am sure that you will appreciate what is meant when I say that many of the newer schools tend to make little or nothing of organized subject-matter of study; to proceed as if any form of direction and guidance by adults were an invasion of individual freedom, and as if the idea that education should be concerned with the present and future meant that acquaintance with the past has little or no rôle to play in education. . . . But the mere removal of external control is no guarantee for the production of self control. It is easy to jump from the frying-pan into the fire. . . . Traditional education tended to ignore the importance of personal impulse and desire as moving springs. But this is no reason why progressive education should identify impulse and desire with purpose and thereby pass lightly over the need for careful observation, for wide range of information, and for judgment, if students are to share in the formation of the purposes which activate them. . . . It is a ground for legitimate criticism, when the ongoing movement of progressive education fails to recognize that the problem of selection and organization of subject-matter for study and learning is fundamental. . . . Nothing can be more absurd educationally than to make a plea for a variety of active occupations in the school while decrying the need for progressive organization of information and ideas. . . . I am not, I hope and believe, in favor of any ends or any methods simply because the name progressive may be applied to them.[11]

The chief defect of progressive education is that it presupposes an ideal situation that is seldom present. It calls for small groups of carefully selected, high-grade students who have an initial interest in educating themselves. To thrust the non-disciplinary, self-motivated system into a typical classroom of elementary, secondary, or collegiate grade is a highly precarious venture, and even where it has been tried in favorable situations its success has not been convincing. Its danger lies in its "informal" character, which in many cases is demoralizing in its abandonment of all set standards and organized curricula. Unhindered and unguided "self-expression" in the school and home has resulted in the *loss* of character rather than its discovery.

Fear of indoctrination on the part of "progressives" has

---

[11] *Experience and Education*, pp. 9, 75, 83, 95, 105, 115. (Quoted by permission of The Macmillan Co., publishers)

left them without convictions, standards, and affirmations. Revolting from the older rigid system with its categorical answers, the advocates of the new school are reluctant to come to any conclusion. The rabid "progressive," holding that method is more important than content, asserts that it is better for a teacher to have taken courses in the method of teaching physics than to have amassed a knowledge of physics itself.

The benefits of a "useful" education sooner or later reach the point of diminishing returns when the activity-minded person has to stop *doing* things and ask himself if he has anything besides a specific training for a certain job. Utilitarianism and the experimental method are theoretically sound and represent the modern liberal tradition, but where this viewpoint is applied in an extreme fashion and to the exclusion of other methods, the result is little more than a trade-school education. Under the influence of this "virus of immediacy" teacher training is overdone; teacher education is undone. Teachers are trained in the educational techniques of the age rather than educated in the wisdom of the ages. The college graduate expecting to teach has been so pre-occupied getting credits demanded by the various States that he has neglected to take courses in the subject he proposes to teach. The fact stands that today a mediocre student who has fulfilled all the picayune requirements in educational ramifications can obtain a teaching position; but it is impossible for a high-ranking graduate of Johns Hopkins or Harvard—regardless of his brilliance, common sense, or fine personality—to qualify for a position in a grammar school.

All of which argues for a sane balance between professionalism in education and classicism. Somewhere between the prosaic statistics of the vocationally trained man and the medievalism of President Hutchins and Mortimer

Adler there is a happy combination of "useful" and "useless" education necessary for the complete man.

In the American Tradition

As the foremost philosopher of American democracy, Dewey worships at the shrine of Thomas Jefferson. "I am not under-estimating Jefferson's abilities as a practical politician," he writes, "when I say that this deep-seated faith in the people and their responsiveness to enlightenment properly presented was a most important factor in enabling him to effect, against great odds, 'the revolution of 1800.' It is the cardinal element bequeathed by Jefferson to the American tradition. . . . The terms in which Jefferson expressed his belief in the moral criterion for judging all political arrangements and his belief that republican institutions are the only ones that are morally legitimate are not now current. It is doubtful, however, whether defense of democracy against the attacks to which it is subjected does not depend upon taking once more the position Jefferson took about its moral basis and purpose, even though we have to find another set of words in which to formulate the moral ideal served by democracy." [12]

The Jeffersonian principle can be applied today in spite of the social and economic revolution that has intervened. Economic and cultural changes demand new imperatives for democracy: universal public education, cooperation between producer and consumer, social security, proper distribution of hours of labor and wages, academic freedom, civil liberties, and the application of the scientific method in economic and civic planning. That is what the Jeffersonian principle means for the twentieth century. Contrary

[12] *Thomas Jefferson*, pp. 18, 25. (Quoted by permission of Longmans, Green & Co.)

to the opinion of his critics, the pragmatic temper with Dewey refers to the scientific interest in method and techniques rather than the end result of commercial success. "Typically American" with them means the *fait accompli* of material possession; with him the phrase has to do with the habit of scientific inquiry. The American way is to try things out; it is the way of the frontier. Dewey would ascertain the possibilities of new ideals by scientific analysis and then would apply them relevantly to the present world.

With liberalism and democracy under fire Dewey today refuses to be a defeatist. Nor is he afraid of being called an optimist. Freedom is still a possibility for America if Americans will understand and have faith in its real meaning and are also willing to pay the price for it. As the philosopher of American democracy Dewey represents the liberal-minded person in every walk of life. The worker who desires voluntary cooperation with employer, the teacher for whom academic freedom is the soul of existence, the preacher who opposes legalism and obscurantism in all its forms—all who are willing to run the risks in order to receive the blessings of democracy.

Dewey believes that liberalism must be organized for social action and recover its fighting faith. "I for one do not believe," he said in the Page-Barbour Lectures, "that Americans living in the tradition of Jefferson and Lincoln will weaken and give up without a whole-hearted effort to make democracy a living reality." [13] The method of intelligence and experimental control of which Dewey so often speaks must be further applied to political and social action or Western culture will revert to barbarism. That application is the immediate task of organized American liberalism.

[13] *Liberalism and Social Action*, p. 92.

XIV

Twentieth-Century Naturalism

Naturalistic Humanism

A PANORAMIC PICTURE of contemporary thought shows four main streams of influence: supernaturalism, idealism, romanticism, and naturalism. These four varieties of philosophy, ranging from the extreme right to the extreme left, represent traditional tendencies which have persisted through the years.[1] Supernaturalism is authoritarian and intransigent in temper, and emphasizes revelation, tradition, and dogmatic belief. Idealism and Romanticism are comparatively liberal in their shift to the ethical and historical point of view but cling to absolutism and intuition in various forms. Naturalism continues the empirical tradition and relies solely on the scientific method.

The present crisis has tended to merge these four groups into two as representatives of the two middle modernistic groups find themselves compelled by the conflicts of the machine age to take one of two positions: Neo-Supernaturalism or Naturalistic Humanism. This is the new battle line, replacing the former Fundamentalist-Modern-

[1] For this classification see Wieman and Meland: *American Philosophies of Religion.*

ist issue. The Neo-Supernaturalists are recruited from erstwhile liberals who deplore the intellectual chaos introduced by the Renaissance and the Reformation, and despairing of any cultural solution of the modern social, economic, and religious conflicts, return to the absolutism of medieval theocracy. The ranks of the Neo-Supernaturalists are made up of former progressives in theology who have called a halt in the march of liberalism and now re-emphasize the dogmatic, revelational philosophy which they once found invalid. The chief European expression of this tendency is Barthianism which demands of its adherents the non-rational submission to the will of a deity who is utterly unknown but who dictates every thought of the individual. The milder American form of Barthianism, represented by Reinhold Niebuhr, is a peculiar combination of economic radicalism and theological conservatism. Led by one of the keenest thinkers of America, the semi-Barthians talk much of total depravity and divine grace. Like Kierkegaard, Niebuhr makes great use of the paradox as a theological method. "The good news of the Gospel," he declares, "is not the law that we ought to love one another. The goods news is that there is a resource of divine mercy which is able to overcome a contradiction within our own souls, which we cannot ourselves overcome." Again he sees "the whole of human history as involved in guilt" and finds no release from this guilt "except in the grace of God." [2]

The Anglo-Catholicism of T. S. Eliot, another form of Neo-Supernaturalism, denying every progressive idea since Galileo and Erasmus, offers the security and unity of the medieval Church as the only hope for the twentieth century. Mr. Eliot's nostalgia is an illustration of romantic

[2] *Christianity and Power Politics*, p. 2.

liberalism living on borrowed time. Just how much unity or security, for instance, was there in feudal Europe? Medievalism was, in point of fact, a static type of society with fixed grades, a society in which individual autonomy was impossible. It was a security of regimentation. The revolt against reason is further typified by D. H. Lawrence who becomes a partner in the Nietzschean-Hitler ethic when he writes: "We can go wrong in our minds; but what our blood feels and believes and says is always true." Another contemporary asks us to recover our morality "by turning from the perverted doctrine of the 'Enlightenment' and from its recrudescence in modern humanitarianism to a larger and higher philosophy." [3]

Religious authoritarianism has indeed assembled some strange bed-fellows. In the writings of Barth, Berdyaev, Belloc, T. S. Eliot, Ralph Adams Cram, Paul Elmer More, Christopher Dawson, Maritain, and Peter Oliver lie the seeds of philosophical totalitarianism. These are the enemies of the liberal spirit, for they all agree that man is hopeless and that the only path to a better world is through the intervention of God. They have abandoned reason and experience. The evangelical ideology of the Reformation stood for the competence of the individual. The typical Protestant philosophy as contrasted to Thomism is experiential. Neo-Supernaturalism, in short, betrays the best thought of the last four hundred years.

The crisis of the twentieth century has likewise forced into being an extension of the naturalistic left-wing known as Scientific Humanism. Humanism carries nineteenth-century relativism and James' pragmatism to their logical conclusion in the social and religious field. The term itself has been used to describe the revival of learning in the

[3] Paul Elmer More: *Aristocracy and Justice*, p. 214.

Renaissance as seen chiefly in the study of Greek and Latin literature. Like Christianity itself, Humanism crystallized into a static worship of Greek and Latin as ends in themselves with the result that the word later became synonymous with orthodox classicism of which the More-Babbitt movement is a modern recrudescence. Contemporary naturalistic Humanism stems from Locke's Empiricism, Voltaire's Deism, Comte's Positivism, Hume's Skepticism, James' Pragmatism, and modern left-wing Unitarianism. To confuse the reactionary Humanism of the literary group with Scientific Humanism reveals either an appalling ignorance of the facts or a deliberate perversion of the same.

Scientific Humanism has been defined as "the doctrine that men, through the use of intelligence, directing the institutions of democratic government, can create for themselves, without aid from 'supernatural powers', a rational civilization in which each person enjoys economic security and finds cultural outlets for whatever normal human capacities and creative energies he possesses." [4] Related explicitly to religion, Humanism is "a faith in the supreme value and self-perfectability of human personality." [5]

A more detailed definition of Naturalistic Humanism is given by Corliss Lamont in the following five propositions:

First, a belief, based mainly on the sciences of biology, psychology and medicine, that man is an evolutionary product of the nature that is his home and an inseparable unity of body and personality having no possibility of individual immortality.

Second, a metaphysics or world-view that rules over all

[4] Oliver Leslie Reiser: *The Promise of Scientific Humanism*, p. 241.
[5] See Charles Francis Potter: *Humanism, a New Religion*, pp. 14 ff.

forms of the supernatural and that regards the universe as a dynamic and constantly changing system of events which exists independently of any mind or consciousness and which follows a regular cause-effect sequence everywhere and at all times.

Third, a conviction that man has the capacity and intelligence successfully to solve his own problems and that he should rely on reason and scientific method to do so.

Fourth, an ethic that holds as its highest aim the this-earthly happiness, freedom and progress, both economic and cultural, of all humanity, regardless of nation or race, religion or occupation, sex or age.

Fifth, a far-reaching social program that stands for the establishment throughout the world of peace and democracy on the foundations of a cooperative economic order, both national and international.[6]

Scientific and Religious Humanism indicates therefore a smaller division under the more comprehensive term Naturalism. The naturalistic view, in contradistinction to the older dualism, holds that personality is a part of nature, an organism affecting as well as being affected by its environment. In the cosmic field the naturalistic position shows the influence of contemporary physics which has given noticeable impetus to the organismic philosophy. The evolutionary theists, of whom Wm. Pepperell Montague serves as an example, believe that the universe is the expression of a Cosmic Mind or Divine Intelligence and that emergent evolution substantiates that belief. Cosmic theists, such as Alfred N. Whitehead and Albert Einstein, identify the ultimate reality with the process of nature and God as the Cosmic Consciousness. Cosmic theists are·more naturalistic and less theological than the evolutionary theists.

[6] *The Humanist*, Vol. 11, No. 2, p. 42.

Neither group would be considered genuinely theistic by orthodoxy and both are favorable to the third type of naturalism—Scientific Humanism. Proponents of this Leftist philosophy hold as their initial proposition that while human beings live and have their being within the bounds of the physical world and are controlled in part by natural laws, yet they can progress in the increasing control of natural forces.

But more important than the scientific control of nature is the possible advance in social control without which civilization will experience an unprecedented retrogression. It is at this point that Religious Humanism enters with both an abstract philosophy and a practical program. The distinguishing characteristic of this movement of thought is its shift from the theocentric to the anthropocentric position. The chief emphasis is on man, not God. As a scientific religion, Humanism deals only with phenomena which are known. With regard to metaphysical and supernatural questions, therefore, it maintains an agnostic attitude. More strictly speaking, Humanists can be divided into three groups: theistic, agnostic, and anti-theistic or atheistic. From the standpoint of conservative religion, or even "Modernism," all Humanists are atheists because they reject the supernaturalism of traditional Christianity. The cosmic deity of Einstein, for instance, would not be recognized either by a Bishop Manning or a Harry Emerson Fosdick. Some Humanists are not willing to sever connections with theism completely but hold to a Spinozistic conception of deity. But all three classes are agreed that the most important object in the universe is man and that religion must devote itself entirely to his improvement, individually and socially.

While Naturalistic Humanism has not had a widespread

appeal (for reasons not far to seek), it has received the wholehearted support of such leading thinkers as the following: Max C. Otto, Roy W. Sellers, A. Eustace Haydon, John Dewey, Edwin A. Burtt, Oliver Leslie Reiser, Harry Nelson Wieman, and Edward Scribner Ames among philosophers; Albert Einstein, J. B. S. Haldane, and Julian Huxley among scientists; Thomas Mann, H. G. Wells, Lin·Yutang, and Walter Lippmann among journalists and authors; Max Lerner, Harry Elmer Barnes, Robert Morss Lovett, John Herman Randall, Jr., James H. Leuba, and J. A. C. F. Auer among educators; John H. Dietrich, Curtis W. Reese, John Haynes Holmes, Charles Francis Potter, and Edwin H. Wilson, among the clergy.

On the whole, then, while not necessarily atheistic, Religious Humanism can be considered negative in regard to traditional religion and philosophical theism. There is no need, it is felt, for transcendental support for social ideals. Nor does the evolutionary scheme presuppose any supernatural causation. The religion of the future must be concerned only with man's "outreach for satisfying values." The high religion, according to Walter Lippmann, is the achievement of "regenerate and mature personality." Since it expects no miracles and has no naïve desires about the universe, it cannot be upset by science. "A religion," writes Lippmann, "which rests upon particular conclusions in astronomy, biology, and history may be fatally injured by the discovery of new truths. But the religion of the spirit does not depend upon creeds and cosmologies; it has no vested interest in any particular truth. It is concerned not with the organization of matter, but with the quality of human desire. . . . In the realm of the spirit, blessedness is not deferred; there is no future which is more auspicious than the present; there are no compensations later for evils now. Evil is to be overcome now and happiness is to be achieved now, for the kingdom of God is within you. The life of the spirit is not a commercial transaction in which the profit has to be anticipated; it is a kind of experience which is inherently profitable." [7]

It is a mistake for empirical theists and liberal idealists to look upon Humanism as a menace and as something beyond the pale. It would be far better to recognize the humanistic emphasis as a salutary influence in contemporary religion and to assimilate the positive elements while discarding the negative. That liberal theism has nothing to lose and much to gain by taking a sympathetic attitude toward Scientific and Religious Humanism is attested in the recent writings of such progressive thinkers as Edgar Sheffield Brightman, James Bissett Pratt, Julius Seelye Bixler, Alfred North Whitehead, and Harry A. Overstreet, who, while not classified as Humanists, nevertheless are hospitable towards the movement both in its philosophical method and its practical program.

The future of Humanism rests largely on the outcome of the present world struggle. If America is headed for totalitarianism, authoritarian religion will prevail. If democracy survives, naturalistic religion will grow, and its growth will aid the progress of democracy, for Humanism is committed to those aspects of democracy which make for a free society. Naturalistic Humanism aims at a philosophy of individual and social action. Its leaders understand that philosophy is not just an intellectual attitude towards life but a dynamic enterprise capable of changing society and its institutions. The social program of Humanism calls for the cultivation of international and inter-racial amity, the

[7] *Preface to Morals*, pp. 327. 329.

legalizing of birth control, the improvement and extension
of education, the defense of freedom of speech, the improvement of penology, the improvement of industrial
conditions, the extension of social insurance, the legislation
of child-welfare measures, the purification of politics, the
abolition of special privilege, and the conservation of
natural resources for the people.[8] Such a program chal-
lenges all liberals, theistic or non-theistic.

Is Religious Certainty Necessary?

It seems to be the fashion for erstwhile liberals to be-
moan in a wistful manner the loss of religious certainty.
Those who analyze the present religious situation griev-
ously lament the passing of absolutism, and yearn for that
sense of security which their intellects no longer allow them
to harbor. They ask for some "basic belief" which will
bring order and meaning to life. They regret that they do
not have the "definite pattern" that their believing grand-
fathers had, and conclude that "we can see the necessity of
living by imperatives and we contemplate with some envy
those generations integrated by orthodox patterns of
thought."

Is this general concern for some absolute or authoritative control justified? Would the relinquishing of supernatural sanctions necessarily mean a loss in religious
values? Does the intelligent man need security theologically as he does economically?

The scientific attitude towards life should not only precipitate a fresh discussion concerning the infallibilities of
religion, but should raise the question as to whether a fixed
intellectual authority is at all necessary for the religious

[8] See Potter: *Op. cit.*, pp. 123 ff.

life. Edwin Arlington Robinson's remark that the world is a "kind of spiritual kindergarten, where millions of bewildered infants are trying to spell God with the wrong blocks" apears sadly appropriate when one surveys the successive shifts in the history of religious authority. We cannot be blamed for playing with the blocks, of course; the trouble comes in thinking that each combination we have set up is eternally fixed and unchangeable. Therein is the fallacy of the infallible, the futility of external religious authority. The fact that the blocks have been rearranged so many times in the history of civilization ought to engender some doubt regarding the validity of *any* absolute prior authority.

Religious or philosophical certainty has been spelled in a great variety of ways in different ages: the Torah, Jehovah, Jesus Christ the Saviour, God the Omnipotent, the finite God, the Church, the Bible, the Trinity, the Christ of Faith, the Jesus of History, Categorical Imperatives, the Absolute Truth, the Universal Spirit, the Life Force, and the Conscience. In spite of this periodic shift in infallibilities, many still hold that absolutism in religion is necessary. Dr. Reinhold Niebuhr and others rejecting all forms of relativism, fall back upon medieval absolutism. What he wants is "the assurance of grace." Rejecting liberalism, which believes in men's ability to improve, he prefers the Calvinistic doctrine of the total depravity of man. The right about face of the former liberals is the result of their unwillingness to carry through beyond modernism. Perhaps they have not realized that modernism at best was only a half-way house. Apprehensive of freedom, they take refuge in faith. Disappointed in man's failure to transform the social order, the Neo-Supernaturalists withdraw to another world, the realm of divine revelation. In a period of insecurity men move in one of two directions: they either discover a new self-confidence or they look to some authority to solve their problems and give them assurance. In terms of religious philosophy this means that those who have been in the middle party of liberalism either press on to a humanistic position or revert to a supernaturalistic one. The more shaky the economic and political world becomes, the more emphatic will be the movement towards theological and philosophical authoritarianism.

Relativity should apply not only to physics but to ethics. Absolutism in the form of Mosaic law, papal encyclicals, biblical inspiration, or Kantian imperatives is simply naïve in the face of the complex, shifting contemporary scene. Ethical standards are relative to the particular civilization in which one lives and to the particular situation in that civilization. Questions of morals should be solved by determining what is good for the individual and society in the long run. Those standards handed down to us from the past which fit and are valid must be followed, not because they are revealed law, absolute truth, but because they are found to be useful. "The things universally forbidden," says Ludwig Lewisohn, "are not wrong because they are forbidden; they are forbidden because they are impossible, because they do not work for human beings."

The idea of finality presupposes a pre-existent, immutable truth, the "perfect reality," towards which we grow and to which we conform. But is there any such reality? Is it not a purely subjective or speculative construction? Christianity, inheriting the idea of revelation and absolutism from its Semitic sources, became a religion of infallible authorities rather than an experiential morality, as it had started; hence the persistent tendency to hark back to a fixed, antedecent, heaven-born reality. The new scientific outlook proved detrimental to the infallibilities which had been worshiped in the prescientific era, but the metaphysicians simply shifted the blocks and spelled their words differently.

"As it was in the beginning" has been an all too prominent factor in religion. The fact that fifty or a hundred million people believe a thing which has been believed for a thousand years does not make it true. The idea still persists, however, even among liberals, that tradition itself lends authority or sanction to certain forms and dogmas, although the ideas or practices are manifestly untenable.

If the only justification for religious authority is the validation of the moral life, its usefulness can seriously be questioned. It is here that religion can profit by the scientific method in rejecting superimposed, traditional authorities and regarding all standards as instrumental and subject to change rather than as ends in themselves and final. The basis of certainty should be pragmatic and experiential. The fallacy of traditional authority is that it is purely a dogmatic assumption divorced from action. The authority for the good life should be qualitative rather than quantitative; it should consist of verifiable values rather than metaphysical beliefs. This, we take it, is what Professor Dewey means by his term "actability." If one objects to this as mere expressionism, coldly intellectual, he is reminded that it is nothing more or less than the acid test of Jesus—"by their fruits ye shall know them." Whatever moral judgments we hold as valid must come from lives under fire. Then and then only can moral standards command the loyalty of intelligent people.

Another weakness of infallibility is that it makes people look backward instead of forward, back to some deified person or to some supernatural revelation. With human values as the norm, the moral person is not committed to any antecedent theory of the universe—which is likely to be overthrown—but faces the more exacting demands of the present. He is not defending the faith; he is trying it out. The traditional theory that the problems of the ever changing present life can be settled automatically by reference to a fixed and ancient authoritative belief is a violation of the scientific method in religion. Such a commitment results in nothing short of complete mental paralysis. Growth, not finality, is the sign of a healthy religion. "Churches," as Kirsopp Lake says, "are not societies for the preservation of ancient opinions, but for the furtherance of a living religion." The preacher is not the curator of a theological museum but a prophet of change, defining religion not in terms of the past alone but of its potentialities.

The religion of the spirit has within its own self authority for the moral life. The achievement of human values, the consciousness of improving self and society—that should be sufficient sanction. It is independent of, and compatible with, scientific truth because it is not tied up to the biological, historical, or astronomical world, as the traditional authorities have been. The ultimate test of value is its own witness within.

If divinity of character is measured in terms of moral achievement, then religious authority is found in moral values, which are ends in themselves to be achieved not for the glory of the supernatural but for the survival and improvement of man.

Neo-Liberalism

The manifest inadequacy of the old individualistic liberalism in the modern world of conflicts and new social organization has led to the belief that the liberal outlook in its entirety is dated. Along with this misunderstanding is the uncertainty of the times, a factor which makes countless converts to authoritarian philosophies. These two factors account for the so-called defeat of liberalism, but that defeat need be considered neither vital nor permanent. The principles for which liberalism has always stood—academic freedom, tolerance of heresies, the idea of human perfectibility, civil liberties, the scientific method of free inquiry, and the life of reason—are not incapacitated but await their proper adjustment to the contemporary scene.

Traditional liberalism was obsessed with the individual's freedom from governmental restraint and from ecclesiastical tyranny. This obsession, carried over into a new order, has paralyzed liberalism itself because it has been played into the hands of reaction. The liberalism of the future, as Max Lerner suggests, must be concerned not so much with *freedom from* as with *freedom for*. "We have never needed an affirmative liberal attitude more than today," he writes, "because we have never needed freedom more—freedom for a huge collective economic effort, freedom for the contrivance of new political forms to carry the burden of that effort, freedom to take the leisure that technology has brought us and build it into our culture." [9]

In refusing to make the jump, passive liberals have lost their liberalism. The next step for liberalism in the socio-economic world is the adaptation of the seventeenth- and eighteenth-century liberal philosophy to the emerging

[9] *It is Later Than You Think*, p. 18.

democratic collectivisim of our own day. It must be willing to change its political and economic form from individual freedom to cooperative enterprise and its spirit from apology to militancy.

"Rugged individualism," "*laissez faire,*" "natural rights," once genuinely liberal tendencies, have in the last hundred years been perverted in the interest of the *status quo.* The slogans of a former liberalism have been exploited in recent years in the interests of economic royalism and anti-social legislation. Social change has been balked by legislative or judicial appeal to "natural rights." Political aspirants have boasted of their "liberalism" when they were Rightists at heart. "Liberty Leagues" are formed to safeguard the freedom of the vested interests. Free discussion has often taken the form of filibustering to stifle some progressive measure or social reform.

It is not the fault of true liberalism as a philosophy that individual economic power took the place of the earlier individual political power; that the robber baron succeeded the feudal baron; or that the principal of *laissez faire* eventually brought economic slavery rather than free opportunity for all. The saying in theological circles that the heresy of today becomes the orthodoxy of tomorrow is no less true in the case of liberalism itself. Nineteenth-century liberalism is not, or should not be, twentieth-century liberalism. The danger is that the liberalism of one generation carries over into the next as a mere legalism or formality, a nineteenth-century ghost in a twentieth-century world. Liberalism cannot be frozen in any given age.

When people speak of the failure of religion, they have in mind certain modes and expressions which have become outmoded. We cannot say that religion is dead any more than we can say that philosophy, economics, politics, education, or art is dead. All of these must, sooner or later, "leave their outgrown shell by life's unresting sea" and take on new forms. The same holds true of liberalism as a way of life. Just because some of its manifestations are no longer serviceable is no reason for thinking that liberalism itself is extinct. It is just as unfair to equate liberalism with *laissez faire* as it is to identify science wth technology, or democracy simply with a form of government.

The crisis in liberalism, as Dewey says, "proceeds from the fact that after early liberalism had done its work, society faced a new problem, that of social organization. Its work was to liberate a group of individuals, representing the new science and the new forces of productivity, from customs, ways of thinking, institutions, that were oppressive of the new modes of social action, however useful they may have been in their day." [10] The chief weakness of liberalism, then, is lack of organization. Nor is there anything startling about that; liberal-minded people are not easily regimented, for the genius of the free mind is independence. Nevertheless the forces of liberalism will have to be organized if the precious values of our heritage are to survive. Nothing is wrong with the values of liberalism as a philosophical attitude towards life. It is for a renascent liberalism to relate these values relevantly to contemporary institutions. Take the concept of liberty which is basic to historic liberalism. The abstract concept will always be valid but its concrete application is relative to any given situation which contains institutions deemed oppressive or totalitarian. Every century in human history has witnessed some kind of battle between freedom and slavery. Today the world is in the grip of the most important conflict of the last thousand years—a life-and-death struggle for human freedom. It is primarily an ideological conflict,

[10] *Liberalism and Social Action*, p. 53.

economic determinists to the contrary notwithstanding. For complacent isolationists to insist that the whole war is nothing but another struggle of power politics, a fight in which there is no appreciable difference between either side, is in itself an unliberal form of absolutism.

The earlier liberalism foundered on the shoals of "rugged individualism." According to Locke, the government exists to protect the rights of the individual. Bentham rendered obsolete the Lockian idea of natural rights. In Green, and later progressive thinkers, liberalism came to be dissociated from the principle of *laissez faire*. But liberalism as a whole was too slow in dropping the idea of natural rights and in recognizing that rights must always be accompanied by responsibilities. The idea persists that through these natural rights the state owes us a living. This assumption minus all moral obligation is humorously illustrated by Professor Hocking. "I recall," he writes, "a good Italian woman who had been burned out in the fire of 1906 in San Francisco. Her home had been on Telegraph Hill; and the Relief Committee had intrusted me with the task of putting up for her a temporary home on that site. During this operation she told me some of her experiences, one of which related to a consignment of bags of flour which had been sent to the priest of that parish for distribution among the refugees. She had gone to the parish house to claim her bag of flour. There was some small argument on the score of her residence; but the claim was allowed. And then, as she said with a touch of pride, 'I go to the nearest street corner, and empty my flour into the gutter. To bake my own bread, I never do it. But I have my rights!' " [11]

Another virtue which came dangerously close to being a

[11] William Ernest Hocking: *The Lasting Elements of Individualism*, pp. 53, 54. (Quoted by permission of the Yale University Press)

vice was the emphasis on tolerance, a principle upon which liberalism was founded. The two terms are for that matter synonymous. And yet the respect for persons, so typical of liberalism, and the recognition that each man is as good as the next degenerated into a flabby idea that everybody is right. When tolerance of people turned into complacency about convictions, liberalism lost its leadership and handed it over to the forces of authoritarianism. This loss of the power of discrimination made for mediocrity and smugness. If everybody was right there was nothing to fight for.

Liberalism also lost its earlier emotional appeal and its zest for fighting. It became too affable and agreeable, if not romantic. It relied on the idea that everything would come out all right. Meanwhile it became so self-effacing that it lost faith in itself, became tongue-tied and paralyzed. Liberalism must now learn not only to "take it" but to take its own part. The new liberalism must devote itself to the educational task of producing a cooperative scheme of production and distribution and organized social and economic planning for the end result of maximum living for all and cultural growth for every individual. The critics and betrayers of liberalism have failed to distinguished between means and ends. Liberalism can, nay must, change its means without changing its ends. The belief that the new order of organized social control is not a continuation of historic liberalism comes from an ignorance of the nature of true liberalism. Individual economic initiative as the guarantee of social progress was once the liberal way. Today organized social control as the guarantee of the individual's progress is the liberal way. But to attain this the new liberalism must organize for action. Liberals must acquire the ability to move together with a common purpose. The alternatives for the future are not Communism and Fascism. There is a third choice—socialized, democratic Liberalism; but before it can be actualized, there must be an effective organization, widespread scientific education, and intelligent legislation. There must be a fundamental change in the economic substructure. The temporary palliatives that "saved" the country in an emergency must give way to a socialized and planned economy. The Machine Age minus social control means a victory of Rossum's Universal Robots and the collapse of western civilization. Archaic social thinking can no longer be tolerated alongside of the scientific futurama.

Neo-Liberalism demands as the solution of the contemporary cultural conflict more science rather than less and an advance in the use of human intelligence and reason rather than a retreat to primitivism. Neo-Liberalism insists on a non-Aristotelian pattern of thought that unifies personality within itself and with nature, that does away with all forms of dualism, unreason, and absolutism. It asserts that religion must adapt itself to the modern temper and think its way through to a serious philosophy that fits the scientific concepts of this age and one that does not set the heart in conflict with the intellect or practical experience with theoretical belief. The new liberalism envisages a world in which the economic and social organization will serve the ends of individual liberty, a world in which every person has the opportunity to grow to the limit of his capacities and to pursue the highest values of life. A revivified liberalism is the only alternative to chaos. It is the sole means of transition to the only wave of the future that has meaning for America—a social order resting on rational religion, civil liberties, planned economy, and democratic collectivism.

Bibliography

CHAPTER ONE

ORIGEN

Primary Sources

Crombie, Frederick: *The Writings of Origen (Ante-Nicene Library)*. Edinburgh. T. and T. Clark. 1878

de Faye, E.: *Origene: sa vie, son œuvre, sa pensée*. 3 Vols. 1923–1928

Secondary Sources

Bigg, Charles: *The Christian Platonists of Alexandria*. Oxford. Clarendon Press. 1886

Butterworth, G. W.: *Origen on First Principles*. London. S. P. C. K. 1936

Fairweather, William: *Origen and Greek Patristic Theology*. New York. Scribner. 1901

Farrar, Frederic William: *Lives of the Fathers*. Vol. 1. Edinburgh. A. & C. Black. 1889

Redepenning, E. R.: *Origenes: Eine Darstellung seines Lebens und seine Lehre*. 2 Vols. Bonn. 1844–46

Westcott, B. F.: *Origen and the Beginnings of Christian Philosophy*. 1891

CHAPTER TWO

EARLY CHRISTIAN RADICALISM

Primary Sources

Ayer, Joseph Cullen: *A Source Book for Ancient Church History*. New York. Scribner. 1913

Kruger, Gustav: *History of Early Christian Literature*. Translated by Charles R. Gillett. New York. Macmillan. 1897

Migne, J. P.: *Patrologiae Graecae*. 161 Vols. Paris. 1857–66

Secondary Sources

Angus, Samuel: *The Religious Quests of the Graeco-Roman World*. New York. Scribner. 1929

Bigg, Charles: *The Christian Platonists of Alexandria*. New York. Macmillan. 1886

Farrar, Frederic W.: *Lives of the Fathers*. New York. Macmillan. 1889

Glover, T. R.: *The Conflict of Religions in the Early Roman Empire*. London. Methuen. 1920 (9th ed.)

Goodspeed, Edgar J.: *A History of Early Christian Literature*. Chicago. University of Chicago Press. 1942

Harnack, Adolf: *History of Dogma*. (Vol. 2, 3) Translated by Buchanan. Boston. Roberts Brothers. 1897

Harnack, Adolf: *The Mission and Expansion of Christianity in the First Three Centuries*. Translated by James Moffatt. 2nd. ed., 2 Vols. New York. Putnam, 1908

McGiffert, Arthur Cushman: *A History of Christian Thought*. Vol. 1. *Early and Eastern*. New York. Scribner. 1932

Schaff, Philip: *History of the Christian Church*. (Vol. 2, 3) New York. Scribner. 1896

Tollinton, Richard B.: *Clement of Alexandria. A Study in Christian Liberalism*. 2 Vols. London. Williams & Norgate. 1914

CHAPTER THREE

ERASMUS

Primary Sources

Erasmus: *Praise of Folly*. Edited by Peter Eckler. New York. Eckler. 1922

The Epistles of Erasmus. Edited by F. M. Nichols. 3 Vols. 1901–19

Erasmus: *The Whole Familiar Colloquies*. Translated by Nathan Bailey. London. Hamilton, Adams. 1877

Opus Epistolarum Des. Erasmi Roterodami. Edited by P. S. Allen. Oxford. Clarendon Press. 1906

Secondary Sources

Allen, P. S.: *The Age of Erasmus*. Oxford. Clarendon Press. 1914

Emerton, Ephraim: *Desiderius Erasmus of Rotterdam*. New York. Putnam. 1899

Froude, James A.: *Life and Letters of Erasmus*. New York. Scribner. 1894

Hollis, Christopher: *Erasmus*. Milwaukee. Bruce. 1933

Huizinga, J.: *Erasmus*. Translated by F. Hopman. New York. Scribner. 1924

Mangan, J.: *Life, Character and Influence of Erasmus*. New York. 1927

Siebohm, F.: *The Oxford Reformers: John Colet, Erasmus, and Thomas More*. London. 1911

Smith, Preserved: *Erasmus: A Study of his Life, Ideals, and Place in History*. New York. Harper. 1923

Zweig, Stefan: *Erasmus of Rotterdam*. Translated by Eden and Cedar Paul. New York. Viking. 1934

Chapter Four

RENAISSANCE HUMANISM

Primary Sources

Galileo: *Dialogues Concerning Two New Sciences*. Translated by H. Crew and A. de Salvio. 1914

The Notebooks of Leonardo da Vinci: Edited by Edward Mac-Curdy. New York. Reynal & Hitchcock. 1939

Smith, Preserved: *The Life and Letters of Martin Luther*. Boston, Houghton, Mifflin. 1911

The Urquhart-LeMotteux Translation of the Works of François Rabelais: Edited by Albert J. Nock and Catherine Rose Wilson. New York. Harcourt, Brace. 1931

The Works of Francis Bacon: 10 Vols. Edited by Spedding, Ellis, and Heath. Boston. Taggard. 1861

Secondary Sources

Burckhardt, Jakob Christoph: *The Civilization of the Renaissance in Italy.* New York. Harper. 1929

The Cambridge Modern History: Edited by A. W. Ward, G. W. Prothero, Stanley Leathes. Cambridge. The University Press. 1902–12

Fletcher, Jefferson B.: *Literature of the Italian Renaissance.* New York. Macmillan. 1934

Funck-Brentano, Frantz: *The Renaissance.* New York. Macmillan. 1936

Hulme, Edward Maslin: *The Renaissance, the Protestant Revolution and the Catholic Reformation in Continental Europe.* New York. Century. 1914

Lindsay, Thomas M.: *A History of the Reformation.* New York. Scribner. 1906–7

Lipsky, Abram: *Martin Luther, Germany's Angry Man.* New York. Stokes. 1933

McGiffert, Arthur C.: *Protestant Thought before Kant.* New York. Scribner. 1911

McGiffert, Arthur C.: *Martin Luther, the Man and his Work.* New York. Century. 1911

Roeder, Ralph: *The Man of the Renaissance.* New York. Viking. 1933

Smith, Preserved: *Age of the Reformation.* New York. Holt. 1920

Smith, Preserved: *Luther's Table Talk: a Critical Study.* New York. Columbia University Press. 1907

Symonds, James A.: *The Renaissance in Italy: the Revival of Learning.* London. Smith, Elder. 1909

Symonds, James A.: *A Short History of the Renaissance, in Italy.*
    New York. Holt. 1893
Tawney, Richard Henry: *Religion and the Rise of Capitalism.*
    New York. Harcourt, Brace. 1926
Taylor, Henry Osborn: *Thought and Expression in the Sixteenth
    Century.* 2 Vols. New York. Macmillan. 1920
Taylor, Rachel Annand: *Leonardo the Florentine.* New York.
    Harper. 1927
Weber, Max: *The Protestant Ethic and the Spirit of Capitalism.*
    Translated by Talcott Parsons. London. Allen & Unwin.
    1930

CHAPTER FIVE

VOLTAIRE

Primary Sources

Letters of Voltaire and Frederick the Great, Translated by
    Richard Aldington. New York. Brentano. 1927
Voltaire: *Candide.* Translated by Henry Morley. New York.
    Dutton. 1922
The Works of Voltaire: Edited by Tobias Smollett. Translated
    by W. F. Fleming. New York. E. R. DuMont. 1901

Secondary Sources

Aldington, Richard: *Voltaire.* New York. Dutton. 1925
Brailsford, Henry N.: *Voltaire.* London. Butterworth. 1935
Brandes, Georg: *Voltaire.* Translated by Otto Kruger and Pierce
    Butler. New York. Boni. 1930
Desnoireterres: *Voltaire et la Societe Francaises au XVIII Siecle.*
    Paris. Didier.
Maurois, André: *Voltaire.* Translated by Hamish Miles. Edin-
    burgh. Davies. 1932
Morley, John: *Voltaire.* New York. Macmillan. 1903
Noyes, Alfred: *Voltaire.* New York. Sheed and Ward. 1936

Sainte-Beuve, Charles Augustine: *Portraits of the Eighteenth Century*. New York. Putnam. 1905

Strachey, G. Lytton: *Books and Characters*. New York. Harcourt, Brace, 1922

Tallentyre, S. G.: *The Life of Voltaire*. London. Smith and Elder. 1903

Torrey, Norman Lewis: *The Spirit of Voltaire*. New York. Columbia University Press. 1938

CHAPTER SIX

FRENCH RATIONALISM

Primary Sources

Bolingbroke, H. St. John: *Works*. Edited by D. Mallet. London. 1754

Hume, David: *Essays, Literary, Moral, and Political*. London. Routledge. 1894

Locke, John: Essay *Concerning Human Understanding*. Edited by Fraser. Oxford. 1894

Newton, Isaac: *Mathematical Principles of Natural Philosophy*. London. 1803

Rousseau, Jean Jacques: *Confessions*. London. Gibbings. 1907

Rousseau, Jean Jacques: *The Social Contract*. Translation and Introduction by G. D. H. Cole. London. Dent. 1938

Secondary Sources

Becker, Carl: *The Heavenly City of the Eighteenth Century Philosophers*. New Haven. 1932

Bury, J. B.: *A History of Freedom of Thought*. New York. Holt. 1913

Josephson, Matthew: *Jean Jacques Rousseau*. New York. Harcourt, Brace. 1931

Lecky, W. E. H.: *History of the Rise and Influence of the Spirit of Rationalism in Europe*. New York. Appleton. 1866

Martin, Kingsley: *French Liberal Thought in the Eighteenth Century*. London. Benn. 1929

McGiffert, Arthur Cushman: *The Rise of Modern Religious Ideas*. New York. Macmillan. 1915

McGiffert, Arthur Cushman: *Protestant Thought before Kant*. New York. Scribner. 1922

Morais, Herbert M.: *Deism in Eighteenth Century America*. New York. Columbia. 1934

More, Louis Trenchard: *Isaac Newton, A Biography*. New York. Scribner. 1934

Morley, John: *Rousseau*. London. Macmillan. 1923

Randall, John Herman, Jr.: *The Making of the Modern Mind*. Boston. Houghton, Mifflin. 1926 (Rev. Ed. 1940)

Schapiro, J. Salwyn: *Condorcet and the Rise of Liberalism*. New York. Harcourt, Brace. 1934

Smith, Preserved: *A History of Modern Culture*. Vol. 2: *The Enlightenment*. New York. Holt. 1934

Strachey, G. Lytton: *Landmarks in French Literature*. New York. Holt. 1912

Stephen, Leslie: *A History of English Thought in the Eighteenth Century*. New York. Putnam. 1876

CHAPTER SEVEN

PAINE

Primary Sources

Conway, Moncure Daniel (Editor): *The Writings of Thomas Paine*. New York. Putnam. 1894

Paine, Thomas: *The Age of Reason*. Edited by Moncure D. Conway. New York. Putnam. 1924

Paine, Thomas: *The Rights of Man*. Introduction by G. J. Holyoake. New York. Dutton. 1915

Wheeler, Daniel E. (Editor): *Life and Writings of Thomas Paine*. New York. Parke. 1915

Secondary Sources

Best, Mary Agnes: *Thomas Paine, Prophet and Martyr of Democracy*. New York. Harcourt, Brace. 1927

Conway, Moncure Daniel: *The Life of Thomas Paine*. New York. Putnam. 1892

Creel, George: *Tom Paine—Liberty Bell*. New York. Sears Publishing Company. 1932

Fast, Howard: *Citizen Tom Paine*. New York. Duell, Sloan & Pearce. 1943

Gould, Frederick James: *Thomas Paine*. Boston. Small, Maynard. 1925

Pearson, Hesketh: *Tom Paine, Friend of Mankind*. New York. Harper. 1937

Smith, Frank: *Thomas Paine, Liberator*. New York. Stokes. 1938

Chapter Eight

AMERICAN DEISM

Primary Sources

Allen, Ethan: *Reason, the Only Oracle of Man*. Bennington. Haswell & Russell. 1784. New York. 1936

Blount, Charles: *The Oracles of Reason*. London. 1693

Chauncy, Charles: *The Benevolence of the Deity*. Boston. Powars and Willis. 1784

Franklin, Benjamin: Writings. Edited by Albert H. Smyth. New York. Macmillan. 1905–7

Jefferson, Thomas: *Writings*. Edited by Ford. 10 Vols. New York. Putnam. 1892 ff.

Stiles, Ezra: *The Literary Diary of Ezra Stiles*. Edited by Franklin B. Dexter. 3 Vols. New York. Scribner. 1901

Secondary Sources

Becker, Carl L.: *The Heavenly City of the Eighteenth-Century Philosophers*. New Haven. Yale University Press. 1932

Dewey, John: *Thomas Jefferson.* (*Living Thoughts Library*) New York. Longmans, Green. 1940

Fay, Bernard: *Franklin, the Apostle of Modern Times.* Boston. Little, Brown. 1929

Jones, Howard Mumford: *America and French Culture, 1750– 1848.* Chapel Hill. University of North Carolina Press. 1927

Koch, G. Adolph: *Republican Religion: The American Revolution and the Cult of Reason.* New York. Holt. 1933

Morais, Herbert M.: *Deism in Eighteenth Century America.* New York. Columbia University Press. 1934

Parrington, Vernon Louis: *Main Currents in American Thought, an Interpretation of American Literature from the Beginnings to 1920.* Vol. 1: *The Colonial Mind;* Vol. 2: *The Romantic Revolution in America.* New York. Harcourt, Brace. 1927

Pell, John: *Ethan Allen.* Boston. Houghton, Mifflin. 1929

Riley, I. Woodbridge: *American Philosophy, the Early Schools.* New York. Dodd, Mead. 1907

Sweet, William Warren: *The Story of Religions in America.* New York. Harper. 1930

Smith, Preserved: *A History of Modern Culture.* Vol. 2: *The Enlightenment.* New York. Holt. 1934

Van Doren, Carl: *Benjamin Franklin.* New York. Viking. 1938

CHAPTER NINE

PARKER

Primary Sources

American Unitarian Association: *Works.* 15 Vols. Boston. 1913

Cobbe, Frances: *The Collected Works of Theodore Parker.* 14 Vols. London. 1874

The Complete Works of Ralph Waldo Emerson. 12 Vols. (Riverside Ed.) Boston. Houghton, Mifflin. 1883–1894

The Journals of Ralph Waldo Emerson. 10 Vols. Boston. Houghton, Mifflin. 1909–1914

The Works of William Ellery Channing. 6 Vols. Boston. Beacon Press. 1881

Weiss, John: *The Life and Correspondence of Theodore Parker.* 2 Vols. Boston. Appleton. 1864

Secondary Sources

Chadwick, John White: *Theodore Parker, Preacher and Reformer.* Boston. Houghton, Mifflin. 1900

Commager, Henry Steele: *Theodore Parker: Yankee Crusader.* Boston. Little, Brown. 1936

Dean, Peter: *Life of Theodore Parker.* 1877

Frothingham, Octavius Brooks: *Theodore Parker, a Biography.* Boston. Osgood. 1874

The Life of William Ellery Channing by William Henry Channing. Boston. Beacon Press. 1899

Reville, Albert: *Life and Writings of Theodore Parker.* 1865

CHAPTER TEN

NEW ENGLAND UNITARIANISM

Primary Sources

Channing, William Ellery: *Works.* 6 Vols. Boston. Monroe. 1848

Complete Works of Emerson. (Riverside Edition) 12 Vols. Boston. Houghton, Mifflin. 1892–95

Perry, Bliss (Editor): *The Heart of Emerson's Journals.* Boston. Houghton, Mifflin. 1926

Writings of Thoreau: Walden Edition, 20 Vols. Boston. Houghton, Mifflin. 1907

Secondary Sources

Allen, Joseph Henry: *Our Liberal Movement in Theology.* Boston. American Unitarian Assoc. Press. 1882

Allen, Joseph Henry and Eddy, Richard: *A History of the Unitarians and the Universalists in the United States.* New York. Scribner. 1894

Brooks, Van Wyck: *The Flowering of New England:* 1815–1865. New York. Dutton. 1936

Brooks, Van Wyck: *New England: Indian Summer; 1865–1915.* New York. Dutton. 1940

Brooks, Van Wyck: *The Life of Emerson.* New York. Dutton. 1932

Canby, Henry Seidel: *Thoreau.* Boston. Houghton, Mifflin. 1939

Chadwick, John White: *William Ellery Channing, Minister of Religion.* Boston, Houghton, Mifflin. 1903

Cooke, George Willis: *Unitarianism in America; a History of its Origin and Development.* Boston. American Unitarian Association. 1902

Eliot, Charles William: *Four American Leaders.* Boston. American Unitarian Association. 1906

Eliot, Samuel Atkins: *Heralds of a Liberal Faith.* Boston. American Unitarian Association. 1910

Parrington, Vernon Louis: *The Romantic Revolution in America; 1800–1860. (Main Currents in American Thought.* Vol. 2) New York. Harcourt, Brace. 1927

CHAPTER ELEVEN

DARWIN

Primary Sources

Darwin, Charles: *The Origin of Species by Means of Natural Selection.* New York. Appleton. 1925 (Authorized Edition)

Darwin, Charles: *The Descent of Man and Selection in Relation to Sex.* New York. Appleton. 1930 (Second Edition, Revised and Augmented)

Darwin, Charles: *Journal of Researches into the Natural History and Geology of the Countries Visited during the Voyage of the H.M.S. Beagle.* New York. Appleton. 1896

Darwin, Charles: *The Expression of the Emotions in Man and Animals.* New York. Appleton. 1873

Darwin, Charles: *The Voyage of the Beagle.* New York. Collier. 1909

Darwin, Francis: *Life and Letters of Charles Darwin.* (Including an Autobiography of Darwin) 2 Vols. New York. Appleton. 1896

Darwin, Francis: *More Letters of Charles Darwin.* 2 Vols. New York. Appleton. 1903

Secondary Sources

Barzun, Jacques: *Darwin, Marx, Wagner: Critique of a Heritage.* Boston. Little, Brown. 1941

Bradford, Gamaliel: *Darwin.* Boston. Houghton, Mifflin. 1926

Huxley, Thomas: *Darwiniana.* New York. Appleton. 1893

Dorsey, George A.: *The Evolution of Charles Darwin.* New York. Doubleday, Page. 1927

Fifty Years of Darwinism: (American Centenary Essays, Auspices of American Association for the Advancement of Science) New York. Holt. 1909

Huxley, Julian: *Darwin.* (*The Living Thoughts Library* edited by James Fisher). New York. Longmans, Green. 1939

Seward, Albert Charles (Editor): *Darwin and Modern Science.* Cambridge University Press. 1909

Ward, Charles Henshaw: *Charles Darwin, The Man and His Warfare.* Indianapolis. Bobbs-Merrill. 1927

Wells, Geoffrey Harry: *Charles Darwin, A Portrait.* New Haven. Yale University Press. 1938

CHAPTER TWELVE

THE NINETEENTH-CENTURY AGE OF CRITICISM

Primary Sources

Barton, George A.: *Archaeology and the Bible.* Philadelphia. American Sunday School Union. 1916

Cobern, Camden McCormick: *The New Archaeological Discoveries and their Bearing upon the New Testament.* New York. Funk & Wagnalls. 1929 (9th ed.)

Kenyon, Frederic George: *The Bible and Archaeology.* London. Harrap. 1940

Marx, Karl: *Capital; a Critique of Political Economy.* Chicago. Kerr. 1906–09

Marx, Karl: *A Contribution to the Critique of Political Economy.* Translated by N. I. Stone. New York. International Library Publishing Company. 1904

Marx, Karl: *Manifesto of the Communist Party.* Edited by Frederick Engels. Chicago. Kerr. 1902

Nietzsche, Friederich Wilhelm: *Beyond Good and Evil.* New York. Macmillan. 1923 (4th ed.)

Nietzsche, Friedrich Wilhelm: *Ecce Homo and the Birth of Tragedy.* Translated by Clifton P. Fadiman. New York. Modern Library. 1927

Nietzsche, Friedrich: *Thus Spake Zarathustra.* Translated by Thomas Common. New York. Macmillan. 1930

Philosophy of Nietzsche. New York. Modern Library. 1937

Rogers, Robert William: *Cuneiform Parallels to the Old Testament.* New York. Eaton & Mains. 1912

Spencer, Herbert: *First Principles of a New System of Philosophy.* New York. Appleton. 1877

Secondary Sources

Beer, Max: *The Life and Teaching of Karl Marx.* Translated by Parrington and Stenning. Boston. Small. 1924

Bober, Mandell Morton: *Karl Marx's Interpretation of History.* Cambridge. Harvard University Press. 1927

Brandes, Georg: *Friedrich Nietzsche.* London. Heinemann. 1914

Briggs, Charles Augustus: *General Introduction to the Study of the Holy Scripture.* New York. Scribner. 1899

Bury, J. B.: *A History of Freedom of Thought.* New York. Holt. 1913

Cheyne, Thomas Kelly: *Founders of Old Testament Criticism.*
New York. Scribner. 1893

Cole, G. D. H.: *What Marx Really Meant.* New York. Knopf.
1934

Conger, G. P.: *New Views of Evolution.* New York. Macmillan.
1929

Dawson, Marshall: *Nineteenth-Century Evolution and After.*
New York. Macmillan. 1923

Dewey, John: *The Influence of Darwin on Philosophy.* New
York. Holt. 1910

*Experience, Reason, and Faith, A Survey in Philosophy and
Religion.* Edited by Eugene G. Bewkes. New York. Harper.
1940

Gabriel, Ralph Henry: *The Course of American Democratic
Thought. An Intellectual History Since 1815.* New York.
Ronald. 1940

Gilbert, George Holley: *Interpretation of the Bible; a Short
History.* New York. Macmillan. 1908

Hook, Sidney: *Towards the Understanding of Karl Marx.* New
York. John Day. 1933

Latourette, Kenneth Scott: *The Great Century. (A History of the
Expansion of Christianity.* Vol 4) New York. Harper. 1941

Lull, R. S.: *Organic Evolution.* New York. Macmillan. 1936

McFadyen, John Edgar: *Old Testament Criticism and the Christian Church.* New York. Scribner. 1903

McGiffert, Arthur Cushman: *The Rise of Modern Religious
Ideas.* New York. Macmillan. 1915

McNeill, John Thomas, *et al.*: *Environmental Factors in Christian History.* Chicago. University of Chicago Press. 1939

Moffatt, James: *An Introduction to the Literature of the New
Testament.* New York. Scribner. 1911

Morgan, C. Lloyd: *Emergent Evolution.* New York. Holt. 1923

Parrington, Vernon Louis: *The Beginnings of Critical Realism in
America. (Main Currents in American Thought.* Vol. 3)
New York. Harcourt, Brace. 1930

Pfeiffer, Robert Henry: *Introduction to the Old Testament.* New York. Harper. 1941

Robertson, J. M.: *A History of Free Thought in the Nineteenth Century.* 2 Vols. New York. Putnam. 1930

Robertson, John M.: *A Short History of Free Thought.* 2 Vols. New York. Putnam. 1906

Thompson, J. A.: *Concerning Evolution.* New Haven. Yale University Press. 1925

Trattner, Ernest Robert: *Unravelling the Book of Books.* New York. Scribner. 1929

White, Andrew D.: *A History of the Warfare of Science with Theology.* 2 Vols. New York. Appleton. 1899

CHAPTER THIRTEEN

DEWEY

Primary Sources

Dewey, John: *A Common Faith.* New Haven. Yale University Press. 1934

Dewey, John: *Democracy and Education: an Introduction to the Philosophy of Education.* New York. Macmillan. 1917

Dewey, John: *Education Today.* New York. Putnam. 1940

Dewey, John: *Experience and Education.* New York, Macmillan. 1938

Dewey, John: *Freedom and Culture.* New York. Putnam. 1939

Dewey, John: *Liberalism and Social Action.* New York. Putnam. 1935

Dewey, John: *Philosophy and Civilization.* New York. Minton, Balch. 1931

Dewey, John: *The Quest for Certainty.* New York. Minton, Balch. 1929

Dewey, John: *Reconstruction in Philosophy.* New York. Holt. 1920

Secondary Sources

Hook, Sidney: *John Dewey, an Intellectual Portrait.* New York. John Day. 1939

Ratner, Joseph: *The Philosophy of John Dewey.* New York. Holt. 1928

Schilpp, Paul Arthur, (Editor): *The Philosophy of John Dewey.* Evanston. Northwestern University Press. 1939

Thomas, Wendell Marshall: *A Democratic Philosophy.* New York. Correlated Enterprises. 1938

CHAPTER FOURTEEN

TWENTIETH CENTURY NATURALISM

References combining source material and description of current thought.

Ames, Edward Scribner: *Religion.* New York. Holt. 1929

Aubrey, Edwin Ewart: *Present Theological Tendencies.* New York. Harper. 1936

Auer, J. A. F. C.: *Humanism States its Case.* Boston. Beacon Press. 1933

Bewkes, Eugene G. (Editor): *Experience, Reason, and Faith.* New York. Harper. 1940

Bixler, Julius Seelye: *Religion for Free Minds.* New York. Harper. 1939

Braden, Charles Samuel: *Varieties of American Religion.* Chicago. Willett, Clark. 1936

Dewey, John: *A Common Faith.* New Haven. Yale University Press. 1934.

Dewey, John: *The Quest for Certainty.* New York, Minton, Balch. 1929

Haydon, A. Eustace: *The Quest of the Ages.* New York. Harpers. 1929

Hocking, W. E.: *Types of Philosophy.* New York. Scribner. 1939

Krutch, J. W.: *The Modern Temper*. New York. Harcourt, Brace. 1929

Lake, Kirsopp: *The Religion of Yesterday and Tomorrow*. Boston. Houghton, Mifflin. 1926

Lerner, Max: *It is Later Than You Think*. New York. Viking. 1939

Lippmann, Walter: *A Preface to Morals*. New York. Macmillan. 1929

More, Paul Elmer: *Aristocracy and Justice*. Boston, Houghton, Mifflin. 1915

Niebuhr, Reinhold: *Christianity and Power Politics*. New York. Scribner. 1940

Niebuhr, Reinhold: *Moral Man and Immoral Society*. New York. Scribner. 1932

Niebuhr, Reinhold: *Reflections on the End of an Era*. New York. Scribner. 1934

Otto, Max C.: *Things and Ideals*. New York. Holt. 1924

Overstreet, Harry A.: *The Enduring Quest*. New York. Norton. 1931

Perry, Ralph B.: *Recent Philosophical Tendencies*. New York. Longmans, Green. 1912

Potter, Charles Francis: *Humanism: A New Religion*. New York. Simon and Schuster. 1930

Reese, Curtis W.: *Humanism*. Chicago. Open Court. 1926

Reiser, Oliver L.: *Humanism and New World Ideals*. Antioch. Antioch Press. 1933

Roberts, David E. and Van Dusen, Henry P.: *Liberal Theology, an Appraisal*. New York. Scribner. 1942

Sellars, Ralph W.: *Evolutionary Naturalism*. Chicago. Open Court. 1921

Sellars, Ralph W.: *Religion Coming of Age*. New York. Macmillan. 1928

Smith, Gerald B.: *Current Christian Thinking*. Chicago. University of Chicago Press. 1928

Tillich, Paul: *The Religious Situation*. New York. Holt. 1932

Watson, John B.: *Behaviourism.* New York. People's Institute Publishing Co. 1926

Whitehead, Alfred North: *Adventures of Ideas.* New York. Macmillan. 1933

Whitehead, Alfred North: *Process and Reality.* New York. Macmillan. 1929

Whitehead, Alfred North: *Science and the Modern World.* New York. Macmillan. 1925

Wieman, Henry Nelson: *Religious Experience and Scientific Method.* New York. Macmillan. 1926

Wieman, Henry Nelson and Bernard Eugene Meland: *American Philosophies of Religion.* Chicago. Willett, Clark. 1930

Index

are independent but is not usually at linear in any environment. Page 53